The New

RELIGIOUS
HUMANISTS

A Reader

Edited by

GREGORY WOLFE

THE FREE PRESS

New York   London   Toronto   Singapore   Sydney

THE FREE PRESS
A Division of Simon & Schuster Inc.
1230 Avenue of the Americas
New York, NY 10020

THE FREE PRESS and colophon are trademarks
of Simon & Schuster Inc.

Designed by Carla Bolte

Manufactured in the United States of America

10   9   8   7   6   5   4   3   2   1

Library of Congress Cataloging-in-Publishing Data
The new religious humanists : a reader / edited by Gregory Wolfe.
        p.   cm.
    Includes bibliographical references.
    ISBN 0–684–83254–2
    1. Humanism, Religious.   I. Wolfe. Gregory.
BL2747.6.N49   1997   97-37196
211′.6—dc21   CIP

To the memory of

GERHART NIEMEYER

CONTENTS

INTRODUCTION

In the history of the West, religious humanism has made only infrequent appearances and has rarely occupied center stage. It is a mode of thought that tends to arise when cultural cohesion is threatened by large social and intellectual upheavals. By and large, religious humanists are men and women of letters who command no legions, and who go about their work without much taste for manifestos and movements. Indeed, they often come under attack from all sides of the ideological spectrum. But it is arguable that they are like the thirty-six just men of Jewish legend, without whom the world would come to an end.

Take, for example, the life and career of one of history's great religious humanists, Erasmus of Rotterdam. The recovery of the literature and culture of classical antiquity that took place in the Renaissance had no more brilliant exponent than this witty, erudite author, who was a master of an elegant Latin prose style. Unlike many humanists of his time, Erasmus was not satisfied with merely aesthetic pleasures; at some point early in his literary career, he experienced a quiet but intense conversion to a deeper, more authentic Christian faith. From that moment on he worked tirelessly to bring about reform in the church.

Erasmus took the humanist passion for going "back to the sources" and directed it toward the Bible. His dissatisfaction with the many errors and conundrums in the Latin vulgate impelled him to translate the New Testament from the original Greek in order to recover what he believed to be the clarity and simplicity of the gospel message. A harsh critic of the abuses of the medieval church, Erasmus never tired of mocking empty rituals, superstitious practices, and the irrelevance of scholastic thinkers arguing interminably over philosophical abstractions. When Martin Luther launched the Protestant Reformation, both sides of the conflict tried to recruit Erasmus as their champion. Caught between his sympathy for Protestant criticisms and a firm loyalty to a Catholic Church that he thought was still reformable, Erasmus held out for many years before finally writing against Luther. By that time the course of events had overtaken him. He died, embittered by the controversies of his later years and still appalled that events had taken such a tragic turn.

That the tragedy proceeded to its inevitable conclusion hardly invalidates the seminal contribution Erasmus made to his own time and to subsequent generations. As the author of an enduring classic of comic irony *(The Praise of Folly),* the father of modern biblical criticism, and the first thinker who successfully synthesized the newly emergent classicism with the Christian faith, Erasmus remains a beacon of wisdom—a peacemaker who steadfastly refused to be co-opted by the ideological extremes of his own day.

Our own tumultuous time is not unlike that of Erasmus. Deep fault lines in American culture have cracked through the surface of public life as the twentieth century draws to a close. Racked by incessant "culture wars," our social order has fallen prey to forms of tribalism. Religious, ethnic, racial, and gender-based groups have withdrawn into political enclaves from which they raise the shrillness of their rhetoric to an ever-higher pitch.

The sociologist James Davison Hunter argued in his book *Culture Wars* (1991) that this struggle is essentially between traditionalists and progressives. The deepening divisions in the few short years since Hunter's book was published seem to bear him out, as the Right has begun to experience the sort of internecine struggles that have long plagued the Left. The fragile coalition of libertarians, populists, and neoconservatives that came together in 1980 to elect Ronald Reagan is unraveling. Political categories, it seems, are becoming ever more confused. This much can be said with confidence: nearly every sector of our common life has become a minefield strewn with explosive political conflicts, from our schools and churches to popular culture and the media through which this culture is transmitted.

As Hunter has pointed out, essentially philosophical and theological issues have become thoroughly politicized. Genuine debate and reflection have been replaced by the clash of factions fighting for ideologically pure visions. Thus the culture wars are fought out in the political realm. In a recent interview, Hunter concluded that "the only thing left to order public life is power. This is why we invest so much in politics."

In this spectacle of ideological warfare we are witnessing the final collapse of an experiment that was begun not long after Erasmus died. The rise of modern philosophy, as exemplified by thinkers like Descartes and Hobbes, was a reaction to the terrible bloodshed and chaos that the religious wars of the sixteenth century left in their wake. Since the competing truth claims of various sects had led to these conflicts, philosophers like Descartes proposed to ground knowledge on human reason unaided by biblical revelation. The rise of modern science and technological progress helped to sustain the belief that secular humanism would bring about peace and prosperity.

Standing as we do on the far side of this four-hundred-year-old experiment, it is hard not to admire the scope of its accomplishments, especially the dramatic progress of modern science and technology. But as the late novelist Walker Percy pointed out, the triumph of rationalistic science has not been paralleled by greater social and psychic harmony; rather, it has been marked by an increasing sense of malaise. Every attempt to ground human nature in some rational, secular truth—from Marx's class conflict to Darwin's natural selection to Freud's subconscious—has failed to sustain itself in either the theoretical or practical realm. As Robert Royal writes in his essay in this anthology, "Our moment is one in which the central doubters have been subjected to doubt, and no definite replacements have emerged." These efforts to construct new "master narratives" to replace the old Judeo-Christian story no longer give meaning to our lives.

To put our situation in some perspective, consider that in 1968 *Time* magazine published a cover story that asked, "Is God Dead?" That story, which generated a sizable amount of discussion, was considered by many to be something of a cultural watershed. By way of contrast, in the last five years *Time* and *Newsweek* each have devoted several cover stories to such topics as the existence of angels and the resurgent interest in religion and spirituality. It would appear that a large segment of our society is aware, at some level of consciousness, of the malaise that Percy named. Many Americans are desperately searching for something beyond the Enlightenment dream of the rational, autonomous individual who is free to acquire property and pursue happiness.

In short, there are numerous signs, both at the polls and in the culture at large, that the Enlightenment project (which served as the foundation of modern liberalism) has driven into a dead end. There is a widespread feeling that liberalism has liberated too much, that the centrifugal force of relativism and an undiluted faith in rationalism have left the nation without a moral rudder.

But if liberalism is exhausted, conservatism—at least in its dominant forms—is hardly a vibrant intellectual force. Neither of its two major branches, libertarianism and populism, has much to say to the current crisis of social fragmentation. Libertarians are merely liberals who believe in the unfettered free market: both schools of thought conceive of the person as an autonomous individual whose only moral obligation is to refrain from directly injuring others. Ironically, both also espouse a form of economic determinism: libertarians believe that social problems will be solved by the spontaneous actions of the market, while liberals are convinced that capitalism always goes wrong and must be ameliorated by the paternalistic state.

To be sure, libertarianism has a certain appeal for those who feel oppressed by a bloated and immobile government. The libertarian vision of privatizing everything touches a deep chord in the American character, celebrating the anarchic energy of the marketplace in which individuals are free to pursue private visions of happiness.

Populist conservatism, though it may often defend venerable institutions and moral traditions, has forfeited much of its relevance and persuasive power. Traumatized by the string of victories that secular liberals have won in the legislatures and especially the courts, populists have fallen back on the rhetoric of righteousness and outrage. This brand of populism is not so much conservative as it is reactionary. A conservative is committed (in theory, at least) to preserving a living tradition through the inevitable changes that history brings, but a reactionary has a more brittle and static concept of social order. Reactionaries spend most of their time fighting rear-guard actions, using the boycott and the filibuster to stave off defeat. Even a political figure with the savvy and apparent goodwill of one-time Christian Coalition director Ralph Reed has found it difficult to communicate a positive vision of the society he wishes to promote. That he has struggled to do so is a sign of recognition that negative movements soon run out of steam.

Within the last decade a host of proposed solutions for our deep cultural divisions have been put forward, from "communitarianism" to the "politics of meaning" to the search for a "new civility." Some of these movements have involved little more than a repackaging of old political agendas, but many others have made significant contributions. The communitarian thinkers, for example, have reminded us of the need to preserve mediating institutions that help individuals develop personal identity, responsibility, and a sense of civic participation.

As valuable as these movements are, however, it is necessary to sink deeper wells if we are to strive for authentic cultural renewal. Those wells can be found, I believe, in the tradition of religious humanism.

What do I mean by religious humanism? The theologian Max Stackhouse recently provided a simple but suggestive definition. "Humanity," Stackhouse wrote, "cannot be understood without reference to God; and neither God nor God's revelation can be understood except through the lens of thought and experience."

On the face of it, the term religious humanism seems to suggest a tension between two opposed terms—between heaven and earth, so to speak. But this is a creative, rather than a deconstructive, tension. Perhaps the best analogy for understanding religious humanism comes from the Christian doctrine of the Incarnation, which holds that Jesus was both human and divine. In the paradoxical meeting of Christ's two natures is the pattern by which we can begin to understand the many dualities we experience in life: flesh and spirit, nature and grace, God and Caesar, faith and reason, justice and mercy.

When emphasis is placed on the divine at the expense of the human (the conservative fault), Jesus becomes an ethereal authority figure who is remote from earthly life and experience. When he is thought of as merely human (the liberal error), he becomes nothing more than a superior social worker or popular guru.

The religious humanist refuses to collapse paradox in on itself. This has an important implication for how he or she approaches the world of culture. Those who make a radical opposition between faith and the world hold such a negative view of human nature that the products of culture are seen as inevitably corrupt and worthless. In contrast, those who are eager to accommodate themselves to the dominant trends of the time baptize nearly everything, even things that may not be compatible with the dictates of faith. But the distinctive mark of religious humanism is its willingness to adapt and transform culture, following the dictum of an early church father, who said that "Wherever there is truth, it is the Lord's." Because religious humanists believe that whatever is good, true, and beautiful is part of God's design, they have confidence that their faith can assimilate the works of culture. Assimilation, rather than rejection or accommodation, constitutes the heart of the religious humanist's vision.

One might ask why the incarnational balance of the human and the divine is not so obvious as to be universally accepted. The truth is that human beings find it difficult to live with paradox. It is far easier to seek a resolution in one direction or the other; indeed, making such choices often seems to be the most principled option. Perhaps the best illustration of religious humanism I've come across can be found in the film *The Mission*. It tells the story of the Jesuit missionaries who attempted bring their faith to the remotest tribes in South America. As the film opens, we see a series of missionaries ejected from the tribe in a gruesomely ironic fashion: each of them is tied to a cross and sent over the edge of a huge waterfall. Evidently these missionaries had tried to preach at the tribesmen and had been rejected. But the Jesuit played by Jeremy Irons enters a clearing near where the tribe lives, sits down on a rock, and begins playing an oboe. This simple gesture enables the tribespeople to recognize what is human in him. They arrive with their spears raised but they soon accept him—and ultimately, convert to Christianity. (Another reason to admire *The Mission* is that it departs from the standard Hollywood stereotype of the missionary as a smug, sexually repressed fanatic.)

Someone noting these references to paradox and ambiguity might object that I am speaking in quintessentially liberal terms, refusing to state my allegiance to the particularities of the faith. In fact, the majority of religious humanists through the centuries have been deeply orthodox (which is not to say that they don't struggle with doubt or possess highly skeptical minds). This is a phenomenon that liberals tend to ignore; it doesn't tally with their notion that religious dogma are somehow lifeless and repressive. But dogma are nothing more—or less—than restatements of the mysteries of faith. Theological systems can become calcified and unreal (giving rise to "dogmatism"), but dogma exist to protect and enshrine mystery. Flannery O'Connor, one of the great religious humanists of the twentieth century, wrote of the effect her faith had on her writing: "There is no reason why fixed dogma should fix anything that the writer sees in the world. On the contrary, dogma is an instrument for penetrating reality. Christian dogma is about the only thing left in the world that surely guards and respects mystery." In a similar vein one need only think of modern Jewish thinkers like Martin Buber and Emmanuel Levinas, who have joined their passionate love of Hasidic mysticism to such modern philosophic schools as personalism and existentialism.

So we arrive at yet another paradox: the religious humanist combines an intense (if occasionally anguished) attachment to orthodoxy with a profound spirit of openness to the world. This helps to explain why so many of the towering figures of religious humanism—from Gregory of Nyssa, Maimonides, Dante, and Erasmus to Fyodor Dostoevsky, T. S. Eliot, and Flannery O'Connor—have been gifted writers. The intuitive powers of the imagination can leap beyond the sometimes leaden abstractions with which reason must work. Because the imagination is always searching to move from conflict to a higher synthesis, it is the natural ally of religious humanism, which struggles to assimilate the data of the world into a deeper vision of faith.

The assimilative power of religious humanism enables it to balance the changing circumstances of history with what T. S. Eliot called the "permanent things." One of the most luminous explanations of this balance was written by John Henry Newman, a Victorian theologian who eventually became a cardinal in the Catholic church. His book on the "development of doctrine" argues that the unfolding of history enables us to see—and respond to—new facets of meaning in the ancient dogma. Newman's concept of doctrinal development has been cited by many scholars as the underlying inspiration for the Second Vatican Council, with its stress on the need for a dialogue between the church and the modern world.

Religious humanism has flourished within the Jewish, Islamic, Catholic, Orthodox, and Protestant traditions at various times. More often than not, it emerges as a response to periods dominated by ideological strife. In the century between 350 and 450 C.E., when the Roman Empire was breathing its last, a remarkable group of church fathers was at work: Augustine wrote the *Confessions,* the first autobiography, and *The City of God,* which provided the blueprint for the medieval polity; Jerome was translating the Bible from Greek into Latin; and the Cappadocian fathers were busy adapting the last major pagan system of philosophy (Neoplatonism) for Christian purposes. With the decay of the medieval order came a series of humanists who incorporated the philosophy of Aristotle into their own traditions: the Arab thinkers Averroes and Avicenna, the Jewish leader Maimonides, and the Catholic Thomas Aquinas. Two centuries later, during the tumult of the Renaissance and Reformation, Nicholas of Cusa, Erasmus, and Thomas More struggled to purify the Catholic church while a number of Protestant thinkers, John Calvin in particular, sought to create their own new theological syntheses. With the Romantic reaction to the Enlightenment, figures as diverse as Samuel Taylor Coleridge, François Chateaubriand, and the Oxford Tractarians (including John Henry Newman) worked to reunite faith, reason, and the imagination.

Since the roots of religious humanism go so far back into the European past, a skeptic might wonder whether such a mode of thought has ever been grafted onto American culture. After all, America is still a relatively young nation, and its Puritan and pragmatic strains—neither particularly hospitable to humanism—are ingrained in our history. Without intending to scant the contributions of earlier religious thinkers, I believe that the leading American representatives of religious humanism have been imaginative writers. Nathaniel Hawthorne's insistence on the reality of evil, the inexorable presence of the past, and a tragic sense of life stood in stark contrast to Emerson's optimism and utopianism. Throughout his career, Hawthorne struggled to achieve a more sacramental perspective, which placed the self in relation to the transcendent, and which encompassed a vision of redemptive suffering. It is possible to draw a direct line from Hawthorne to such modern American writers as Eliot, O'Connor, and Walker Percy.

In the twentieth century, religious humanism has manifested itself in two distinct waves. The first emerged after World War I and was largely centered in Europe, though many of its leading lights emigrated to the United States. These religious intellectuals were aghast at the catastrophic effects of the war and determined to waken the churches out of what they felt was a bourgeois, provincial torpor. Above all, they wanted to bring their faith into a dialogue with modernity. Philosophers like Gabriel Marcel and Nicholas Berdyaev engaged existentialism, while Jacques Maritain and Etienne Gilson brought Thomas Aquinas into the context of contemporary problems. Theologians like Reinhold Niebuhr and Paul Tillich struggled to find in historic Protestantism the resources to address such overwhelming questions as the rise of modern totalitarian ideologies. Georges Rouault, Eric Gill, Marc Chagall, and Jacob Epstein created paintings and sculptures with biblical subjects that broke decisively with the sentimentality of nineteenth-century religious iconography. In the realm of literature, religious humanists abounded in the form of Paul Claudel, Georges Bernanos, François Mauriac, T. S. Eliot, David Jones, Evelyn Waugh, Graham Greene, Sigrid Undset, Allen Tate, Flannery O'Connor, Thomas Merton, Isaac Bashevis Singer, and Bernard Malamud. Many other writers (including W. H. Auden, Robert Lowell, and John Berryman) experienced intense, if sometimes fleeting, periods of religious belief.

The scope of the intellectual and artistic contributions made by these figures is astonishing. No less remarkable, from the perspective of the present, is how thoroughly these religious humanists were integrated into the public life of their own time. They taught at Harvard, Princeton, and Columbia, were invited to deliver the Mellon Lectures at the National Gallery of Art, and wrote for *The Partisan Review* and even occasionally for the *Saturday Evening Post*. They were, in short, representatives of a now-endangered species known as the public intellectual. Writing in *The Atlantic,* the cultural critic Cullen Murphy recently bemoaned the loss of this class of thinkers. Describing the environment in which the first wave of religious humanists flourished along with their secular counterparts, Murphy laments the virtual disappearance of . . . people like Dewey and Trilling and Howe and Niebuhr who were generalists and inhabited the outside world . . . as much as or more than they inhabited academe. They displayed a broad knowledge of the culture as a whole . . . and wrote widely of what they saw in a style that Irving Howe once characterized as "free-lance dash, peacock strut, and knockout synthesis." One thinks of them almost as circuit riders, keeping disparate segments of the national culture—segments that sometimes may not have been talking—informed about one another. Whatever their conclusions, they engaged moral and religious considerations with respect, and helped preserve the public role of these things.

As late as 1950, Murphy notes, the *Partisan Review* was willing to devote a major symposium to the subject of "religion and the intellectuals."

With the massive social, political, and cultural upheavals of the next generation, though, the era of the public intellectual—and the religious humanist—seemingly came to an end. Brilliant as the first wave of twentieth-century religious humanists were, they lived in a time (like that of Erasmus) when the tectonic plates of culture were shifting under their feet, driven by pressures that had been building up for decades if not centuries. Secular liberalism made huge strides in the 1960s and 1970s, transforming government, academia, and social mores as well as having a profound impact on churches and synagogues. Young theologians like Harvey Cox got swept up in the spirit of the time. Cox's *The Secular City* neatly encapsulated the drift of liberal theology: having lost confidence in the traditional doctrines of sin, grace, and redemption, theologians from all sectors of the religious community hastened to celebrate the secular. A corollary of this movement was a heightened involvement in politics. While this step led to some constructive and necessary engagements, including the civil rights movement, many liberal theologians and clerics went on to defend such dubious causes as financial support for Marxist guerrillas around the globe.

What these secularizing crusaders failed to understand was that they were, in essence, defining themselves out of their jobs. Swept along in these social changes, they found that the secular city really had no need for them. Moreover, a series of Supreme Court decisions limiting the presence of religion in schools and other institutions helped to create an atmosphere that banished faith from the public square. From the mid-1950s to the mid-1980s there were few magazine symposia on "religion and the intellectuals," because it was widely assumed that the two never mixed.

The battle lines of our current culture wars were also set out in the personal, psychic experiences of many young intellectuals of the 1960s. Hardened by the fires of that ideological decade, many of these thinkers underwent political conversion experiences—most from Left to Right (including, of course, the neoconservatives), but with a few (such as Garry Wills) in the opposite direction. One cannot help but admire the steady stream of books, journals, and organizations that have been produced by these culture warriors. Nevertheless, there is something tragic about the way their politicized rhetoric has narrowed the range of our public discourse. Today, rather than the circuit-riding public intellectuals of an earlier generation, we have road shows by political performance artists. The religious community, far from being exempt from this trend, has been deeply implicated in it. Take, for example, the seemingly respectable world of thoughtful religious magazines and journals. Whereas these publications once gained their distinctiveness from their theology, the majority of them today are known—and read—primarily for the side of the political fence on which they come down.

And yet, despite the harshness of our cultural climate, a new generation of religious humanists is making its presence known. Many of the most dynamic of these thinkers were born a generation after the one that experienced the divisiveness of the 1960s. While these younger thinkers care passionately about the issues at the heart of the culture wars, they seek a less apocalyptic and political role for religion. To a great extent they draw their inspiration from the first wave of twentieth-century religious humanists, who were assimilators rather than warriors, but there is a significant difference. Whereas thinkers like Eliot could still rely on a social order in which religion was entrenched, contemporary thinkers face a cultural situation that can only be described as post-Christian. This has given rise to a whole new series of cultural and intellectual approaches.

The new religious humanists have a number of things going for them. Now that the baby boomers have arrived at middle age, fully aware for the first time of their mortality and concerned about their children's moral and physical well-being, we have witnessed a wave of interest in religion, ranging from fascination with New Age pantheism to nostalgia for traditional rites and moral codes. Indeed, religious humanism must compete with the Wal-Mart of spiritual and therapeutic nostrums available today. Even if much of this can be discounted as sentimental religiosity, there is a spirit of openness that can, and must, be addressed.

There is no "school" of religious humanism, no centralized office or publication that represents it to the worlds of politics or the media, no platform with readily identifiable political planks. However, there are subtle but powerful threads that link many of the most distinguished minds of our time. In philosophy, Alasdair MacIntyre and Charles Taylor have brought the existence of God and the idea of "the good" back into serious discussion. Theologians such as the American Jesuit Avery Dulles, the German Lutheran Wolfhart Pannenberg, and the late Hans Urs von Balthasar and his followers have demonstrated that faithfulness to the ancient teachings of the church can inspire nuanced and creative thought. There are also a growing number of scholars who have been meditating on the relationship between religion and science, including Stanley Jaki, John Polkinghorne, and Langdon Gilkey.

One clear lesson that these thinkers have learned from the culture wars is that the process of politicization endangers the ability of religion to permeate and renew the very culture that is being fought over. The culture wars might be likened to two gardeners who spend all their time spraying rival brands of pesticide while forgetting to water the plants and fertilize the soil. Perhaps the most frightening thing about this syndrome is that it seems to betoken a pervasive despair about the very possibility of cultural renewal. To cite just one example of this from my personal experience: The vast majority of conservatives I have encountered are firmly convinced that almost nothing of value has been produced in Western culture for over a hundred years. There is an element of simple philistinism here, but there is also the despair of those who can only look backward.

Yet another paradox of religious humanism is that it combines a tragic sense of life—an awareness of our fallenness and the limits of human institutions—with a strain of persistent hope. T. S. Eliot once said that there are no lost causes because there are no gained causes. The religious humanist refuses to give in to apocalyptic fears, believing that grace is always available, and that the life-giving soil of culture is often seeded with suffering. If, as I believe, faith and imagination are the two primary sources of culture, then even in the darkest time it is possible to make poems and prayers out of our travails.

The new religious humanists know that culture shapes and informs politics far more powerfully than the other way around. They recognize that symbolism, imagery, and language play a crucial role in forming attitudes and prejudices, and have devoted themselves to nourishing the imaginative life. At a time when the model of Enlightenment rationalism is crumbling under the weight of postmodern cynicism and nihilism, the religious imagination can speak meaningfully into the void.

In fact, it is the novelists and poets who are at the heart of the resurgence of religious humanism in our time. An entire bookshelf of anthologies could be gleaned from such writers as Elie Wiesel, John Updike, Czeslaw Milosz, Richard Wilbur, Chaim Potok, Reynolds Price, Garrison Keillor, Anne Tyler, John Irving, Denise Levertov, Dana Gioia, Andre Dubus, Frederick Buechner, Louise Erdrich, Larry Woiwode, Tobias Wolff, Mark Helprin, Ron Hansen, Doris Betts, James Lee Burke, Michael Malone, Madeleine L'Engle, Sue Miller, Jon Hassler, J. F. Powers, Edward Hirsch, and Paul Mariani. Internationally, writers like Torgny Lindgren from Sweden, Tim Winton and Les Murray from Australia, the late Japanese novelist Shusaku Endo, and Geoffrey Hill, Muriel Spark, Piers Paul Read, and Susan Howatch from England have created a rich and enduring body of work. In the world of classical music, nearly half a dozen contemporary Christian composers have been on the bestseller lists, including Arvo Pärt from Estonia, Henryk Górecki of Poland, and John Tavener and James Macmillan from Britain. A few years ago I founded *Image: A Journal of the Arts and Religion,* a quarterly publication that gathers together the wealth of material that is emerging from this aesthetic renaissance. And yet, despite all this outpouring of creativity, many critics still make dour comments about the lack of serious religious writers and artists.

Unlike the culture warriors, with their short-term political strategies, the new generation of religious humanists are not afraid that the sky will fall any time soon; they are, in fact, willing to devote themselves to the slower rhythms of real cultural change. For example, in her essay in this anthology on "Abortion and the Search for Common Ground," Frederica Matthewes-Green reports on a remarkable dialogue that is now taking place between some members of the pro-life and pro-choice communities. Or take Wilfred McClay's essay on the role of religious faith in American higher education, which contains wisdom that, if heeded, could bring about lasting change in one of our most troubled institutions. In his essay "Second Genesis: The Biotechnology Revolution," Andrew Kimbrell demonstrates an ability to combine his environmental activism with a sacramental theory of nature and the body.

This anthology of writing by contemporary religious humanists is intended to demonstrate the vitality of their ideas, the imaginative depth and resonance of their vision, and the diversity of their interests. All of these writers are making active contributions to American culture. They include some of our most eloquent and sagacious thinkers, including Robert Coles, Wendell Berry, and Annie Dillard, as well as several outstanding representatives of the younger generation. Here, I would submit, are some of the true public intellectuals of our time.

A word about the organization of the book. The first section, "Faith and Doubt," contains a group of personal narratives that exemplify the spirit of religious humanism and anchor it in concrete experience. The next two sections, "Past and Present" and "Sacred and Profane," demonstrate the ways in which religious humanism recovers the wisdom of the past and seeks to apply it to contemporary crises. "Heaven and Earth" and "Nature and Grace" explore the role of religion in politics and culture. The last section, "Flesh and Spirit," focuses on such topics as environmentalism, biotechnology, abortion, and euthanasia; religious humanism, it seems to me, is particularly well-suited to addressing these issues of the human body and the "world's body." Although the essays in this collection span a wide range of subjects, I have resisted the temptation to supply extensive commentaries and connective material. My hope is that readers will sense for themselves the unity of vision that lies at the heart of this book.

Finally, I believe this collection proves that the old political categories of Left and Right are increasingly irrelevant. By returning to the traditional sources of their religious traditions, these writers have found themselves addressing the present in new ways. Having sought out the perennial truths of religious faith, they return to the present and find themselves sharing, often unexpectedly, spiritual and intellectual common ground. In a culture as fragmented and contentious as ours, this may be the most heartening news this generation of thinkers can bring us.

I dedicate this anthology to the memory of Gerhart Niemeyer, a scholar who has been for me, as he was for the generations of students who have been privileged to know him, a model of religious humanism.

This book is the product of conversations that I have been carrying on for more than a decade. I would like to thank Mitch Horowitz, for giving me the chance to make the results public. I also owe a great deal to my agent, Carol Mann, who knows when to give a timely pep talk. Richard Wilkinson, the managing editor of *Image,* has not only discussed the meaning of religious humanism with me but has worked tirelessly to sustain the journal we edit. My colleagues at the Intercollegiate Studies Institute (Ken Cribb, John Lulves, and Jeffrey Nelson) have been both understanding and supportive.

I would like to single out two friends—Wilfred M. McClay and Robert Royal—not only for taking the time to help me refine my understanding of religious humanism, but for exemplifying it in their own lives. I would also like to thank the following for keeping up a lively and ongoing conversation: Doris Betts, Annie Dillard, John Farina, Harold Fickett, Dana Gioia, Ron Hansen, A.G. Harmon, Russell Hittinger, Deal Hudson, Andrew Kimbrell, John Lukacs, Paul Mariani, Fr. James Massa, Frederica Mathewes-Green, Kenneth Myers, Virgil Nemoianu, Virginia Stem Owens, Paul Vitz, and Dan Wakefield.

I find it impossible to thank my wife, Suzanne, for the same reason that I don't thank my legs for carrying me about; she has been so much a part of my mental and spiritual growth that we are as much one mind as we are one flesh. There's no doubt, however, that Suzanne is the person responsible for humanizing me. Finally, I would like to thank my children—Magdalen, Helena, Charles, and Benedict—for placing mercy ahead of justice in putting up with their preoccupied father.

Part I

FAITH AND DOUBT

Believing in a Postmodern Age

ANNIE DILLARD

Annie Dillard won the Pulitzer Prize for her first book, *Pilgrim at Tinker Creek,* a personal narrative that has been frequently compared to another famous meditation on the relationship between the human and the natural worlds, Henry David Thoreau's *Walden.* She has written fiction, poetry, and memoir, as well as extended reflections on reading imaginative literature and the writing life. A convert to the Roman Catholic Church, Dillard's Christian faith has been seamlessly woven into all her writings. This excerpt is taken from her second book, *Holy the Firm* (1977), a series of brief narratives and *pensées* growing out of a period in her life when she lived alone on the Puget Sound of Washington state.

Holy the Firm

I KNOW ONLY enough of God to want to worship him, by any means ready to hand. There is an anomalous specificity to all our experience in space, a scandal of particularity, by which God burgeons up or showers down into the shabbiest of occasions, and leaves his creation's dealings with him in the hands of purblind and clumsy amateurs. This is all we are and all we ever were; God *kann nicht anders.* This process in time is history; in space, at such shocking random, it is mystery.

A blur of romance clings to our notions of "publicans," "sinners," "the poor," "people in the marketplace," "our neighbors"—as though of course God should reveal himself, if at all, to these simple people, these Sunday-school watercolor figures, who are so purely themselves in their tattered robes, who are single in themselves, while we now are various, complex, and full at heart. We are busy. So, I see now, were they. Who shall ascend into the hill of the Lord? Or who shall stand in his holy place? There is no one but us. There is no one to send, nor a clean hand, nor a pure heart on the face of the earth, nor in the earth, but only us, a generation comforting ourselves with the notion that we have come at an awkward time, that our innocent fathers are all dead—as if innocence had ever been—and our children busy and troubled, and we ourselves unfit, not yet ready, having each of us chosen wrongly, made a false start, failed, yielded to impulse and the tangled comfort of pleasures, and grown exhausted, unable to seek the thread, weak, and involved. But there is no one but us. There never has been. There have been generations which remembered, and generations which forgot; there has never been a generation of whole men and women who lived well for even one day. Yet some have imagined well, with honesty and art, the detail of such a life, and have described it with such grace that we mistake vision for history, dream for description, and fancy that life has devolved. So. You learn this studying any history at all, especially the lives of artists and visionaries; you learn it from Emerson, who noticed that the meanness of our days is itself worth our thought; and you learn it, fitful in your pew, at church.

There is one church here, so I go to it. On Sunday mornings I quit the house and wander down the hill to the white frame church in the firs. On a big Sunday there might be twenty of us there; often I am the only person under sixty, feeling as though I'm on an archaeological tour of Soviet Russia. The members are of mixed denominations; the minister is a Congregationalist and wears a white shirt. The man knows God. Once, in the middle of the long pastoral prayer of intercession for the whole world—for the gift of wisdom to its leaders, for hope and mercy to the grieving and pained, succor to the oppressed, and God's grace to all—in the middle of this he stopped and burst out, "Lord, we bring you these same petitions every week." After a shocked pause, he continued reading the prayer. Because of this, I like him very much. "Good morning!" he says after the first hymn and invocation, startling me witless every time, and we all shout back, "Good morning!"

The churchwomen all bring flowers for the altar; they haul in arrangements as big as hedges, of wayside herbs in season, and flowers from their gardens, huge bunches of foliage and blossoms as tall as I am, in vases the size of tubs and the altar still looks empty, irredeemably linoleum, and beige. We had a wretched singer once, a guest from a Canadian congregation, a hulking blond girl with chopped hair and big shoulders, who wore tinted spectacles and a long lacy dress, and sang, grinning, to faltering accompaniment, an entirely secular song about mountains. Nothing could have been more apparent than that God loved this girl; nothing could more surely convince me of God's unending mercy than the continued existence on earth of the church.

The higher Christian churches—where, if anywhere, I belong—come at God with an unwarranted air of professionalism, with authority and pomp, as though they knew what they were doing, as though people in themselves were an appropriate set of creatures to have dealings with God. I often think of the set pieces of liturgy as certain words that people have successfully addressed to God without their getting killed. In the high churches they saunter through the liturgy like Mohawks along a strand of scaffolding who have long since forgotten their danger. If God were to blast such a service to bits, the congregation would be, I believe, genuinely shocked. But in the low churches you expect it any minute. This is the beginning of wisdom.

Today is Friday, November 20. Julie Norwich is in the hospital, burned; we can get no word of her condition. People released from burn wards, I read once, have a very high suicide rate. They had not realized, before they were burned, that life could include such suffering, nor that they personally could be permitted such pain. No drugs ease the pain of third-degree burns, because burns destroy skin: the drugs simply leak into the sheets. His disciples asked Christ about a roadside beggar who had been blind from birth, "Who did sin, this man or his parents, that he was born blind?" And Christ, who spat on the ground, made a mud of his spittle and clay, plastered the mud over the man's eyes, and gave him sight, answered, "Neither hath this man sinned, nor his parents: but that the works of God should be made manifest in him." Really? If we take this answer to refer to the affliction itself—and not the subsequent cure—as "God's works made manifest," then we have, along with "Not as the world gives do I give unto you," two meager, baffling, and infuriating answers to one of the few questions worth asking, to wit, What in the Sam Hill is going on here?

The works of God made manifest? Do we really need more victims to remind us that we're all victims? Is this some sort of parade for which a conquering army shines up its terrible guns and rolls them up and down the streets for the people to see? Do we need blind men stumbling about, and little flamefaced children, to remind us what God can—and will—do?

I am drinking boiled coffee and watching the bay from the window. Almost all of the people who reef net have hauled their gears for the winter; the salmon runs are over, days are short. Still, boats come and go on the water—tankers, tugs and barges, rowboats and sails. There are killer whales if you're lucky, rafts of harlequin ducks if you're lucky, and every day the scoter and the solitary grebes. How many tons of sky can I see from the window? It is morning: morning! and the water clobbered with light. Yes, in fact, we do. We do need reminding, not of what God can do, but of what he cannot do, or will not, which is to catch time in its free fall and stick a nickel's worth of sense into our days. And we need reminding of what time can do, must only do; churn out enormity at random and beat it, with God's blessing, into our heads: that we are created, *created,* sojourners in a land we did not make, a land with no meaning of itself and no meaning we can make for it alone. Who are we to demand explanations of God? (And what monsters of perfection should we be if we did not?) We forget ourselves, picnicking; we forget where we are. There is no such thing as a freak accident. "God is at home," says Meister Eckhart, "We are in the far country."

We are most deeply asleep at the switch when we fancy we control any switches at all. We sleep to time's hurdy-gurdy; we wake, if we ever wake, to the silence of God. And then, when we wake to the deep shores of light uncreated, then when the dazzling dark breaks over the far slopes of time, then it's time to toss things, like our reason, and our will; then it's time to break our necks for home.

There are no events but thoughts and the heart's hard turning, the heart's slow learning where to love and whom. The rest is merely gossip, and tales for other times. The god of today is a tree. He is a forest of trees or a desert, or a wedge from wideness down to a scatter of stars, stars like salt, low and dumb and abiding. Today's god said: shed. He peels from eternity always, spread; he winds into time like a rind. I am or seem to be on a road walking. The hedges are just where they were. There is a corner, and a long hill, a glimpse of snow on the mountains, a slope planted in apple trees, and a store next to a pasture, where I am going to buy the communion wine.

How can I buy the communion wine? Who am I to buy the communion wine? Someone has to buy the communion wine. Having wine instead of grape juice was my idea, and of course I offered to buy it. Shouldn't I be wearing robes and, especially, a mask? Shouldn't I *make* the communion wine? Are there holy grapes, is there holy ground, is anything here holy? There are no holy grapes, there is no holy ground, nor is there anyone but us. I have an empty knapsack over my parka's shoulders; it is cold, and I'll want my hands in my pockets. According to the Rule of St. Benedict, I should say, Our hands in our pockets. "All things come of thee, O Lord, and of thine own have we given thee." There must be a rule for the purchase of communion wine. "Will that be cash, or charge?" All I know is that when I go to this store—to buy eggs, or sandpaper, broccoli, wood screws, milk—I like to tease a bit, if he'll let me, with the owners' son, two, whose name happens to be Chandler, and who himself likes to play in the big bins of nails.

And so, forgetting myself, thank God: Hullo. Hullo, short and relatively new. Welcome again to the land of the living, to time, this hill of beans. Chandler will have, as usual, none of it. He keeps his mysterious counsel. And I'm out on the road again walking, my right hand forgetting my left. I'm out on the road again walking, and toting a backload of God.

Here is a bottle of wine with a label, Christ with a cork. I bear holiness splintered into a vessel, very God of very God, the sempiternal silence personal and brooding, bright on the back of my ribs. I start up the hill.

The world is changing. The landscape begins to respond as a current upwells. It is starting to clack with itself, though nothing moves in space and there's no wind. It is starting to utter its infinite particulars, each overlapping and lone, like a hundred hills of hounds all giving tongue. The hedgerows are blackberry brambles, white snowberries, red rose hips, gaunt and clattering broom. Their leafless stems are starting to live visibly deep in their centers, as hidden as banked fires live, and as clearly as recognition, mute, shines forth from eyes. Above me the mountains are raw nerves, sensible and exultant; the trees, the grass, and the asphalt below me are living petals of mind, each sharp and invisible, held in a greeting or glance full perfectly formed. There is something stretched or jostling about the sky which, when I study it, vanishes. Why are there all these apples in the world, and why so wet and transparent? Through all my clothing, through the pack on my back and through the bottle's glass I feel the wine. Walking faster and faster, weightless, I feel the wine. It sheds light in slats through my rib cage, and fills the buttressed vaults of my ribs with light, pooled and buoyant. I am moth; I am light. I am prayer and I can hardly see.

Each thing in the world is translucent, even the cattle, and moving, cell by cell. I remember this reality. Where has it been? I sail to the crest of the hill as if blown up the slope of a swell. I see, blasted, the bay transfigured below me, the saltwater bay, far down the hill past the road to my house, past the firs and the church and the sheep in the pasture: the bay and the islands on fire and boundless beyond it, catching alight the unraveling sky. Pieces of the sky are falling down. Everything, everything, is whole, and a parcel of everything else. I myself am falling down, slowly, or slowly lifting up. On the bay's stone shore are people among whom I float, real people, gathering of an afternoon, in the cells of whose skin stream thin-colored waters in pieces that give back the general flame.

Christ is being baptized. The one who is Christ is there, and the one who is John, and the dim other people standing on cobbles or sitting on beach logs back from the bay. These are ordinary people—if I am one now, if those are ordinary sheep singing a song in the pasture.

The two men are bare to the waist. The one walks him into the water, and holds him under. His hand is on his neck. Christ is coiled and white under the water, standing on stones.

He lifts from the water. Water beads on his shoulders. I see the water in balls as heavy as planets, a billion beads of water as weighty as worlds, and he lifts them up on his back as he rises. He stands wet in the water. Each one bead is transparent, and each has a world, or the same world, light and alive and apparent inside the drop: it is all there ever could be, moving at once, past and future, and all the people. I can look into any sphere and see people stream past me, and cool my eyes with colors and the sight of the world in spectacle perishing ever, and ever renewed. I do; I deepen into a drop and see all that time contains, all the faces and deeps of the worlds and all the earth's contents, every landscape and room, everything living or made or fashioned, all past and future stars, and especially faces, faces like the cells of everything, faces pouring past me talking, and going, and gone. And I am gone.

For outside it is bright. The surface of things outside the drops has fused. Christ himself and the others, and the brown warm wind, and hair, sky, the beach, the shattered water—all this has fused. It is the one glare of holiness; it is bare and unspeakable. There is no speech nor language; there is nothing, no one thing, nor motion, nor time. There is only this everything. There is only this, and its bright and multiple noise.

I seem to be on a road, standing still. It is the top of the hill. The hedges are here, subsiding. My hands are in my pockets. There is a bottle of wine on my back, a California red. I see my feet. I move down the hill toward home.

RICHARD RODRIGUEZ

Richard Rodriguez is an essayist for "The NewsHour with Jim
Lehrer," an editor at Pacific News Service, and a contributing editor for *Harper's* magazine, *U.S. News & World Report,* and the Sunday Opinion section of the *Los Angeles Times.* He has written for
the *New York Times,* the *Wall Street Journal,* the *American Scholar,*
Time, and the *New Republic,* among other publications. He is the
author of two books, *Hunger of Memory* and *Days of Obligation: An
Argument With My Mexican Father.* This excerpt from his autobio-
graphical work *Hunger of Memory* (1982) deals with the development of his religious convictions from his childhood as the son of
Mexican immigrants to his career as a writer and scholar.

Credo

THE STEPS of the church defined the eternal square where children
played and adults talked after dinner. He remembers the way the
church building was at the center of town life. She remembers the way one
could hear the bell throughout the day, telling time. And the way the town
completely closed down for certain feastdays. He remembers that the
church spire was the first thing he'd see walking back into town. Both my
parents have tried to describe something of what it was like for them to
have grown up Catholic in small Mexican towns. They remember towns
where everyone was a Catholic.

With their move to America, my mother and father left behind that
Mexican church to find themselves (she praying in whispered Spanish) in

an Irish-American parish. In a way, they found themselves at ease in such a church. My parents had much in common with the Irish-born priests and nuns. Like my parents, the priests remembered what it was like to have been Catholic in villages and cities where everyone else was a Catholic. In their American classrooms, the nuns worked very hard to approximate that other place, that earlier kind of religious experience. For a time they succeeded. For a time I too enjoyed a Catholicism something like that enjoyed a generation before me by my parents.

I grew up a Catholic at home and at school, in private and in public. My mother and father were deeply pious *católicos;* all my relatives were Catholics. At home, there were holy pictures on a wall of nearly every room, and a crucifix hung over my bed. My first twelve years as a student were spent in Catholic schools where I could look up to the front of the room and see a crucifix hanging over the clock.

When I was a boy, anyone not a Catholic was defined by that fact and the term *non-Catholic.* The expression suggests the parochialism of the Catholicism in which I was raised. In those years I could have told you the names of persons in public life who were Catholics. I knew that Ed Sullivan was a Catholic. And Mrs. Bob Hope. And Senator John F. Kennedy. As the neighborhood newspaper boy, I knew all the names on my route; as a Catholic, I noted which open doors, which front-room windows disclosed a crucifix. At quarter to eight Sunday mornings, I saw the O'Briens and the Van Hoyts walking down the empty sidewalk past our house and I knew. Catholics were mysteriously lucky, 'chosen' by God to be nurtured a special way. Non-Catholics had souls too, of course, and somehow could get to heaven. But on Sundays they got all dressed up only to go to a church where there was no incense, no sacred body and blood, and no confessional box. Or else they slept late and didn't go to church at all. For non-Catholics, it seemed, there was all white and no yolk.

In twelve years of Catholic schooling, I learned, in fact, very little about the beliefs of non-Catholics, though the little I learned was conveyed by my teachers without hostility and with fair accuracy. All that I knew about Protestants was that they differed from Catholics. But what precisely distinguished a Baptist from a Methodist from an Episcopalian, I could not have said. I surmised the clearest notion of Protestant theology from discussions of the Reformation. At that, Protestantism emerged only as deviance from Catholic practice and thought.

Judaism was different. Before the Christian era Judaism was *my* religion, the nuns said ('We are all Jews because of Christ'). But what happened to Judaism after Christ's death to the time the modern state of Israel was founded, I could not have said. Nor did I know a thing about Hinduism or Buddhism or Islam. I knew nothing about modern secular ideologies. In civics class a great deal was said about oppressive Soviet policies; but at no time did I hear classical Marxism explained. In church, at the close of mass, the congregation prayed for "the conversion of Russia."

It is not enough to say that I grew up a ghetto Catholic. As a Catholic schoolboy, I was educated a middle-class American. Even while grammar school nuns reminded me of my spiritual separateness from non-Catholics, they provided excellent *public* schooling. A school day began with prayer—the Morning Offering. Then there was the Pledge of Allegiance to the American flag. Religion class followed immediately. But afterward, for the rest of the day, I was taught well those skills of numbers and words crucial to my Americanization. Soon I became as Americanized as my classmates—most of whom were two or three generations removed from their immigrant ancestors, and all of whom were children of middle-class parents.

When we were eleven years old, the nuns would warn us about the dangers of mixed marriage (between a Catholic and a non-Catholic). And we heard a priest say that it was a mortal sin to read newspaper accounts of a Billy Graham sermon. But the ghetto Catholic Church, so defensive, so fearful of contact with non-Catholics, was already outdated when I entered the classroom. My classmates and I were destined to live in a world very different from that which the nuns remembered in Ireland or my parents remembered in Mexico. We were destined to live on unhallowed ground, beyond the gated city of God.

I was in high school when Kennedy's picture went up on the wall. And I remember feeling that he was "one of us." His election to the presidency, however, did not surprise me as it did my father. Nor was I encouraged by it. I did not take it as evidence that Catholics could, after all, participate fully in

American public life. (I assumed that to be true.) When I was a senior in high school, consequently, I did not hesitate to apply to secular colleges.

It was to be in college, at Stanford, that my religious faith would seem to me suddenly pared. I would remain a Catholic, but a Catholic defined by a non-Catholic world. This is how I think of myself now. I remember my early Catholic schooling and recall an experience of religion very different from anything I have known since. Never since have I felt so much at home in the church, so easy at mass. My grammar school years especially were the years when the great church doors opened to enclose me, filling my day as I was certain the church filled all time. Living in a community of shared faith, I enjoyed much more than mere social reinforcement of religious belief. Experienced continuously in public and private, Catholicism shaped my whole day. It framed my experience of eating and sleeping and washing; it named the season and the hour.

The sky was full then, and the coming of spring was a religious event. I would awaken to the sound of garage doors creaking open and know without thinking that it was Friday and that my father was on his way to six-thirty mass. I saw, without bothering to notice, statues at home and at school of the Virgin and of Christ. I would write at the top of my arithmetic or history homework the initials *Jesus, Mary,* and *Joseph.* (All my homework was thus dedicated.) I felt the air was different, somehow still and more silent on Sundays and high feastdays. I felt lightened, transparent as sky, after confessing my sins to a priest. Schooldays were routinely divided by prayers said with classmates. I would not have forgotten to say grace before eating. And I would not have turned off the light next to my bed or fallen asleep without praying to God.

Now. I go to mass every Sunday. Old habits persist. But it is an English mass I attend, a ritual of words. A ritual that seeks to feed my mind and would starve my somewhat metaphorical soul. The mass is less ornamental; it has been "modernized," tampered with, demythologized, deflated. The priest performs fewer gestures. His central role as priest—intermediary between congregation and God—is diminished. Symbols have changed. A reciprocal relationship between people and clergy is dramatized as the congregation takes an active role in the recitation of the mass.

The priest faces the people, his back to the tabernacle. And the effect of this rearrangement is to make the mass seem less a prayer directed to God, more a communal celebration of the Eucharist. There is something occasional about it all, and no occasion for pomp or solemnity. No longer is the congregation moved to a contemplation of the timeless; rather, it is the idiomatic one hears. One's focus is upon this place. This time. The moment. Now.

In the old Latin mass my mother could recite her rosary while still being at one with prayer at the altar. The new English mass is unilinear, lacking density; there is little opportunity for private prayer. The English words enforce attention. Emphasis is on the communal prayer, communal identity. There is a moment just before the Communion when members of the congregation shake hands to dramatize a union. We nod and bow, shake hands like figures on a music box.

I go along with the Kiss of Peace, but paradoxically I feel isolated sitting in half-empty churches among people I am suddenly aware of not knowing. The kiss signifies to me a betrayal of the older ceremonial liturgy. I miss that high ceremony. I am saddened by inappropriate music about which it is damning enough to say that it is not good enough, and not even the best of its authentic kind: folk, pop, quasi-religious Broadway show tunes. I miss the old trappings—trappings that disclosed a different reality. I have left church early, walked out, after hearing the congregation spontaneously applaud its own singing. And I have wondered how the church I loved could have changed so quickly and completely.

I continue to claim my Catholicism. Invariably I arrive late at somebody's brunch or tennis party—the festivities of a secular Sunday. Friends find it peculiar that I still go to mass; most have heard me complain about liturgical changes. Amid the orange juice and croissants I burlesque the folk-mass liturgy ("Kumbaya"), the peppy tambourine. Those listening find my sarcasm amusing. And someone says that my Catholicism is a mere affectation, an attempt to play the Evelyn Waugh eccentric to a bland and vulgar secular age.

I am not surprised. I do not know myself, not with any certainty, how much I really am saying when I profess Catholicism. In a cultural sense, I remain a Catholic. My upbringing has shaped in me certain attitudes that have not worn thin over the years. I am, for example, a materialist largely because I was brought up to believe in the central mystery of the church—the redemptive Incarnation. (I carried the heavy gold crucifix in church ceremonies far too often to share the distrust of the material still prevalent in modern Puritan America.) I am a man who trusts a society that is carefully ordered by figures of authority. (I respond to policemen in the same tone of voice I used years ago, addressing parish priests and nuns.) I realize that I am a Catholic, moreover, when I listen skeptically to a political thinker describe with enthusiasm a scheme for lasting political change. (My historical pessimism was determined by grammar school lessons about sin, especially original sin.)

More important than any of this, I continue to believe the central tenets of the church. I stand at the Creed of the mass. Though it is exactly then, at that very moment in the liturgy, when I must realize how different the church has become in recent years. I stand as a stranger among strangers. For the truth is, it is not only the church that has changed; I've changed as well.

My Catholicism changed when I was in high school. The liturgy was just then beginning to be altered. It was not simply that I found a different church when I went to church; I went to church less often. (My high school was not connected to a neighborhood church the way my grammar school had been. There were, consequently, few school days interrupted by worship.) Liturgy was something for Sunday.

My high school, staffed by the Christian Brothers, offered a more "Protestant" education. My freshman literature teacher and other high school teachers encouraged my intellectual independence. Religious instruction became rigorously intellectual. With excitement I'd study complex Pauline and Thomistic theology, and I'd remember with something like scorn the simple instructions of *The Baltimore Catechism*. In high school I started saying that I *believed* in Catholicism. My faith was buttressed by a book by Jacques Maritain rather than by the experience of worship at a Lenten service with classmates or serving at some old lady's funeral. Those years were marked by the realization that my parents assumed a Catholicism very different from mine. My parents seemed to me piously simple—like the nuns I remembered—and unwilling to entertain intellectual challenges. They would rely on their rosary every night, while in another room I read patristic theology.

In college I had few Catholic friends and fewer Catholic teachers. Most of my friends had been raised as Protestants or Jews; many referred to themselves as agnostics. During my college years I started reading Protestant theology. The church was no longer my sole spiritual teacher. I blended Catholicism with borrowed insights from Sartre and Zen and Buber and Miltonic Protestantism. And Freud.

I was a senior at Stanford during the last year of the Vatican Council. I cheered for the liberal bishops and cardinals at that great convocation. (The villains, in my view, were the conservatives of the Roman Curia.) I welcomed the church's attempts at reconciliation with other religions. I approved of the liberal encyclicals concerning "the church in the modern world." But I was changing rather more quickly than the Council fathers were changing the church. I was already a "new Catholic." I didn't wait for the American bishops to terminate the observance of meatless Fridays before I ate what looked best in the dormitory cafeteria on Friday nights. Nor did I request a dispensation from a priest when a non-Catholic friend asked me to be his best man. I simply agreed and stood beside him in a Methodist church.

I would go to friends for advice when I was troubled; I didn't go to priests anymore. I stopped going to confession, not because my behavior conflicted with the teachings of the institutional church but because I no longer thought to assess my behavior against those standards. A Catholic who lived most of his week without a sense of communal Catholicism, I relied upon conscience as never before. The priest who was the college chaplain would regularly say in his sermons that a Catholic must rely upon conscience as his ultimate guide. It seemed so to me. But I remember feeling uneasy when that priest was later excommunicated for having been secretly married.

Throughout college and graduate school, I thought of myself as an orthodox Catholic. I was a liberal Catholic. In all things save the liturgy I was a liberal. From the start I despised the liturgical reformation. In college chapels I would listen to folk singing and see plain altars draped with bright appliqué banners: JOY! GOD IS LOVE. One Sunday I would watch dancers in leotards perform some kind of ballet in front of the altar; one

Sunday there would be a rock mass; one Sunday the priest encouraged us to spend several minutes before the Offertory introducing ourselves, while a small, bad jazzy combo punched out a cocktail mix. I longed for the Latin mass. Incense. Music of Bach. Ceremonies of candles and acolytes.

Over the last several years, I have visited many Catholic churches in the several cities I have lived in: Palo Alto, New York, Berkeley, Los Angeles, London, San Francisco. I have wandered on Sundays from church to church. But in all the churches I have had to listen to the new English mass. The proclamation of faith, the Creed, I hear recited by the congregation around me. "We believe in God. . . ." In the abandoned Latin service it was the priest alone who spoke the affirmation of faith. It was the priest who said, "Credo . . ." using the first person singular. The differences between the old service and the new can be summarized in this change. At the old mass, the priest's Credo ("I believe") reminded the congregation of the fact that each person stands before God as an individual, implying at the same time—because the priest could join all voices in his—the union of believers, the consolation of communal faith. The listener was assured of his membership in the church; he was not alone before God. (The church would assist him.) By translating credo into the English first person plural, the church no longer reminds the listener that he is alone. "We believe," the congregation is encouraged to say, celebrating community—but only that fact.

I would protest this simplification of the liturgy if I could. I would protest as well the diminished sense of the sacred in churches today. I would protest the use of folk music and the hand-holding. Finally, though, I cannot. I suspect that the reason I despise the new liturgy is because it is mine. It reflects and attempts to resolve the dilemma of Catholics just like me. The informal touches; the handshaking; the folk music; the insistence upon union—all these changes are aimed at serving Catholics who no longer live in a Catholic world. To such Catholics—increasingly alone in their faith—the church says: You are part of a community of believers. You are not single in your faith. Not solitary. We are together, Catholics, *We* believe. We believe. We believe. This assurance is necessary because, in a sense, it no longer is true.

The Catholic Church of my past required no such obvious reminders of community as smiles and handshakes before the Communion. The old mass proceeded with sure, blind pomp precisely because Catholics had faith in their public identity as Catholics; the old liturgy was ceremonial because of the Church's assumption that worship is a public event. The lack of high ceremony in church today betrays a loss of faith in communal Catholicism. In obvious ways everyone in the congregation seems closer and more aware of each other. As a group, throughout mass, the congregation responds to the priest with various prayers; one listens to a steady flow of prayers said in English. But there is scant opportunity for private prayer. The church cannot dare it.

A priest I once heard in a white middle-class parish defended the reformed liturgy by saying that it had become necessary to "de-Europeanize" the Roman Catholic Church. He said that Catholicism must translate God's word into the many languages and cultures of the world. I suppose he is right. I do not think, however, that the primary impetus for liturgical reformation came from Third World Catholics. I think rather that it came in response to a middle-class crisis of faith in North America and Western Europe. The new liturgy is suited especially to those who live in the secular city, alone in their faith for most of the week. It is not a liturgy suited to my parents or grandparents as much as to me.

When I go to church on Sunday I am forced to recognize a great deal about myself. I would rather go to a high ceremonial mass, reap for an hour or two its communal assurance. The sentimental solution would be ideal: to remain a liberal Catholic and to worship at a traditional mass. But now that I no longer live as a Catholic in a Catholic world, I cannot expect the liturgy—which reflects and cultivates my faith—to remain what it was. I will continue to go to the English mass. I will go because it is my liturgy. I will, however, often recall with nostalgia the faith I have lost. And I will be uneasy knowing that the old faith was lost as much by *choice* as it was inevitably lost. My education may have made it inevitable that I would become a citizen of the secular city, but I have come to *embrace* the city's values: social mobility, pluralism, egalitarianism, self-reliance. By choice I do not confine myself to Catholic society. Most of my friends and nearly all of my intimates are non-Catholics. With them I normally will observe the politesse of secular society concerning religion—say nothing about it. By choice I do not pray before eating lunch in a downtown restaurant. (My public day is not divided by prayer.) By choice I do not consult the movie ratings of the Legion of Decency, and my reading is not curtailed by the Index. By choice I am ruled by conscience rather than the authority of priests I consider my equals. I do not listen to papal pronouncements with which I disagree.

Recently, bishops and popes who have encouraged liturgical reforms have seemed surprised at the insistence of so many Catholics to determine for themselves the morality of such matters as divorce, homosexuality, contraception, abortion, and extramarital sex. But the church fathers who initiated rituals that reflect a shared priesthood of laity and clergy should not be surprised by the independence of modern Catholics. The authoritarian church belonged to another time. It was an upper-class church; it was a lower-class church. It was a hierarchical church. It was my grandparents' church.

If I ask questions about religion that my grandparents didn't ask, it is not because I am intellectually advanced. I wonder about the existence of God because, unlike my grandparents, I live much of my day in a secular city where I do not measure the hours with the tolling bells of a church. As a boy, I believed in God by believing in His church. Now that my faith in communal Catholicism is so changed, my faith in God is without certain foundation. It occurs to me to ask that profound question of modern agnosticism: Is God dead?

I would cry into the void. . . . If I should lose my faith in God. I would have no place to go to where I could feel myself a man. The Catholic church of my youth mediated with special grace between the public and private realms of my life, such was the extent of its faith in itself. That church is no longer mine. I cling to the new Catholic Church. Though it leaves me unsatisfied, I fear giving it up, falling through space. Even in today's Catholic Church, it is possible for me to feel myself in the eye of God, while I kneel in the presence of others.

If God is dead, where shall I go for such an experience? In this modern post-religious age, secular institutions flounder to imitate the gift that is uniquely found in the temple and mosque and church. Secular institutions lack the key; they have no basis for claiming access to the realm of the private. When they try to deny their limits, secular institutions only lie. They pretend that there is no difference between public and private life. The worst are totalitarian governments. They respect no notion of privacy. They intrude into a family's life. They ignore the individual's right to be private. They would bulldoze the barrier separating the public from the private. They create the modern nightmare of institutional life.

If God is dead I will cry into the void.

There was a time in my life when it would never have occurred to me to make a confession like this one. There was a time when I would never have thought to discuss my spiritual life, even with other Catholics I knew intimately. It is true that in high school I read Augustine's *Confessions,* but that extraordinary autobiography did not prompt my imitation. Just the reverse: There seemed to me something non-Catholic about the *Confessions.* I intuited that such revelations made Augustine a Protestant church father more than a Catholic father.

Years after, in college, I remember reading the diaries of seventeenth-century Puritans. To encounter "simple" people—a tradesman, a housewife, a farmer—describing their spiritual lives in detail amazed me. The Protestant confession was boldly different from the Catholic sacrament of Confession. The Protestants were public about their spiritual lives in a way that I, as a Catholic schoolboy, could never have been. Protestants were so public because they were otherwise alone in their faith. I marveled at the paradox implied by their writings. Those early "pure" English Protestants, strangers to ceremony, and for their own reasons alien from the institutional church, were attempting to form through their writings a new kind of Christian community—a community of those who share with each other only the experience of standing alone before God. It was then that I began to realize the difference separating the individualistic Protestant from the institutional Catholic. Now I realize that I have become like a Protestant Christian. I call myself a Christian.

My own Catholic Church in recent years has become more like a Protestant church. Perhaps Protestants will teach Catholics like me how to remain believers when the sense one has for so much of one's day is of being alone in faith. If, in fact, my spiritual fathers are those seventeenth-century Puritans, there is one important difference between their writings and mine. I am writing about my religious life, aware that most of my readers do not consider themselves religious. With them—with you—I am making this admission of faith. It is appropriate that I do so. The resolution of my spiritual dilemma, if there is to be one before death, will have to take place where it began, among persons who do not share my religious convictions. Persons like my good friends now, those who, smiling, wonder why I am more than an hour late for their Sunday brunch.

GERALD EARLY

Gerald Early is Merle Kling Professor of Modern Letters in the Department of English in Arts and Sciences at Washington University in St. Louis, where he is also director of the African and Afro-American Studies Program in Arts and Sciences. He is the author of *The Culture of Bruising: Essays on Prizefighting, Literature, and Modern American Culture,* which won the National Book Critics Circle Award, and *One Nation Under a Groove: Motown and American Culture.* He also edited the anthology *Lure and Loathing: Essays on Race, Identity, and the Ambivalence of Assimilation.* The material below is excerpted from his book *Daughters: On Family and Fatherhood* (1994). In the first section, Early speaks of his faith and his concern, as a father and a cultural critic, to search out and celebrate the existence of "righteousness." In the second section, he recounts his lifelong passion for baseball, and describes an attempt to tell his daughters about his own childhood.

Faith and Fatherhood

I MIGHT ADD here simply that this book is suffused with a kind of Christian thought (but nothing for which I would use such an elevated term as *theology*). Let us say that this book has a certain subtle preoccupation with, to use a quaint word, righteousness, and, to use a more quaint word, mercy. And it would seem that a family is as good a place to be concerned about these matters as, say, society at large or this incredibly unjust world as we know it. This, I suppose, is hardly surprising for a man whose personal hero is Edmund Campion—whom my daughters call Champion and whom my wife thought for a goodly time was the hero of mystery novels. My children are not, in fact, Christians, in the sense that they have never been baptized, although they do attend a church on a fairly regular basis. In other words, I like to think of this book, in part, as a story of family and its faith struggle. I suppose that I am deeply devoted to my religion, to the faith—that is, if I might ever learn to be worthy of it.

I remember as a boy hearing the Bells of Joy sing a song played on the black gospel radio station nearly every Sunday called "Let's Talk About Jesus" and other groups such as the Harmonizing Four singing "All things Are Possible (If You Only Believe)," the Dixie Hummingbirds' "In the Morning (When the Dark Clouds Roll Away)," the Davis Sisters, the Caravans, Mahalia Jackson's "How I Got Over," a favorite of my mother, and the Golden Gate Gospel Quartet singing a song I learned in Sunday School:

> Children, Go Where I Send Thee,
> O, How Shall I Send Thee?
> Well, I'm gonna send you
> Five by Five
> Five for the five that came back alive
> Four for the four that stood at the door
> And Three for the Hebrew children
> And Two for Paul and Silas
> And One for the little, bitty baby
> Born, Born, Born in Bethlehem.

I thought as a boy that there could be no greater life than to sing praise to God. There could be no greater life than kneeling—without pad, to be more holy—as an altar boy at the small black Episcopal church of my boyhood listening to our old Bahamian priest—all of us Bahamian-descended black folk belonged to three Episcopal churches in the city—intone in a richly accented sing-songy chant from the *Book of Common Prayer:*

> All glory be to thee, Almighty God, our heavenly Father, for that thou, of thy tender mercy, didst give thine only Son Jesus Christ to suffer death upon the Cross for our redemption; who made there (by his one oblation

of himself once offered) a full, perfect, and sufficient sacrifice, oblation, and satisfaction, for the sins of the whole world; and did institute, and in his holy Gospel command us to continue, a perpetual memory of that his precious death and sacrifice until his coming again. . . .

And the hazy, incensed, sunlit silence would break when I had rung the bell, signaling the transubstantiation, and I would think to myself in that mystic moment, "O God, never let me leave this place." Then I would look at Victor Pettijohn—our thurifer, then our master of ceremonies— every Sunday, with his cool saintly professionalism with the censer, with his aiding of the priest, with his supervision of the other acolytes and, thrilled beyond telling, beyond ordinary measure, would just say to myself, "Boy!" I was disappointed to learn that when Rosalind took my *Book of Common Prayer* it was not to read but to fill a space in her bookshelf, as its unusual size gave her collection symmetry. "I'm glad she's not into that voodoo nonsense of watered-down Catholicism anyway," Ida the Baptist says, truly spoken by someone who spent six years in a segregated Catholic school in Dallas.

Ida, my wise counsel, is as dedicated to virtue, and to the possibilities and expressiveness of sheer goodness, as perhaps any human being I have ever met. She understands intuitively the human heart. I, on the other hand, am more conflicted, even, sometimes, confounded by such matters. But this admission about faith struggle should hardly be striking for an author who reads passages from *The Confessions of Augustine* and Bunyan's *Grace Abounding to the Chief of Sinners* nearly every week.

I doubt if my children believe anything remotely Christian. I have read significant chunks of the Bible to them, and their response is that it is a nice story but, as Rosalind put it, "Who can believe that stuff?" And Ida has been more than a little annoyed at the three of us in church, making doodles, and suffocating laughs from private jokes when the minister is delivering his sermons. "You act more like a kid than they do; you are shaming me in church," she scolded. For periods of time, I will straighten up, chastising Rosalind and Linnet for not paying attention to the sermon, for acting disruptive during the service, but this enforcement does not last long. There is something about church, its sanctified boredom, that brings out the kid in me that was suppressed when I was a kid, and I am very glad to have my children for company when I am there. In fact, I hate the idea of going without them.

"Why do the faithful go to church?" asked a Catholic priest once of Linnet when she, having a sudden urge to investigate Catholicism, went with me to a nearby Catholic church to find out about it.

"Well," said Linnet nervously, put on edge by the inquisitorial nature of the discussion, looking desperately at me for a sense of the right answer.

"Tell him why *you* go to church," I said quietly.

And she seemed at once markedly relieved by having the question placed in the personal.

"Oh, I go to church," she said, "to make friends and have a good time."

The priest thought this to be a fairly, well, lackluster answer, bordering between childishness and improper parental instruction.

"Did I give the wrong answer?" Linnet asked sheepishly when we left.

"No," I said, laughing. "That's the most sensible answer I've ever heard for joining a church."

"I mean," Linnet continued, "when the priest started talking about sacraments and catechism and all that stuff I didn't understand, I thought, well, it kinda sounded like school. I don't want to join a church if it's just like being in school. I felt maybe I wouldn't be smart enough for that religion, because I'm L.D. [Learning Disabled].

"I don't want to struggle and feel dumb trying to learn a religion. But would you have taken me to a Catholic church if I had wanted to go?"

"Yes," I said, "I would have gone with you for as long as you wanted to go."

"But you wouldn't have become Catholic?" she asked.

"No," I said. "But I would have supported you if that was what you really wanted to do."

So ended the adventure with Catholicism.

"I'll believe if you do," Linnet said once after I read the story of the Resurrection from Mark.

A long time passed before I answered.

"Do you believe it?" she asked again. "Do you, Daddy?"

"Yes," I said at last. "But you shouldn't believe just because I do. Don't ever say that again." And I shut the Bible and walked away from the table.

"Your children love you very much," Ida said. "They admire you. They worship the ground you walk on. You hurt them when you say something like that. You could go a long way toward making them believers. What's wrong with them believing because you do?"

"Because," I said to Ida, "I might be wrong. I might be a hypocrite. I might be a liar. Because of all the things I know I never can be and all the base things that I know that I am, they cannot believe *through* me. Who knows? One day their relationship with me might change for the worse, and that shouldn't determine the question of their faith. Mark Twain was right when he said that if religion were truly a matter of freedom of conscience and not family conformity, then any given family should be a mixture of Christians, agnostics, Buddhists, Jews, and anything else. Rosalind and Linnet must believe on their accord and in their own way."

"Okay, but don't make this business too intellectual or too spiritual," Ida warned. "After all, the fact that you believe should mean something to them. You know that old blues song you like to play, 'You're Gonna Need Somebody on Your Bond.' People need the assurance that other people believe."

This book then is the story of a faith struggle, of how the members of a family come to believe in each other and, through this, I think, to believe in that which not only makes belief in ourselves possible, but makes it matter. Ida was right: We're all gonna need somebody on our bond. It is also a story where race, oddly, plays only a very small role; class is a great deal more important. But mostly this is a tale that turns on the mundane events of our lives: how people living together understand and support each other—even take joy in knowing each other—despite petty annoyances, blatant misunderstandings, embarrassments, ordinary but stressful trials, numerous insensitivities, moments of utter cowardice, and both inadvertent and willful ignorance.

"Do you like being a parent—you know, being a father, having children and all?" Linnet once asked me.

"Yes," I said, after a moment. "It's like dancing with a partner. It takes a lot of effort to do it well. But when it's done well it's a beautiful thing to see."

". . . To Know You're Alive"

For I have the blessing of God in the three Points of manhood,
of the pen, of the sword, & of chivalry.
—Christopher Smart, *Rejoice in the Lamb*

Stretched out against a blue, hard, indifferent sky.
Taut and poised as a dancer's muscled stillness.
As a mouse upon a cat's bare, bloody throat,
As the bloody lines of empire dimly netting the throes.
As the distant church-spire pressed tight against the wire.
Is the season of our joy and pain flung in its dimensions
Of balls and strikes and fouls and errors and outs and pauses,
Boredom and spit, a soft, soft waster of time, the irrelevant
Gallantry of outfielders outstretched for catches: The Game.
And this we watch—o splendid errand—against the blue, hard sky,
The men below in a child's game that only, then,
Those men, magically, can play to provide, in grace,
For us, the throng, at last, the will to outlast that sorrow
Against which this dubious contentment is our only flight
To a tremulous childhood of tumultuous peace, that, spoken in the
Tragic speech of prayer, alas, can bring us, rejoicing in that
Regeneration abounding (This, then, the only love that's left
In that stolen expanse of our glory!), fairly struck in the sunlit
Reaches of our grievance and our divine repair.
—Gerald Early, "The Green Fields of America (Paths of
Our Republic)"

There is a certain sweet but taut madness that descends upon the culture during the late summer and early fall. Those who are lovers of baseball know this as the "pennant chase." In the dead of summer, the long season moves along with a bit of contented leisure, with the assurance that, after all, for everyone, players and fans alike, there is always another game. But suddenly with the advent of autumn, there is the ferocious realization that not only will it end but it must end—what might be called, to borrow a term from a famous musician, a ferocious longing to come to its own resolution at last. And it is during these days, when light is less, that watching a baseball game is a bit like taking the final measurement of an unavoidable metaphysical truism: namely, that enacted on the field is the proposition that the urgency of an implacable fate always thwarts the expectancy of a well-tempered design. In other words, nature is not bound to obey any plan, no matter how wonderfully constructed. It is the old saw about man proposing but God disposing. It is a rule that I learned from being a passionate lover of baseball since I was a boy.

If I could have run around as a boy with a tin whistle, a water pistol, a foldable kite, a large collection of bats and sticks and gloves for baseball and stickball, and my newspapers and shopping bags, I would have been ecstatically happy and I could have died at the age of twelve and never felt I missed anything in life—not sex, not education, not adulthood, not marriage, not family.

"My sister Rosalind first taught me about the game of baseball—not playing it, but following the pro game," I told Linnet and Rosalind. "She taught me about a team called the Milwaukee Braves and about players named Hank Aaron, Eddie Mathews, and Joe Adcock. I must have been about six or seven, because it was the late fifties, when the Braves were a championship team. I have always had an interest in them ever since because of that. She also gave me baseball cards and taught me how to read a box score."

"You learned about baseball from a girl?!" Rosalind said, "From my Aunt Rosalind? That's something."

> *The single desire that dominated my search for delight was*
> *simply to love and to be loved.*
> —Saint Augustine, *The Confessions*

There was a week where I took first Rosalind, then Linnet, to baseball games with me. I have had season's tickets to the St. Louis Cardinals now for a few years, but my daughters do not go to the games with me very often. I dreamed of teaching them how to score the games and making them fans, but at the games themselves they take very little interest. I showed them how to score: Rosalind picked it up fairly easily but was soon very bored with it. Linnet never truly understood it and I did not press the matter as, after all, there was no need, in my mind, to make attending a baseball game something like going to school all over again. What always interested them about going to the games, aside from the food (children, I suppose, will always be thrilled at the chance of eating bad, cheap, greasy food somewhere outside home), was my own love of the game. I could sometimes feel them looking at me, hunched in my seat, watching the game with a kind of tension that would not indicate love at all but agony and anxiety. I never cheer plays, never boo failure; indeed, except at moments when I provide them with some commentary on what is going on, I am usually silent.

One afternoon during a particular week when we had seen games nearly back-to-back, they were looking at a picture of me when I was boy of about eight. It is the only picture they have seen of me as a boy (so few were taken, and most of those were lost). I am standing, with three other boys, in front of the altar of my church. We are all in our Sunday best, but I am the only one wearing a coat—a trench coat, buttoned to my throat. I remember the coat well and the day of the picture. It was an Easter Sunday. I am smiling to beat the band in the picture.

"You were a cute little boy," Linnet said, holding the picture out to me.

"Yeah," said Rosalind, laughing, "big happy smile, big block head."

"I wish I could have known you when you were a boy," Linnet said, almost with a tone of poignant regret.

"Me, too," said Rosalind. "I bet you were a nice little boy."

"You guys don't even like boys," I said grinning. "Besides, you wouldn't have liked me. I was a boring little boy. All I liked was baseball. It was all I thought about as a boy. It was all I wanted to play. I loved to play it and I loved to watch the professionals play it."

"Why did you like baseball so much, Daddy?" Linnet asked.

"You know," I said, casting my mind back a bit, "there would be these days, terribly hot summer days, and no one when I was a boy had air-conditioning except the movie houses, a few corner grocery stores, and a couple of the Italian homeowners in the neighborhood. Well, on those days especially, there would be a group of us black boys who would get together to play baseball, softball, stickball, anything, somewhere in the heat. All day long that is what we would do. And before each game, just as we saw done in the major-league games, we would sing the national anthem, the whole bunch of us, before we played a game. Can you imagine that? A group of black boys out in some lot in the heat singing the national anthem? We didn't even like the song and most of us didn't like to sing but we did because that was how the professionals did it. Well, it was at those moments of singing the national anthem like that, a bunch of raggedy black boys, that I really loved baseball most of all because it made me feel like an American. I felt like I was part of the country."

They were silent for a time, I suppose more impressed by this response than they should have been.

"But," I said suddenly, "that's not all. That's not quite it. I mean, I loved baseball, watching the pros play because I was a fatherless boy without brothers and so I could watch those young men and imagine one of them as an older brother or as my father. I loved baseball as a boy because . . ."

As I was saying this my thoughts drifted back to my father and how much I, when I was a boy, wished I could have known him, not as a man, but when he was a boy. I wished that I could have grown up with him, that he could have been my best friend, that we could have sung the national anthem together, and could have gone to games. My father and I would walk arm in arm, a fantasy so intense that I would sometimes see him before me, imagine him there, talk to him. So intense a fantasy was it that at times as a child I thought my make-believe was a sure sign that I was crazy. Whose little boy are you? For years, I lied to my childhood friends, telling them that my father wanted to name me after him, wanted to name me Henry.

"He wanted to," I would say proudly, "but my mom wouldn't let him." But I knew, all along, the story that he hated his name, that he would never have given it to me. But all children wish to know their parents as children, wish to know the origin of these people who rather spring upon them fully grown, fully developed, fully being what they are.

I finished my thought to my daughters: ". . . because it made me feel less lonely."

"Well," said Linnet, after a moment, "we still wish we could have known you as a boy. You were probably real nice. Not like the boys we know. I bet it would have been fun going to a baseball game with you when you were a boy."

"Yea," said Rosalind, "going to a baseball game with that smiley little boy with the big block head. That would have been fun."

I remembered what I had once read in the Richard Wright novel *The Outsider*, about the tragic protagonist, Cross Damon: "It was the restrictions of marriage, the duties to children, obligations to friends, to sweethearts, and blood kin that he had struck at so blindly and—gallantly?" But it was in the very "restrictions of marriage" and of family life that I had gained the greatest sense of freedom and the highest form of liberation. For it was through being bound to others that I found that I could lose myself, escape the entrapment of solipsism, cease the restless search for that fulfillment of myself simply through acts of absorption.

During a tense moment in our marriage, many years ago, Ida and I sat across from one another, I on a crate and she on a piano bench. It was a Sunday afternoon. We had just come from church, and it was then that I had to decide if I wanted to stay married.

"Do you want a life," she asked me, "or just the trappings of a life? Do you want to grow or do you simply wish to say, 'I had these things, some experiences with women.' You're not wrong if you want something else, Gerald. But dammit, you've got to want what you want."

"I want my children," I said, quietly, and after a moment, "to understand the qualities of devotion and virtue."

"Well, you can live it, hope for the best, and be called a fool. Or not live it, hope for the best, and be called a hypocrite," Ida said.

Later that same afternoon, while Ida sat at the kitchen table flipping through catalogues and I rummaged through the pots and pans to begin making Sunday dinner, I felt for a moment—considering the scene—how much life goes on, that a certain kind of serenity, ironically, transcends even the greatest domestic turbulence. I turned to Ida, measuring my words with some care:

"I'm ashamed to admit it but I have not always *tried* to be a good man. There were times when it was easier not to be and I took the easy way. And although I tried much harder, I have sometimes failed as a husband and I'm sure you've been disappointed in me from time to time. But I have never *not* tried to be a good father. Never! I may not always have succeeded, but I've never stopped *trying* to be a good father. I can bear the price I must pay for my lack of vigilance in some aspects of my life, but never for any lack of vigilance as a father."

And Ida, legs crossed, tilted her head as the late afternoon sun came through the kitchen window, tinting her hair, splashing on the table like a light water, and, without looking directly at me, smiled. It was the first time in a while that she had done that, and I smiled too.

"Try?" she said softly. "Try? *Anybody* can try. Trying is nothing. Succeeding is everything in this world and in this life."

I cocked my head a bit, recognizing my own rhetoric—exactly the same words I would say to myself when I had not done well on some writing project or in the classroom, exactly the same words I would say to Linnet or Rosalind to goad them to achieve. I had been told as a boy that Babe Ruth had once said those same words to Joe Louis shortly before Louis fought for the title. It had always stayed with me.

Her smile had broadened to a grin. She was simply badgering me in a playful way with my own bromides. She looked almost happy, and very girlish—like someone, some pink-dressed girl, a boy would ask to dance.

"Some people have succeeded more than they think they have," she said. "Besides, don't put too much pressure on yourself to be more than anybody's got a right to expect. I wouldn't be much of a woman if I couldn't deal with some disappointments and you wouldn't be much of a man if you couldn't deal with them either.

"You know," she continued, out of the blue, "I could never play Pinochle. Could never learn to play the game. At least, not with you Philadelphia Negroes. The cards moved too fast and I was always getting my head rubbed."

"I guess I'm not a typical Philadelphia Negro. I could never play it either. The same thing happened to me," I said musingly.

"Well, what's for dinner?" she asked.

Shortly after this conversation with Ida, I thought of my mother, who during all of her years of widowhood, all my growing-up years, adolescent years, young-adult years, had never had a man spend the night in our

house. I had been permitted to grow up free from the emotional entangle-
ments of her life, never burdened with how my mother felt about some
man, or if she suffered. I had been free to think only and constantly about
myself. Such a wonderful gift to give to a child! When I became an adult I
thought this such a sacrifice.

"Listen," my mother said to me once recently, "why make your life
harder than you have to? I sacrificed, but I never denied myself anything."
What I learned in this conversation with my mother was that you do what
you have to, not so that you can do what you want but because doing what
you have to is what you want. There was no trace of sentimentality when
she said this, and I realized there was none because, after all, she had done
this as much for herself as for her children, because she had never, once,
felt an ounce of sentimentality about having children or living with them.

And so I thought as well, then, at that moment, thinking about my
mother, *Why make my life harder than I have to?*

I looked at my daughters, and my boyhood picture, and appreciated the
gift of parenthood, at that moment, more than any other gift I have ever
been given. For what person, except one's own children, would want so
deeply and sincerely to have shared your childhood? Who else would
think your insignificant and petty life so precious in the living, so rich in its
expressiveness, that it would be worth partaking of what you were to understand what you are? And so in the end I fulfill my needs by discovering
that I mean this much to my children, more than I could possibly mean to
anyone else. Sidney Poitier once wrote, "The word 'Daddy' held some
magical connotations for me." But it was the absence of the word in my
own life, never having called anyone that, that made me think it less a
naming of a category than the unstoppable expression of an artifice that
imagines itself an aspiration. That someone would call me what I had always yearned to call someone else was not a fulfillment but a triumphant
disquietude, a quirky, spotty redemption.

I could not stop laughing at the sheer wonder of the thought. So I
laughed and laughed, though my daughters, nonplussed, did not, I am
sure, think that the picture of the big-headed boy smiling to beat the band
was as funny as all that.

Mr. Rogers is right: It *is* such a good feeling to know you're alive.

KATHLEEN NORRIS

Kathleen Norris burst onto the literary scene with her 1993 memoir *Dakota: A Spiritual Geography,* which became a surprise national best-seller. In it, she describes her return to her childhood Christian faith after a period of agnosticism while trying to live the literary life in New York City. Above all, *Dakota* is a moving tribute to the geography and spirituality of the Great Plains. Norris is also an award-winning poet; her most recent collection is *Little Girls in Church.* This excerpt is taken from *The Cloister Walk,* a collection of interrelated narratives that explain how she, a married Presbyterian woman, has become deeply attached to the Benedictine order and the monastic way of life. Here she considers the role of the imagination in contemporary America and the connections between the poet's use of metaphor and religious faith.

Exile, Homeland, and Negative Capability

Exile, like memory, may be a place of hope and delusion. But there are rules of light there and principles of darkness. . . . The expatriate is in search of a country, the exile in search of a self.
—Eavan Boland,. *Object Lessons*

Negative capability . . . [is being] capable of being in uncertainties, mysteries, doubts without any irritable reaching after fact and reason.
—John Keats

A STRANGE THING happens when I enter an elementary school classroom as a visiting artist, to read some poetry and eventually get the kids to write. It has much less to do with me as an individual than with the power of poetry, and may also be a side effect of the simple fact that I come to the children knowing very little about them. With me, they are suddenly handed a fresh slate. But no matter if the school is rich or poor, in the country, a suburb, or city, I've found that the kids that the teacher might have described as "good students" will inevitably write acceptable but unexceptional poems and stories. The breathtaking poems come from left field, as it were, from bad students, the ones the teachers will say don't usually participate well in classroom activities.

One day, when I was engaged with fifth-graders in a working-class neighborhood in North Dakota, I glanced down at a boy's paper and saw the words "My Very First Dad," and that alerted me that something very personal, very deep was going on. I no longer remember what my assignment had been, but I know it was nothing as invasive as "write a poem about someone in your family." Most likely it was an open-ended challenge to work with similes. Given the freedom to write about anything at all, this boy had chosen to write about his "very first dad," and while I left him alone to work it out, I did have several conversations with him. He was pleased, and surprised, when I pointed out to him that his similes were so good they had quickly led him into the deeper realm of metaphor. He'd written of his father: "I remember him/like God in my heart, I remember him in my heart/like the clouds over head,/and strawberry ice cream and bananas/when I was a little kid. But the most I remember/is his love,/as big as Texas/when I was born."

The boy said, rather proudly, that he had been born in Texas, but otherwise told me nothing of his story. It was his stunned teacher who filled me in. She said things that did not surprise me, given my previous experience as an artist-in-residence—"He's not a good student, he tries, but he's never done anything like this before"—but then she told me that the boy had never known his father; he'd skipped town on the day he was born.

Oddly enough, hearing this was gratifying. Just a poet's presence in that classroom, on behalf of similes and metaphors (officially, to justify my presence in terms recognized by the educational establishment, that's what I was "teaching"), had allowed this boy to tell the adults in his life— his teacher, his mom, his stepfather—something they need to know, that a "very first dad" looms large in his psyche. Like God in his heart, to quote the poem, a revelation from the depths of this boy's soul.

There are no prescriptions, no set of rules that will produce a poem like this; no workshop could teach a method that would replicate exactly what went on between me and the students in that room. But I have some idea as to how and why it happened. A teacher once told me that having an artist come to her classroom was like letting a cat in—and I'll risk a bad pun by saying that I think it's more like dropping a catalyst into a chemical solution in order to stimulate a reaction.

What *is* happening in that classroom, when the poet acts as a catalyst? Well, first of all, before I ask students to write, we always have a long discussion about rules. I tell them that for this adventure of writing poetry, we can suspend many of the normal rules for English class. No, you don't have to write within the margins; no, you don't have to look a word up in the dictionary to make sure you're spelling it right—we'll do that later. For now just write the word the way you think it's spelled so you don't interrupt the flow of writing; you can print or use cursive (that's a *big* issue in third grade); you can doodle on your paper; you can scratch things out (here I show them my own rough drafts, so they can see that I mean it); you can write anonymously or even make up a name for yourself as a poet.

If you're really stuck, I tell them, you can collaborate and work on a poem with someone else who's also stuck. This means you can *talk* in the classroom, so long as you don't disturb your neighbor. As we're working, I often have to reassure a student that it's all right not to finish a poem if you really can't. You can let it sit for a while and maybe come back to it, or maybe not. And if you really get carried away by an assignment, it's all right not to go on to my next one—just keep going with what you're doing; *take your time.* (Often, by this time the students are looking at me gratefully but a bit warily, wondering if they've fallen into the hands of a lunatic.)

We talk about the ways this kind of writing differs from learning spelling or math, where there are right and wrong answers. I tell the kids that in what we'll be doing, there *is* no one right answer, not even a right way or wrong way to do it. And if, in a particular writing assignment, I do suggest some rules to follow, I always say that if you can think of a way to break these rules and still come out with a really good poem—go right ahead. I see this as a way to get beyond paying lip service to children's creativity and encouraging them to practice it. By now the good students may be feeling lost. They're often kids who have beaten the system, who have become experts at following the rules in order to get a good grade. And now, maybe for the first time, they're experiencing helplessness at school, because the boundaries have shifted; without rules to follow, they're not sure how to proceed. They may sulk, or even cry, although they usually come around and have a good time.

But it's the other students, the bad students, the little criminals, who often have a form of intelligence that is not much rewarded in school, who are listening most attentively. It's these kids, for whom helplessness and frustration are the norm at school, and often in life—maybe their mom's boyfriend got drunk and abusive the night before—who take to poetry like ducklings to water. And sometimes, as with that fifth-grade boy, they find that adopting a poetic voice can be a revelation. It's as if they're free to speak with their true voice for the very first time. It is always a gift—to the teacher, the class, and to me—to have a child lead us into the heart of poetry. That boy spoke to our own loneliness and exile and reminded us that our everyday world is more mysterious than we know: who would have guessed that an ordinary boy, in an ordinary classroom in North Dakota, was walking around with a love, and a loss, as big as Texas in his heart?

Often, when I'm working in an elementary classroom, my mind pitches back to my own school days. I enjoyed school wholeheartedly until third grade. My mother was an elementary school teacher, and that may have helped me develop early on a sense of what was expected of me, and the confidence that I could learn new things. Then, as we moved from adding and subtracting to multiplying and dividing, I had my first taste of failure. I'd grown used to counting on my fingers and panicked when the numbers became so big so fast, literally untouchable. I became enormously frustrated trying to grasp concepts that remained tantalizingly out of reach. I still excelled at English and found spelling easy. But I began to fall behind in math.

One day in fourth grade, I had an epiphany about the nature of numbers, and a peculiar taste of otherness—the unmistakable sense that I'd seen something that my teacher, and the other students, could not see. My teacher that year prided herself on being tough. She had warned us on the very first day of school that she expected us to work, and to work hard. That was fine with me; I wanted to learn. As I was one of the better students in English, however, my teacher seemed unable to forgive me for being so backward in mathematics. I believe she thought that if she pressured me enough, even ridiculed me from time to time, I would simply apply myself and learn. Thus, one day, in exasperation at some muddle I'd made with a math problem on the blackboard (an experience that always terrified me), she grabbed my chalk, solved the problem, and said, in a sarcastic voice, "You see, it's simple, as simple as two plus two is always four."

And, without thinking, I said, "That can't be." Suddenly, I was sure that two plus two could not possibly *always* be four. And, of course, it isn't. In Boolean algebra, two plus two can be zero; in base three, two plus two is eleven. I had stumbled onto set theory, a truth about numbers that I had no language for. As this was the early 1950s, my teacher had no language for it either, and she and the class had a good laugh over my ridiculous remark. I staggered away from my epiphany and went back to my seat, feeling certain of the truth of what I'd seen but also terribly confused. Briefly, numbers had seemed much more exciting than I had been led to believe. But if two plus two was always four, then numbers were too literal, too boring, to be worth much attention. I wrote math off right then and there, and, of course, ended up with a classic case of math anxiety.

In a way, though, this experience had a positive side, as the beginning of my formation as a poet. Whenever definitions were given as absolutes, as *always,* I would have that familiar tingle—*that can't be*—and soon learned that I could focus on the fuzzy boundaries, where definitions give way to metaphor. Even though "negative capability," like set theory, was a term I wasn't to hear for years, I had stumbled onto it as a way of being, a way of thinking, a way of intelligence that largely defined me. It was there in that ambiguous world that I resolved to dwell.

I have since met visual artists who as children were so intent on playing with the shapes of numbers and letters that they fell behind in both English and math—to the despair of their teachers, who recognized that these were intelligent children. Yet visual intelligence, even more than poetic intelligence, can be a handicap in this culture. Years ago, when I was a kindergarten aide at a Quaker school, one little girl demonstrated a capacity for attention unusual at the age of five; every afternoon, she would paint huge blocks of color onto newsprint, working for nearly an hour. Then she would ask me to hang the painting to dry so that she could work on it again the next day. The teacher and I were fascinated but soon found that we had to protect her from the other children, who, once they noticed that her paintings didn't "look like anything," made fun of them. The girl, remarkably, was undeterred, already adept at exile.

And once, when I was visiting a second-grade classroom and the children were showing me drawings they'd done in celebration of fall, a restless, untidy little boy reluctantly retrieved his from the bottom of a pile of papers. The drawing depicted a man throwing a football, with the ball shown in every stage of the arc. It was the way an engineer might depict a football pass, but the boy (and I suspect, his teacher) was convinced that he had done the drawing "wrong." I wondered if his exile had begun, and where it would lead him.

Working with children on the writing of poetry has led me to ponder the ways that most of us become exiled from the certainties of childhood; how it is that the things we most treasure when we're young are exactly those things we come to spurn as teenagers and young adults. Very small children are often conscious of God, for example, in ways that adults seldom are. They sing to God, they talk to God, they recognize a divine presence in the world around them: they can see the Virgin Mary dancing among the clouds, they know that God made a deep ravine by their house "because he was angry when people would not love him," they believe that an overnight snowfall is "just like Jesus glowing on the mountaintop." Yet these budding theologians often despise church by the time they're in eighth grade.

In a similar way, the children who unself-consciously make up songs and poems when they're young—I once observed a three-year-old singing a passionate ode to the colorful vegetables in a supermarket—quickly come to regard poetry as meaningless and irrelevant. I began to despise mathematics when I sensed that I was getting only part of the story, a dull, literal-minded version of what in fact was a great mystery, and I wonder if children don't begin to reject both poetry and religion for similar reasons, because the way both are taught takes the life out of them. If we teach children when they're young to reject their epiphanies, then it's no wonder that we end up with so many adults who are mathematically, poetically, and theologically illiterate.

Some teachers still require children to copy bad nineteenth-century verse as a handwriting exercise. And in most classrooms I've been in, the teacher assumes that she is "teaching" the students the ordinary tools of language that are in fact the basis of human intelligence. Once, in a fourth-grade classroom, after I'd talked about metaphor, made up some silly examples on the board, and also read and discussed several deeply metaphorical poems, I asked the students to come up with metaphors of their own. The teacher warned me, "This isn't a subject they've studied," but I replied, "They'll know how to do it, they just don't know the word for it yet." She and I had our own epiphanies that day, and that class turned out to be one of the best I ever worked with.

As children grow older and are asked to analyze poetry, they are taught that separating out the elements in the poem—images, similes, metaphors—is the only way to "appreciate" it. As if the poem is somehow less than the whole of its parts, a frog students must dissect in order to make it live; as if the purpose of poetry is to provide boring exercises for English class. The metaphorical intelligence that has pulled disparate elements together to make the poem is of no consequence. Clearly it has not been taught, in most classrooms I've visited, as one of the more intriguing elements of the human imagination.

And do we do any better when it comes to the teaching of religion? The liturgical scholar Gail Ramshaw makes a valuable distinction between theology and liturgy: theology is prose, she says, but liturgy is poetry. "If faith is about facts," she writes, "then we line up the children and make them memorize questions and answers . . . . But if we are dealing with poetry instead of prose . . . then we do not teach answers to questions. We memorize not answers but the chants of the ordinary; we explain liturgical action . . . we immerse people in worship so that they, too, become part of the metaphoric exchange."

Metaphor has been so degraded in our culture that it may be difficult for people to conceive of worship as a "metaphoric exchange." But as a poet I am willing to explore the implications. How would it change our understanding of worship if, from the time they were small, children were taught to value and explore the possibilities of Keats's "negative capability" in themselves? They might better understand faith as a process, and church tradition as not only relevant but strikingly alive.

The ancient understanding of Christian worship is that, in the words of the liturgical scholar Aidan Kavanagh, it "gives rise to theological reflection, and not the other way around." We can see the obvious truth of this by shifting our attention to poetry, and entertaining the notion that one might grow into faith much as one writes a poem. It takes time, patience, discipline, a listening heart. There is precious little certainty, and often great struggling, but also joy in our discoveries. This joy we experience, however, is not visible or quantifiable; we have only the words and form of the poem, the results of our exploration. Later, the thinkers and definers come along and treat these results as the whole—*Let's see; here she's used a metaphor, and look, she's made up a rhyme scheme. Let's stick with it. Let's teach it. Let's make it a rule.* What began as an experiment, a form of play, an attempt to engage in dialogue with mystery, is now a dogma, set in stone. It is something that can be taught in school.

Let's return to our classroom setting, only this time we'll be exploring faith as well as poetry. A poem, as Mallarmé once said, is not made of ideas but of words, and faith also expresses itself through that which is lived, breathed, uttered, left silent. If faith, like poetry, is a process, not a product, then this class will be messier than we can imagine. To make the poem of our faith, we must learn not to settle for a false certitude but to embrace ambiguity and mystery. Our goal will be to recover our original freedom, our childlike (but never childish) wisdom. It will be difficult to lose our adult self-consciousness (here the discipline of writing can help us), difficult not to confuse our worship with self-expression. (All too often the call for "creativity" in worship simply leads to bad art.)

We will need a powerful catalyst. In any institution, while there's always the sacred "way we've always done it," and certainly a place for the traditions that such an attitude reflects, there is also a spirit at work that has more to do with being than with doing.

Poets are immersed in process, and I mean process not as an amorphous blur but as a *discipline.* The hard work of writing has taught me that in matters of the heart, such as writing, or faith, there is no right or wrong way to do it, but only the way of your life. Just paying attention will teach you what bears fruit and what doesn't. But it will be necessary to revise— to doodle, scratch out, erase, even make a mess of things—in order to make it come out right.

When it comes to faith, while there are guidelines—for Christians, the Bible and the scaffolding of the church's theology and tradition—there is no one right way to do it. Flannery O'Connor once wisely remarked that "most of us come to the church by a means the church does not allow," and Martin Buber implies that discovering this means might constitute our life's work: "All [of us] have access to God, but each has a different access. [Our] great chance lies precisely in [our] unlikeness. God's all-inclusiveness manifests itself in the infinite multiplicity of the ways that lead to him, each of which is open to one [person]." He illustrates this with a story about Rabbi Zusya, who said, a short while before his death, "In the world to come I shall not be asked: 'Why were you not Moses?' I shall be asked: 'Why were you not Zusya?'" The rabbi is not speaking of a vague "personal spirituality" that allows him to be Zusya alone; he knows himself to be a part of the people of Israel.

For myself, I have found that being a member of a church congregation and also following, as I am able, the discipline of Benedict's Rule has helped me to take my path toward God without falling into the trap of thinking of myself as "a church of one." I have also found that the Benedictines are a good illustration of Buber's point. Although their members follow a common way of life, monasteries do not produce cookie cutter monks and nuns. Just the opposite. Monasteries have a unity that is remarkably unrestrained by uniformity; they are comprised of distinct individuals, often memorable characters whose eccentricities live for generations in the community's oral history.

The first time I went to a monastery, I dreamed about the place for a week, and the most vivid dream was of the place as a chemistry lab. Might religion be seen as an experiment in human chemistry? And the breath of the divine as the catalyst that sparks reactions and makes our humble institutions work as well as they do, often despite ourselves? Imagination and reason, those vital elements of human intelligence, are adept at dismantling our delusions; both bring us up against our true abilities and our limitations. But we've gotten ourselves into a curious mess in the modern world. We've grown afraid of the imagination (except as a misguided notion of a "creativity" granted to a few) and yet are less and less capable of valuing rationality as another resource of our humanity, of our *religious* humanity. We end up with a curious spectrum of popular religions, a rigid fundamentalism at one end, and New Age otherworldliness, manifested in "angel channeling workshops," on the other. And even religious institutions—I'll speak here of the Christian churches, because they are what I know—often manifest themselves as anything but Christ's humble body on earth. What gets lost in all of this is any viable sense of the sacred that gives both imagination and reason room to play.

Can poets be of any use here? I believe so, though I'm not sure of the reasons why. I may be doodling. But the sense of the sacred is very much alive in contemporary poetry; maybe because poetry, like prayer, is a dialogue with the sacred. And poets speak from the margins, those places in the ecosystem where, as any ecologist can tell you, the most life forms are to be found. The poet Maxine Kumin has described herself as "an unreconstructed atheist who believes in the mystery of the creative process," while my husband, who is both a lyric poet and a computer programmer, declares himself to be "a scientific rationalist who believes in ghosts." If, as Gail Ramshaw has said, "Christianity requires metaphoric thinking," if, as a Benedictine liturgist once said to me, the loss of the ability to think metaphorically is one of the greatest problems in liturgy today, maybe the voices of poets are the ones we need to hear.

I hear many stories these days from people who are exiled from their religious traditions. They also speak from the margins. Many, like me, are members of the baby-boom generation who dropped religious observance after high school or college, and are now experiencing an enormous hunger for spiritual grounding. One woman wrote to me to say that she felt a great longing for ritual and community; she said she wanted to mark the year with more than watching the trees change. She'd joined some political organizations and a women's service club, but found that it wasn't enough. She was afraid to even think of joining a church—the Bible makes her angry, more often than not—but she thought she might have to.

There is no set of rules for her to follow, but only the messy process of life to be lived. Since what she's seeking is salvation and not therapy, nor political or social relevance, I suspect that she might eventually find what she is looking for in the practice of prayer and in communal worship. And if things work as they should, whatever healing needs to happen, whatever larger social dimension she needs to address will grow organically out of those experiences, that community. But how does she get from here to there?

She may be closer than she knows. The Anglican bishop John V. Taylor has said, "Imagination and faith are the same thing, 'giving substance to our hopes and reality to the unseen.' The whole Bible endorses this, and if believers talked about faith in these terms they would be more readily understood." In the Book of Deuteronomy, the commandment of God is revealed not as an inaccessible mystery but as "something very near to you, already in your mouths and in your hearts; you have only to carry it out" (Deut. 30:14). And in the Gospel of Luke, Jesus says, "The coming of the kingdom of God cannot be observed, and no one will announce. 'Look, here it is!' or, 'There it is.' For, behold, the kingdom of God is within you" (Luke 17:20–21).

The boy who wrote about his absent father had a story to tell. His heart was in exile, and the catalyst of poetry helped it come home. And what of the catalyst of faith? Drawing from both our reason and our capacity for negative capability, faith might help us see that our most valuable experiences are always those which leave us, as the sculptor and critic Edward Robinson has said, with "an unaccountable remainder . . . 2 plus 2 equals 5 experiences," which remind us that our relationships with each other and the world are more mysterious than we care to admit. In the universe God made, the real world we call home, love is bigger than Texas, and even death itself, and 2 plus 2 might be 0, 11, or even 4.

Part II

PAST AND PRESENT

Returning to the Sources

ROBERT L. WILKEN

Robert L. Wilken is William R. Kenan, Jr. Professor of the History
of Christianity, University of Virginia at Charlottesville. Among his
many books are *The Myth of Christian Beginnings* and *The Land
Called Holy: Palestine in Christian History and Thought*. He is a frequent contributor to such publications as *First Things* and *Pro Ecclesia*. This essay was originally published in *Reasoned Faith,* edited
by Frank F. Birtel, and reprinted in a collection of Wilken's essays
entitled *Remembering the Christian Past* (1995).

Tradition and Trust

The Role of Memory in the Christian Intellectual Life

IT IS EASY to get religion, something else to hold onto it. As in dieting, many find it easy to take off weight, but quite another matter to
keep it off. Religion, however, unlike dieting, is not a solitary business. Unless one is an unchastened Jamesian, religion is communal, and for religious men and women, the challenge is not only to keep the faith for
ourselves but also to hand it on to the next generation. Only with difficulty
and imagination can we transmit our experiences to those after us who
feel, think, and act differently than we do. For the task of handing on the
faith, the warm heart is insufficient, as the parent who is "born again" or
"converted" soon realizes when facing the task of giving his or her children
religious instruction.

To be sure, without affections there can be no religious life, as we learn
from thinkers as diverse as Augustine of Hippo, Maximus the Confessor,

and Jonathan Edwards. Affective language permeates the Bible.[1] With the development of early Christian thought, the vocabulary of the spiritual life expanded so that words such as *love, desire,* and *longing* became as familiar as *faith, obedience,* and *knowledge.* The rich imagery of the Bible—for example, "As the deer longs for flowing streams, so longs my soul for you, O God" (Ps. 42)—was complemented by the passionate love of the saints— for example, "My love of you, O Lord, is not some vague feeling: it is positive and certain. Your word struck into my heart and from that moment I loved you" (Augustine).[2]

Although there can be no faith without the affections, in a culture steeped in the jargon of psychology the subtle role of the affections in Christian life is too readily supplanted by a shriveled and subjective notion of faith. Indeed, so often is the term *faith* used to refer solely to the act of believing that in popular speech the object of faith seems irrelevant, as though it is the believing that counts, not what one believes. Faith, in this view, is self-legitimizing, impervious to examination, correction, or argument, and has its home in the private imaginings of the believer or in the sheltered world of religious communities. In the same way, the term *value* is used without reference to the good, as though all values are of equal worth and equal validity.

It is quite possible, however, as our daily experience teaches, to put faith in things that are illusory or false. Faith is only as good as its object; if the object of our faith is trustworthy, then it is reasonable to put our trust in it. If not, then it does not deserve our trust. Credulity is no virtue. A necessary component of faith is reason. The phrase *reasonable faith* was first used in the fourth century by Hilary of Poitiers. He believed that "faith is akin to reason and accepts its aid." When the mind lays hold of God in faith, it knows that it can "rest with assurance, as on some peaceful watch-tower."[3] There is no leap of faith into the unknown for Hilary. In his view, as in the view of all early Christian thinkers, faith was not a subjective attitude or feeling but a reasoned conviction. Whether speaking about faith in human beings or belief in God, the church fathers knew that faith cannot be self-authenticating and that to believe in something false or ignoble is not admirable but foolish, like trusting a person who is an incorrigible liar.

Even a cursory study of the history of Christian thought will show that the charge of fideism caricatures the Christian intellectual tradition. Yet this caricature has become part of the way we tell the story of Western culture. From Edward Gibbon in the eighteenth century to historians of the present, Christianity has been charged with substituting authority and uncritical faith for reason, philosophy, and science. In the eighteenth century the encyclopedist Marquis de Condorcet wrote: "Contempt for the humanities was one of the principal characteristics of Christianity. It had to avenge itself against the insults offered by philosophy. . . . Christianity feared that spirit of investigation and doubt, that confidence in one's own reason, which is the scourge of all religious beliefs. . . . The triumph of Christianity was the signal for the complete decay of the sciences and philosophy."[4]

No doubt one of the reasons why faith has been divorced from reason is that, by laying stress on the attitude of the believer rather than on the truth of the thing believed, it is easier for people to negotiate our diverse and heterogeneous society. That attitude is also thought to discourage religious warfare. If faith is an affair of the believing subject and is self-authenticating, then it is easier for us to tolerate differences and live together in peace and harmony. A genial pluralism offers a protected place for individuals and communities of whatever religious belief to practice their faith without external hindrance.

Yet this form of religious peace has a price, for by acquiescing in a subjective notion of faith, religious people unwittingly empty faith of its cognitive character. When the object of faith becomes secondary to the act of believing, theology becomes reflection on faith, not reasoned speech about God. The theological enterprise may be variously useful or frivolous depending on one's point of view, but it makes no cognitive claims. It is valuable chiefly as an instrument to nurture the identity of a particular community. Hence theology can only speak about meaning "for us" or "for them," that is, whatever works in a particular community, and can make no claim to speak about what is true. This is, of course, a reversal of the classical Christian (and Jewish) view that theology's object is God. Once the object of faith is abandoned, theology's object inevitably becomes human experience. Similarly, when talk of the good gives way to the language of values, we inevitably abandon the notion that some values are better than others, and that the *summum bonum* orders all lesser values.

But it is not my purpose here to elaborate on faith and reason, or on the question of values, at least not in the narrow sense of those terms. I begin with these observations because I want to discuss tradition.

The church is a living community that is the bearer of ancient traditions received from those who have gone before. In the marketplace of ideas, however, particular commitments (that is, traditions) are thought to be limiting and restrictive because they rest on authority and exalt the wisdom of the past over supposed rational insights of the present. Enlightenment thinkers, writes Alasdair MacIntyre, hoped that "reason would displace authority and tradition. Rational justification was to appeal to principles undeniable by any rational person and therefore independent of all those social and cultural particularities which the Enlightenment thinkers took to be mere accidental clothing of reason in particular times and places."[5]

So deeply have these ideas penetrated into our consciousness that even religious thinkers have taken them as axiomatic. The mark of rationality, it is assumed, is autonomy. Unless a thinker is freed from the constraints of inherited beliefs and institutions, he or she cannot engage in the spirit of free inquiry that leads to truth. Only if the scholar frees himself from the claims of tradition and becomes independent of external constraints (i.e., tradition) can he properly carry out his work of research, scholarship, and original thinking.

"The traditional Christian theologian," writes David Tracy, "of whatever tradition, preached and practiced a morality of belief in and obedience to the tradition and a fundamental loyalty to the church-community's beliefs. The modern historian and scientist—whether in natural or social sciences—preaches and practices an exactly contrary morality. For him, one cannot investigate a cognitive claim with integrity if one insists simultaneously that the claim is believable because tradition has believed." Tracy applies these same principles to the theologian: "The fundamental ethical commitment of the theologian qua theologian remains to that community of scientific inquiry whose province logically includes whatever issue is under investigation." In Tracy's view, the theologian must be committed to the "ethical model of the autonomous inquirer."[6]

Now there is something to what Tracy and others like him say. As early as Origen of Alexandria, Christian thinkers claimed that their ideas should be judged by the "common notions" that are at work within the intellectual community. The openness of Christian thinkers in the last two hundred years to modern thinking is a remarkable sign of confidence in reason as well as in the Christian tradition. They believed, rightly, that truth was one and that if one joined with others in the quest for truth, the results could only be beneficial for Christianity. Christian thought has always been a critical and rational enterprise, and at its best has welcomed the wisdom of the world into the household of faith.

Nevertheless, Christian thinkers have also known that they were bearers of a tradition. "That which I have received, I have handed on to you," wrote Saint Paul (1 Cor. 15:3). This tradition, exhibited first in the Scriptures, was later subjected to critical examination, tested in the lives of countless men and women, defended against its critics, and elaborated in myriad social and cultural settings. Hence I am a bit baffled why one should assume, as Tracy apparently does, that reason is to be found only outside of tradition and that genuine rationality requires "autonomy." This premise seems to invite a willful amnesia, a self-imposed affliction that would rob our lives of depth and direction. Yet Tracy believes (or did when he wrote *Blessed Rage for Order*) that the liaison with tradition obstructs the path to enlightenment. To be an intellectual, in this view, is to loosen the moorings that bind one to a particular tradition or a living religious community.

That such ideas could take hold in the academy is evidence of how insular intellectuals can be, even religious ones. In many fields of creative work, immersion in tradition is the presupposition for excellence and originality. Think, for example, of music. On Saturday mornings, I often listen to a jazz show on National Public Radio that features interviews with famous and not-so-famous jazz pianists, saxophonists, drummers, trumpeters, etc., and I am regularly struck at how they speak with such respect of teachers and masters, and how to a person they learned to play the piano by first playing in someone else's style or learned to blow the trumpet by imitating Louis Armstrong or someone else. Similarly, one is impressed with how often a performer like folk singer Jean Redpath speaks about tradition as the necessary condition for making and singing folk music. How often we are admonished not to let the old traditions be forgotten. Why? Surely not for historical or archaeological reasons, but because musicians, like painters and writers and sculptors, know in their fingertips or vocal cords or ears that imitation is the way to excellence and originality.

Without tradition, learning is arduous at best, impossible at worst. In most things in life—learning to speak, making cabinets, playing the violin—the only way to learn is by imitation, by letting someone else guide our movements until we learn to do the thing on our own. I am not sure why this is so, but I suspect a chief reason is that only in the act of doing and participating do we truly know and understand. To do something well, we have to give ourselves over to it. T. S. Eliot made this point about literary criticism: "You don't really criticize any author to whom you have never surrendered yourself. . . . You have to give yourself up, and then recover yourself, and the third moment is having something to say, before you have wholly forgotten both surrender and recovery."[7]

Reason, it seems, is found within rather than outside of things; it is not an abstract quality that exists independently in the human mind—which means, of course, that it is *reasonable* to allow one's hands to be guided by a master, and foolish to go it alone, as though one could learn to play the violin or sculpt a statue by studying a set of instructions. In this context, the ideal of the autonomous individual is glaringly inappropriate, for we recognize that here the true mark of rationality is to apprentice oneself to another rather than to strike out on one's own. To paraphrase Kenny Rogers, 'there'll be time enough' for originality when the apprenticeship is done.

What applies to violin-playing or cabinet-making also applies, *mutatis mutandis,* to the intellectual life. The way we learn to think is by reading good thinkers and letting their thoughts form our thoughts. Matthew Arnold reminds us: "Commerce with the ancients appears to me to produce, in those who constantly practice it, a steadying and composing effect upon their judgment, not of literary works only, but of men and events in general. They are like persons who have had a very weighty and impressive experience; they are more truly than others under the empire of facts, and more independent of the language current among those with whom they live."[8]

From the ancients, we learn to use language in a precise way, to understand the inner logic of ideas, to discern the deeper relation between seemingly disparate concepts, to discriminate between things that appear similar, to know what is central and what is peripheral. And in the process we are tutored in humility, for we see that the things worthy of reception by us have been tested in the fire of human experience. As Charles M. Wood has pointed out, "Concepts . . . are creatures of history: they come into being, are molded and occasionally transformed through their complex and flexible relationships to other concepts and to the particularities of human existence, and may even fade and wither. The lives of concepts are inextricably related to the lives of actual persons and communities."[9] Hence there can be no genuine Christian intellectual life that is not rooted in history.

In the first volume of his *Systematic Theology,* Wolfhart Pannenberg observes that for a long time he had thought it possible to present theology in such a way that its chief themes could be divorced from the "bewildering multiplicity of historical questions." Only then could the systematic unity of Christian theology become evident. Contrary to his own expectations, however, he found that this way of presenting theology had to be discarded. He writes: "Christian teaching is of such a character that it is through and through a historical creation."[10] Its content rests on the historical person of Jesus Christ and on the historical interpretations that arose as a result of his life, death, and resurrection. The language of Christian thought cannot be extracted from its place in history, for without history, language loses particularity, and hence intelligibility.

The first question, then, that a Christian intellectual should ask is not "What should be believed?" or "What should one think?" but "*Whom* should one trust?" Augustine understood this well, and in his early apologetic work, *On True Religion,* he links the appeal to reason with trust in the community and authority. Our notion of authority is so attenuated that it may be useful to look a bit more closely at what Augustine means by authority. For us, authority is linked to offices and institutions, to those who hold jurisdiction, hence to notions of power. We speak of submitting to authority or of obeying authority, and assume that authority has to do with the *will,* not with the *understanding.*

Yet there is another sense of authority that traces its source to the *auctor* in *auctoritas*. Sometimes translated "author," *auctor* can designate a magistrate, writer, witness, someone who is worthy of trust, a guarantor who attests to the truth of a statement, one who teaches or advises. Authority in this view has to do with trustworthiness, with the confidence a teacher earns through teaching with truthfulness, if you will. To say we need authority is much the same as saying we need teachers, or (to use my earlier analogy) that we need to become apprentices.

Augustine expressed his idea of authority in *On True Religion* by saying: "Authority invites trust and prepares human beings for reason. Reason leads to understanding and knowledge. But reason is not entirely absent from authority, for we have got to consider whom we have to believe." In the Library of Christian Classics translation of this passage, the first words are rendered: "Authority demands belief."[11] Translated in this way, especially with the term *demands,* the sentence is misleading. For Augustine is not thinking of an authority that *demands* or *commands* or *coerces* (terms that require an act of will), but of a truth that engenders confidence because of who tells it to us.

Authority resides in a person who by actions as well as words invites trust and confidence. Augustine's model for authority is the relation of a teacher to a student, a master to a disciple, not a magistrate to a subject. The student's trust is won not simply by words but also by actions, by the kind of person the teacher is—in short, by character. When Gregory Thaumaturgus, a young man from Asia Minor, went to Caesarea in Palestine to study with Origen, the greatest intellectual of his day, he said that he did so because he wanted to have "fellowship" with "that man."

Authority rests neither on external legitimization nor on power but on trustworthiness, or in Augustine's words, on truth. Its purpose is to clarify and illuminate, that is, to aid understanding, and its instrument is argument, not coercion. If a teacher is constantly saying "believe me" without giving reasons, the student may for a time assent, but he will not understand nor be convinced, and in time will stop listening. As Saint Thomas wrote, "If the teacher determines the question by appeal to authorities only, the student will be convinced that the thing is so, but will have acquired no knowledge or understanding, and he will go away with an empty mind."[12]

Thus far, I have spoken rather generally about the place of tradition in the intellectual life, but since I have made so much of particularity, it is time to be more specific. Apprenticeship is a purely formal category and, like reason, cannot be discussed in the abstract. Here the point about "whom shall we trust" becomes critical, for just as there are different styles of playing the piano, so there are different ways of thinking. What makes the difference between ways of thinking is not only the subject matter (whether law or biology or mathematics or statecraft or philosophy) but the sources that one draws on.

A particularly acute problem for Christian intellectuals today, especially those who work in philosophy, theology, and related fields, is that they have hired themselves out as apprentices to a body of literature that is drawn almost wholly from the nineteenth and twentieth centuries. For various reasons, we assume that the post-Enlightenment sources formulate the problems that are distinctive to our age, and hence make a unique claim on our attention. Other sources—the Bible, the writings of the church fathers, the treatises of the scholastics—belong to the past and to the domain of historians and biblical scholars.

Further, we assume that the task of the intellectual is to "translate" the substance of the tradition into contemporary language and categories. How, it is asked, are we to speak of God in an age of light bulbs and computers? The assumed answer is that we need to translate the idiom of the Scriptures into the idiom of our own time, to discuss the biblical faith in terms intelligible in the nonbiblical categories of today.

The difficulty with this program of translation is that the language of the Bible is irreplaceable, and more often than not the consequence of "translation" is that the language of the Scriptures is supplanted by another language or relegated to the footnotes. It ceases to be the vehicle of thought. As necessary as it is to "translate" the Bible into the thought patterns of our age, it is also the case that Christians in every generation must learn afresh how to think and imagine *in* the language and idiom of the Scriptures.

Let me illustrate the point with the trinitarian language of Father and Son. My example comes from the dispute between Gregory of Nyssa, the fourth-century bishop, theologian, and spiritual writer, and Eunomius, a second-generation Arian who believed that Christ was "unlike" the Father. Eunomius summed up his doctrine as follows: We believe in the "supreme and absolute being, and in another being existing by reason of the First (the Son), and a third being not ranking with either of these but inferior to the one as to its cause, to the other as to its energy." This was a rather startling argument for a Christian bishop, especially in light of the Council of Nicaea's confession (325 C.E.) that the Son was "of the same substance" as the Father.

Gregory, in response, appeals to the language of Scripture. He says that Eunomius "corrects as it were the expressions of the Gospel, and will not use the words . . . by which our Lord conveyed the mystery [of the Holy Trinity] to us; he suppresses the names of 'Father, Son, and Holy Spirit,' and speaks of a 'Supreme and absolute Being,' instead of the Father, of 'another existing through it, but after it' instead of the Son, and of a 'third ranking with neither of these two' instead of the Holy Spirit."

Now one might reply that Gregory, by simply appealing to the authority of Scripture and the words of Jesus, ignores the real issue: How is the language of Scripture to be understood by people who have been formed in a Hellenistic culture? What point is there in defending the metaphorical language of the Bible in the context of a genuine theological dispute about the relation of the Son to the Father, a dispute, moreover, that has arisen precisely *because* of the imprecision and diversity of the biblical language? Gregory, however, was as much aware of the difficulty as was Eunomius, and so he proceeded to give reasons why the biblical language has to be respected and cherished and used.

The words one uses, Gregory argues, make a difference; terms cannot be indiscriminately exchanged, as though the content of a proposition remains the same no matter what the vehicle. The term *Father,* for example, is quite different from "Supreme and absolute being," and Son from "one existing after the other," says Gregory, because when the words *Father* and *Son* are spoken, we recognize at once "the proper and natural relationship to one another" that the terms imply. These terms signify a relationship that the others do not. By abandoning the terms *Father* and *Son,* Eunomius does not simply jettison the biblical language; he also abandons "the idea of relationship which enters the ear with the words." Similarly,

Eunomius' way of designating the Holy Spirit does not make clear that the Holy Spirit is a "distinct entity."[13]

I pick my illustration from Gregory of Nyssa because he is one of the most philosophical of all early Christian thinkers, a man who rigorously subjected the biblical tradition to critical analysis. Yet he also believed that the Scriptures had come from God and that the language of the Scriptures was not simply the result of historical accident or cultural conditioning. The Scriptures were a firm point of reference, rooted in the apostolic age, and there could be no genuine talk of God that ignored the biblical language. He approached the Scriptures with humility, looked to them for instruction, and believed that he was subject to them, not they to him.

The difficulty with the idea of "translating" biblical truth into nonbiblical language, as Janet Soskice observes in her fine book *Metaphor and Religious Language,* is that it assumes that "revelation exists as a body of free-floating truths." Meaning takes precedence over words, for what is essential, it is claimed, can be had independent of the language, the metaphors, the practices and form of life that have been the bearer of the meaning.[14]

Soskice illustrates her point by reference to the biblical metaphor of water: "Ho, every one who thirsts come to the water" (Isa. 55:1). She shows how this image runs throughout the Scriptures ("fountain of living waters" [Jer. 2:13]; "rivers of living waters" [John 7:37–38]) and Christian tradition (e.g., in the words of Teresa of Avila, who said: "I cannot find anything more apt for the explanation of certain spiritual things than this element of water; for, as I am ignorant and my wit gives me no help, and I am so fond of this element, I have looked at it more attentively than at other things").

The constant repetition of metaphor has gone hand in hand with typological interpretation of the Scriptures. To say that God is a "fountain of living water" or a fortress or vinekeeper or king, Soskice notes, "requires an account not merely of fountains, rocks, vines, and kings, but of a whole tradition of experiences and of the literary tradition which records and interprets them." The Christian imagination is biblical; for this reason, certain emblematic metaphors, ways of speaking, and events are given priority over others. Soskice writes, "The Old Testament's importance is not principally as a set of propositions but as the milieu from which Christian belief arose and indeed still arises, for these books are the source of Christian descriptive language and particularly of metaphors which have embodied a people's understanding of God."[15] Further, the value of the biblical language is not only that it is biblical (that is to say, authoritative), but that it is grounded in the experience of men and women who have known the God about which it speaks.

Language is a vehicle of memory. Few things are more satisfying than to hear old and familiar words spoken or read anew to us. Like the madeleine cake in Proust's *A la recherche du temps perdu,* language not only makes alive (or makes present, to use a sacramental term) what gets lost in the recesses of the mind; it also molds our experience, stirs our imagination, holds before us the same things that were known by earlier generations, and keeps our mind trained on that to which the language refers: the God of Abraham, Isaac, Jacob, and Jesus. A pernicious feature of much historical criticism is that it unravels the cord linking the language of the Bible to the living God, and trains us to look away from the ostensible meaning to meanings that, however interesting, are not rooted in history or experience.

The Christian intellectual tradition, then, is inescapably historical. Without memory, our intellectual life is impoverished, barren, ephemeral, subject to the whims of the moment. Memory locates us in the corporate and the particular. There is no memory that is not rooted in communal experience—a strange fact that we all experience whenever we return to the place where we grew up and talk to family and friends, yet one that is often forgotten in abstract thought. Just as there can be no human life without the bricks and wood, the trees, hills, and rivers, the neighbors and family and friends that make up the world of each of us, so there can be no Christian intellectual life without reference to the writings of the prophets and evangelists, the doctrines of the church fathers, the conceptual niceties of the scholastics, the language of the liturgy, the songs of the poets and hymn writers, the exploits of the martyrs, and the holy tales of the saints.

The Christian intellectual is inescapably bound to those persons and ideas and events that have created the Christian memory, as Dante understood so well. Across the pages of the *Divine Comedy* stride an unparalleled cast of characters: Virgil and Beatrice, the Blessed Virgin, Saint Bernard,

Potiphar's wife, Cato the Elder, King Solomon and Justinian, Pope Gregory the Great—whose views on angels Dionysius the Aeropagite corrected—popes Boniface VIII and John XXII, Saint John examining Dante on love, and Marco Lombardo discoursing on free will—characters presented not as a series of disconnected lives or philosophical ideas, but as part of a grand story held together by one thing: how every person and event and idea stands in relation to the "never ending light."

Dante understood that the Christian intellectual tradition is rooted in concreteness. Christian thinking does not begin with general religious ideas or universal principles, but with a particular history that began in a tiny part of the world called Judea and extends across the generations and centuries in a stately procession of those who look to that light that "once seen, alone and always kindles love." For the mystery that lies at the center of Christian faith is mediated by the men and women whose lives have been illumined by that light. The Christian intellectual, then, knows that he does not traffic in ideas alone, for he perceives, with Dante, that God's ways are "buried from the eyes of everyone whose intellect has not matured within the flame of love."[16]

LEON R. KASS

Leon Kass is Addie Clark Harding Professor in The College and the Committee on Social Thought at the University of Chicago. He is the author of *Toward a More Natural Science: Biology and Human Affairs* and *The Hungry Soul: Eating and the Perfecting of Our Nature*. His essays have appeared in *Commentary, First Things,* and a host of other publications. For over ten years Dr. Kass has been writing a series of brilliant exegeses of biblical texts, such as the essay reprinted below, which is reprinted from *The American Scholar,* Volume 58, Number 1, Winter 1988–89.

What's Wrong With Babel?

THE BOOK of Genesis is largely an account of the beginnings of the people of Israel. Beginning with God's call of Abraham in chapter 12, it narrates the trials of the founders—Abraham, Isaac, and Jacob—and their households, as God Himself directly leads one people to follow His chosen path. But before the coming of this new way, Genesis presents an account of human beginnings universally considered, employing tales of men and women functioning largely on their own and left to their own devices. The last episode of that universal human story is the famous tale of the city and tower of Babel, presented economically in the first nine verses of the eleventh chapter of Genesis. As everybody knows, God disrupts the building of the city, confounding the speech of the builders and scattering them abroad upon the face of the earth.

Here is the story:

1. And the whole earth was of one language and one speech.
2. And as they journeyed about from the east, they found a plain in the land of Shinar, and they settled there.
3. And they said, one man to his neighbor, "Come, let us make bricks, and burn them thoroughly [literally, "to a burning"]";
   And they had brick for stone, and bitumen for mortar.
4. And they said, "Come, let us build for us a city with a tower, with its top [or "head"] in the heavens;
   And let us make for us a name, lest we be scattered abroad upon the face of the earth."
5. But the Lord came down to see the city and the tower, which the children of man [or "children of Adam"—*benêy ha'âdâm*] were building.
6. And the Lord said, "Behold, it is one people, and they have all one language; and this they begin to do: and now nothing will be restrained from them which they have imagined [or "plotted"—*zâmam*] to do.
7. "Come, let us go down and confound their language, that they may not understand one another's speech."
8. So the Lord scattered them from thence upon the face of all the earth; and they ceased to build the city.
9. Therefore is the name of it called Babel [*bâbel*], because the Lord did there confound [*bâlal*] the language of all the earth; and from thence did the Lord scatter them upon the face of the earth.

The building of the city and tower is an expression of powerful human impulses, at first toward safety and permanence, eventually toward full independence and self-sufficiency, and accomplished entirely by rational and peaceful means: by forethought and planning, by arts to transform the given world, and by cooperative social arrangements made possible by common speech and uniform thoughts. This ancient story encapsulates a recurrent human dream of universal human community living in peace and freedom, no longer at the mercy of an inhospitable or hostile nature, and enjoying a life no longer solitary, nasty, poor, brutish, and short. The universal city is the bearer and embodiment of this dream. According to the story, however, God finds this dream a nightmare. Taking strong objection to the city of man, He thwarts its completion by measures designed to make it permanently impossible. Why?

Given that the human beings want the city but God does not, our first impulse is to think that the answer depends on knowing God's reasons or seeing things from His point of view. Of this, all that we know is contained in God's remark, no doubt uttered with a negative judgment, "Now nothing will be restrained from them which they have imagined to do" (verse 6). God, it seems, sees the likely success of the project, but doesn't approve it. He does not approve of the prospect of unrestrained human powers, exercised in support of unlimited imaginings and desires. More generally, He may not like the absence of reverence, the vaunt of pride, the trust in technique, the quest for material power, the aspiration for self-sufficiency, the desire to reach into heaven—in short, the implied wish to be as gods, with comparable creative power. From God's point of view, the city of man is, in its deepest meaning, at best a form of idolatry, and at worst, a great threat to the earth.

Why should we, enlightened readers, take God's view of the matter? Should we not cherish the hopes of our fellows, those first dreamers of the humanistic dream? After all, we are told, all mankind without exception thought the project right and good. Absent a meddlesome God, would there be any reason to disagree? And if a meddlesome God is *truly* absent, would there not be every reason to revive the dream? If there is no city of God, the city of man is not only not idolatry—it becomes our last best hope.

The careful study of the biblical story suggests that this view is mistaken, that God's judgments and actions regarding Babel are entirely fitting, and on grounds accessible to human reason. Pondering the building of Babel, in the context of what precedes and follows, we may ourselves come to see it from God's point of view.

I

The first eleven chapters of Genesis present an unfolding story of the beginnings of human life. Chapter 1 provides a picture of the cosmic whole, man included, the main purpose of which is to teach creation and creation *by God,* and, the crucial corollary, that the sun, the moon, the stars, and all the visible heavens are not gods but creatures. The story of human beginnings proper commences in the second chapter, with life in the Garden of Eden, and proceeds temporally, giving the impression that it constitutes the primordial history of our race: first Adam and Eve; then their sons Cain and Abel; later Noah and the Deluge; afterwards Noah's sons and their descendants; and so on. But the biblical author seems to be using this temporal account to convey something atemporal and nonhistorical— indeed, something permanent and philosophical. Even more important than Genesis's version of historical beginnings is its teaching about anthropological beginnings and about moral beginnings. Thanks to the stories, we learn something about the basic nature of human beings and their primordial associations; and we learn why that nature and those associations are morally troubling. We are shown the beginnings of human life understood as the fundamental elements of human life, psychic and social—speech, questioning, the quest for autonomy, imagination, the love of your own, the arts, ambition, pride-jealousy-anger-and-shame, the love of beauty, the lust for blood and the taste for wine, and the divination of higher powers-that-be and the desire to control them, for example, through sacrifices—and we see quite clearly the troubles they cause us. The artful series of tales unfolds a natural anthropology, naturally evolving; and, by showing vividly the troubles that emerge when human beings act naturally, the same tales provide that most essential human beginning, the beginning of the moral education of the reader.

This moral education is accomplished by taking us vicariously through four major human stages or alternative conditions of human life: first, simple innocence (in the absence of human self-consciousness); second, life without law—that is, anarchy—based on internalized "knowledge" of good and bad; third, life under the primordial law, when man emerges from what later writers will call the state of nature; and fourth, the dispersion of peoples, each living under its own law or customs. Let me briefly review these early "stages" or human alternatives.

First is the condition of simple innocence in the Garden of Eden. Innocence is destroyed when man, his desires enlarged by newly used powers of mind, exercises his autonomy and takes to himself independent knowledge of good and bad; judgmentally self-conscious, he immediately discovers his nakedness, and thus his shame and wounded pride, which he artfully attempts to clothe over. This end of innocence is, literally, the expulsion into the real world, where men live according to their own lights and judgments of good and bad, without imposed law. In this second state, we encounter Eve's proud birth of Cain; Cain's sacrifice, wounded pride, jealousy, and murder of his brother; the line of Cain and the line of Seth, and their ill-fated interbreeding after Adam died in the tenth generation; and the world degenerating into riotous and lewd behavior. The flood completes the dissolution of this anarchic world.

The third state begins after the flood with Noah—righteous and simple Noah, the first man born into the world after Adam dies—when God institutes a new order based on law and covenant. An externally imposed law—to begin with, no murder—is now administered and enforced by men but with divine sanction, against a world order guaranteed to be not hostile to human aspiration by God's covenant never again to destroy the earth. This new state of primitively lawful society was to have been transmitted universally, from fathers to sons, but it was not successfully perpetuated even for one generation: Noah's drunkenness and the irreverent conduct of one of his sons made universal transmission impossible. Dispersion of peoples and election of one, under the direct leadership of God, became the next plan, featuring the nation that begins with Abraham, a people that will be called to carry God's way as a light to all the nations.

One way to speak about this series of states is to say that God keeps trying new plans after the old ones fail, in many cases making concessions to unavoidable and undesirable human weaknesses (for example, in the permission to eat meat granted with Noah). But a better way is to say that, by this means, *we* the readers learn that those other imaginable human possibilities—innocence, anarchy, universal perpetuation of law and covenant through natural lineage—"have been tried" and have failed, which is to say, *they are impossible.* We are educated to believe that the human spirit of righteousness is not strong enough to rule from within but needs outside instruction, legislation, and help. The story of the city and tower of Babel is the culmination of this sequence: it shows the impossibility of transmitting the right way through the universal, technological, secular city.

The more immediate background for the builders of Babel is the Flood. Through this universal cataclysm, human beings encountered the full destructive force of brute nature. After the Flood, God promised "Never again," but it is reasonable to surmise that the memory of the Deluge weighed at least as heavily as the hearsay report of God's promise not to repeat it—especially if one also imagines that the earth remained covered with skeletons of men and animals who died in the Flood. God's first postdiluvian command to Noah to spread out and fill the earth with people might have been a terrifying prospect under the circumstances. The connection of Babel to the antecedent Flood is in fact hinted at by the very last words of chapter 10 immediately preceding the story of Babel:

These are the families of the sons of Noah, after their generations, in their nations; and of these were the nations divided in the earth *after the flood.*

Chapter 10 is, altogether, another and gentler account of the division of mankind, answering in its way these questions: How came there to be many nations? How came there to be many tongues? The answer of chapter 10 is genealogical, beginning with the three sons of Noah, their descendants reflecting to some degree their own very different characters. Among the descendants of Ham, the irreverent son, we find one man who is, in this version, connected with Babel. Nimrod, whose name means "rebelliousness," was the one who began to be a mighty man upon the earth. He was a powerful hunter in the face of God, and for this he became famous; he was also the founder, presumably by conquest, of an empire of cities in the plain of Shinar, and the beginning of his kingdom was Babel. By means of a large kingdom, Nimrod attempts to overcome by force the division of mankind. We should not be too quick to blame him: if what lies behind the human world is only chaos and instability, man must make his own order: Human ordering is the theme of the story of Babel.

II

"*The* whole earth *was of one language and one speech.*" The story of Babel begins with all mankind united as a single, harmonious group, or, as God says later, as "one people." Unlike the previous chapter's account of the differentiation of peoples, descending from the very different sons of Noah (who, though of one family, were not of one mind), this story begins with the entire human race, united and whole; the narrator accentuates the unity by exaggeration, identifying all mankind as "the whole earth." The project they are about to undertake is a universal human project; it is not the work only of Nimrod and the line of Ham. This is the first clue that Babel is not just any city, but is the city, the paradigmatic or universal city, representing a certain universal human aspiration.

"*Of one language.*" The unity of the human race was linguistic or logical, not (merely) genealogical. This means more than sharing uniform sounds and symbols—speaking, say, Aramaic rather than Greek; it means sharing the view of the world embedded in a language. It means sharing a common understanding of the world that any pure language implicitly contains. And, because language also bespeaks the inner world of the speakers, sharing one language means also a common inner life, with simple words accurately conveying the selfsame imaginings, passions, and desires of every human being. To be of one language is to be of one mind about the most fundamental things. This is confirmed by the words that immediately follow in the story.

"*Of one speech.*" The Hebrew words are hard to translate, because there is a grammatical paradox regarding number: the noun, *devâriym,* "words," a plural, is modified by the generally singular adjective, "one," here written as a plural *'achâdiym.* A variety of interpretations have been offered: "few words," implying simple thoughts and communication; "many words but one speech," implying a single plan; or "single words," read as a synonym for a single language. But I wonder whether the strange construction with the impossible plural of "one" might be a literary hint that these people were confused about the being of one and many, and in particular about the unity of the highest One. Such confusion might, in the end, jeopardize the apparent simplicity, singleness of purpose, common understanding, and intelligibility of their thought.

"*They found a* plain *in the land of* Shinar, *and they* settled *there.*" Though mankind was told to disperse and fill the earth, the human race chose rather to settle in one place, a fertile plain in the land of Shinar (that is, in the Euphrates valley), that could accommodate and sustain them all. A fertile plain very likely suggests agriculture, not hunting and gathering; agriculture suggests settlement, rather than wandering, and also forethought, fences, and the arts. It also requires a keen dependence on heaven—on sun and rain, a matter to which we shall return.

"*And they* said, *one man to his neighbor,* 'Come, let us make *bricks.*'" The project for building the city depends on human speech. But whereas human speech has previously been used for a variety of other purposes—naming, self-naming, questioning authority, shifting blame, denying guilt, expressing fear, boasting in song, spreading shame and ridicule, and blessing and cursing—speech is here used by human beings to exhort to action and enunciate a project of *making,* for the first time in Genesis. "Come" (or "go to," *hâbâh*) means "prepare yourself," "get ready to join in our mutual plan." Each man thus aroused his neighbor to the joint venture, "Let us *make.*" Speech is the herald of craft.

"*Make* bricks *and* burn *them thoroughly*" (literally, "to a burning"). Far from the mountains where stones could be had, the men found no ready-made blocks for building, so they started by making their own materials, from scratch. This is the Bible's first mention of bricks. Were bricks, or permanent houses, known previously? It is doubtful: even after the flood, Noah dwelt in a tent. The very *idea* of bricks is itself an invention, a creative act of the resourceful mind. And how and from what does one make bricks? From the ground, from the moistened dust of the ground, by means of fire. Fire is universally the symbol of the arts and crafts, of technology. Through the controlled use of fire's transforming power, human beings set about to alter the world, presumably because, as it is, it is insufficient for human need. Imitating God's creation of man out of the dust of the ground, the human race begins its own project of creation by warming and transforming portions of the earth.

"*And they said, 'Come, let us build for us* a city *with a* tower *with its top* [or 'head'] *in the* heavens.'" Like so much of modern technology, the means precede and generate their own ends: "Now we have bricks. What can we make with them?" Bricks now in hand, the creative imagination proceeds to a new plane: it projects a city with a tower. The meaning of the city is inextricably linked with the meaning and presence of the tower; but also, the meaning of the tower is inextricably linked with the nature and meaning of the city.

Some insight is available through tales of other cities in Genesis. Before Babel, there are only two references to cities. Cain, after killing his brother Abel, is told by God that he would be a fugitive and a wanderer. But Cain settles in the land of Nod and, presumably out of fear, builds there a city, a refuge, once he has a family; and he names that city for his first born, Enoch. (The line of Cain includes the founders of the arts and crafts, implicit in civilization.) After the Flood there is also a brief mention of the great city of the Assyrians, Nineveh, with its cluster of satellite cities (Genesis 10:11–12), whose wickedness Jonah will much later be sent to reprove. Later, we will learn about the supremely wicked Canaanite city of *Sidom,* destroyed by God. Whatever the city means, it seems to be linked, at least in these other cases, with violence, lewdness, and corruption. But none of those features appear tied to the city of Babel—at least not yet—which proceeds through peaceful cooperation under the rule of reason.

The city—every city—is a thoroughly human institution, with settled place and defined boundaries, whose internal plan and visible structures all manifest the presence of human reason and artfulness. The city affirms man's effort to provide for his own safety and needs, strictly on his own. Standing up against the given world, it affirms man's ability to control and master the given world, at least to some extent. Outliving its present inhabitants, the city stands as a memorial to the ingenuity and success of those who have gone before. But at any given moment the city is an expression of the human effort at self-sufficiency, at satisfying by human means alone all of the needs and wants of human life. Born in need, the human city, by meeting and more-than-meeting the needs of its builders, proudly celebrates the powers of human reason.

Perhaps the most celebrated passage on the origins and nature of the city is provided by Aristotle near the beginning of the *Politics:*

> The association constituted in accordance with nature for every day needs is the household. . . . The first association made out of many households for the sake of needs which are not only daily is the village. . . . And the association made out of several villages and complete is the *polis* [the city], having already, so to speak, reached the limit of full self-sufficiency; that is, it comes into being for the sake of living, but it is for the sake of living well.

This argument that roots the city in human need and defines it by self-sufficiency is supported by a second argument, which roots the city in human speech: the city, the ground of self-sufficiency, is the natural home of human beings also because it is the embodiment of, and stage for, human speech and reason. Because men have speech, they live in cities, not just in herds or swarms:

> Man is by nature a *polis*-animal . . . more than any bee or any herding animal. . . . For man alone among the animals has *logos* [thoughtful speech/reason]. . . . But *logos* is for making clear the advantageous and the harmful, and so also the just and the unjust. For this is special to men alone in relation to the other animals; having alone the awareness of good and bad, just and unjust, and the rest. And the community of these things makes a household and a *polis*.

Speaking animal, rational animal, artful animal, political animal, animal knowing good and bad, and opining about the just and the unjust—it is all one package: man becomes truly man only when he lives in a *polis*, providing for himself and ruling himself by his own light of reason, through speech and shared opinions about good and bad, just and unjust. Though the biblical author almost certainly did not read Aristotle's *Politics*, he seems to share a similar view of the meaning of the city—though not of its goodness. Precisely what Aristotle celebrates, Genesis views with suspicion.

And what of the tower? How is this connected with the meaning of the city? The context of the flood suggests a connection with safety: the tower is an artificial high ground providing refuge against future floods and a watchtower for the plain; it is even imaginable that it might be intended as a pillar to hold up heaven, lest it crack open another time. These suggestions, while plausible, do not go far enough. To this we must add what we know of the historical city of Babylon and its tower, the famous ziggurat, *Etemenanki,* in the temple of Marduk.

Marduk was the chief god of Babylon. Originally he seems to have been a god of thunderstorms, but, according to an epic poem, *Enuma elish*, he rose to preeminence after conquering the monster of primeval chaos to become "lord of the gods of heaven and earth," the supreme ruler of all nature, responsible, among other things, for the motion of the stars and for fertility and vegetation. The name of the tower, *Etemenanki,* in Sumerian means "House of the Foundation of Heaven and Earth." The tower, part of the city's temple, is a human effort to link up heaven and earth. According to some accounts, the Babylonian tower was intended to pave a way for a divine entrance to the city; yet even granting such an aspiration, the project is not unambiguously pious. Unless the god or gods explicitly command such a gesture, the tower—any such conduit—must be seen as a presumptuous attempt to control or appropriate the divine, to bring the cosmic origins down into one's own midst, to encompass the divine within one's own constructions. What appears at first glance as submission is in fact, at least partly, an expression of pride.

But there is probably more to the Babylonian tower than its name and its connection with Marduk. The ziggurats of Babylon had more straightforward, even rational, interests in heaven—understood, quite literally, as the place of the sun, moon, and stars, and as the source of rain. Babylon was the place where human beings first began to study the stars and to plot and measure their courses. The towers would, almost certainly, have been the favored sites for astronomical observation—not for the restful and disinterested contemplation of the Greek philosophers, but for an apprehensive yet patient scrutiny and measurement of the motions of the heavenly bodies, in the service of calculation, prediction, and control (and, not least, for rain). The priests ruled the city on the basis of their knowledge— and divination—regarding heaven. The House of the Foundation of Heaven and Earth thus sought to link the city with the cosmos, and to bring the city into line with the heavenly powers-that-be, or perhaps to bring the powers-that-be into line with the goals of the city.

Not every human city has a ziggurat, but every human city orients itself on the basis of some intuition about the cosmic whole. Without some instruction to the contrary, human beings will eventually be inclined to look up to nature and, especially, to heaven, for heaven is the home of those visible powers that matter so much to the life of the city, especially as the city rests on agriculture.

"*And let us* make *for us a* name, lest we be scattered *abroad upon the face of the whole earth.*" The city is a mixture of pride and fear. Its origins, quite likely, are in fear. This immediately post-diluvian population has better reason than most to know and fear nature's wildness and inhospitality and to shrink from standing unarmed and dispersed before the powers that be. Having (at best) hearsay knowledge of God's promise to Noah ("No more floods," no total destruction), these men are inclined rather to trust to self-help for protection against the state of nature and the wide open spaces. They find strength in numbers and unification, and in their ability cooperatively to craft a home in the midst of an indifferent—not to say hostile—world.

But the beginnings in fear gradually give rise to pride. Human craft is its foundation. Beginning low and working from the ground up, men make bricks from the dust of the earth by the transforming power of fire. Lowly materials in hand, their ambition soars, as they conceive next to build a city and a tower, with its top in heaven. The city and tower express the human conquest of necessity, human self-sufficiency, and independence. Above all, the sky-scraping tower—whatever its explicit purpose—stands proudly as a monumental achievement of proud builders, to serve their everlasting glory. The anticipatory vaunt of the builders—"Let us *make* us a *name*"—shows the towering pride, though the fear of dispersion ("lest we be scattered abroad") has not been altogether extinguished.

What is this wish "to *make* us a *name*"? The verb "to make," *'âsâh,* has previously been used only by God either to announce His own makings or to command Noah's building of the ark, or, once, by the narrator to report God's making of coats of skins. The word *name,* hitherto used in relation to particular names, acquires here a new sense for the first time in Genesis. Adam had named the animals, named himself and the woman as woman and man (*'îyshâh* and *'îysh*), and later renamed the woman, "Eve," honoring her powers as mother of all life. People give and receive names that are significant (Noah, for example, the first person born after the death of Adam, gets a name meaning both "comfort" and "lament"). Fame and renown are sought, and some men even boast of their deeds (for example, Lamech, who is poet for his own heroism). But the aspiration to *make* a name goes beyond the desires to *give* oneself a name or to *gain* a name—that is, fame and glory for great success.

To *make* a name for oneself is, most radically, to "make that which requires a name." To make a new name for oneself is to remake the meaning of one's life so that it deserves a new name. To change the meaning of human being is to remake the content and character of human life. The city, fully understood, achieves precisely that. Through technology, through division of labor, through new modes of interdependence and rule, and through laws, customs, and mores, the city radically transforms its inhabitants. At once makers and made, the founders of Babel aspire to nothing less than self-*re*-creation—through the arts and crafts, customs and mores of their city. The children of man (Adam) remake themselves and, thus, their name, in every respect taking the place of God.

"But the Lord came down to see the city and the tower, which the children of man [or "children of Adam," *benêy ha'âdâm*] *were building."* At its midpoint, the story of Babel shifts from the human point of view to God's; but in making the shift, the narrator identifies the builders of the city as "the children of Adam." This could be a simple euphemism for human beings: sons of man, playing at being God. But it also connects the protagonists of this last pre-Abrahamic story with their oldest ancestor, the first or paradigmatic man, Adam (whose name is, in fact, not a proper name at all but rather the generic name for the entire species). The term *Children of Adam* assimilates the meaning of the project of Babel to the first "project" of the first man, the appropriation of autonomous knowledge of good and bad. Here, as in the Garden of Eden, men act in disobedience to distinct commands, Adam to the specific prohibition about the tree of knowledge, the builders of the tower to the post-diluvian command to be fruitful and multiply and to fill the earth. The comparison is apt, for in both cases the very deed means disobedience: in Adam's individual case, autonomy (choosing for yourself) is the opposite of obedience; in the builders' case, independent self-sufficiency (making yourself) is the opposite of obedient dependence, in relation to God or anything else. The road from Adam to the builders of the city is straight and true. As the end of the Garden of Eden story itself makes clear, the "fall of man" is in fact a bittersweet rise into civilization. God's announced future for our race—the so-called sentence pronounced in Genesis 3:14–24—embraces separation from the animals, self-consciousness, division of labor, rule and obedience, agriculture and bread, clothing and the arts, concern with good and bad, and the longing for immortality and lost innocence—in a word, civilization.

Civilization suffers, perhaps, when compared with the innocence and contentment of Eden; but when men come face to face with hostile nature or hostile men in a state of nature, the city appears as a remedy and the universal city a dream of deliverance, peace, and prosperity. In Babel, the universal city, with its own uniform language, beliefs, truths, customs, and laws, the dream of the city holds full sway in the hearts and minds of its inhabitants. Protected by its walls, warmed and comforted in its habitats, and ruled by its teachings, the children of Adam, now men of the city, neither know nor seek to know anything beyond. Contentment reigns, or so it does seem.

III

Can such a project succeed? Can such a city, if successfully founded, long endure? There is some reason to be doubtful. For one thing, the goal of reaching heaven with the tower is impossible; that the Lord had to "come down" to see what the men had done is, in part, a wry comment on the gap between their aspiration and their deed. For another, the materials used by the men were poor substitutes—bricks for stones, slime for mortar— and were unlikely to secure the desired permanence. More fundamentally, the unity of mind that inspired the project of the city could hardly be expected to survive the division of labor that brought the city into being: the oneness of human life would surely be replaced by the many ways of life, as masons and carpenters and farmers and metalworkers acquire different and competing interests. Yet God's single comment would seem to imply that the project would, or at least could, succeed as conceived—that is, that the city was feasible. Its failings, if any, were intellectual or moral or spiritual, not practical. They would be the failings of success.

What might these failings be? The first and most obvious is the matter of piety. What do the men revere? To what do they look up? At first they may look up, quite literally, to heaven, to the "powers that be": the sun, moon, and stars. But implicit in the attempt to know, exploit, and control these powers—through calculation, divination, and perhaps sacrifices—is their belief in their own superiority. The aspiration to reach heaven is in fact a desire to bring heaven into town, either to control it or, more radically, to efface altogether the distinction between the human and the natural or divine. In the end, the men will revere nothing and will look up to nothing not of their own making, to nothing beyond or outside of themselves, in part because they will see no eternal horizon. Content with and confined within "the cave," they will forget about the truly enduring realm beyond.

This charge against the city is not peculiarly biblical, as the allusion to the Platonic allegory of the cave reminds us. In comparing our lives to those of men enchained in caves, Socrates implies that it is the Promethean gift of fire and the enchantment of the arts that hold men unwittingly enslaved, blind to the world beyond the city. Mistaking their crafted world for the whole, men live as cave dwellers, ignorant of their true standing in the world and their absolute dependence on powers not of their making and beyond their control.

Second among their failings is that the men refuse to look not only "up" but down. They seem willfully to forget and deny their own mortality. Unlike Cain, who named his city for his son, the men of Babel want a name for themselves here and now, and give no thought for their offspring. Rational, but proudly unreasonable, these self-made makers forget their animality and the need for procreation. Mind and craft, they implicitly believe, can thoroughly triumph over necessity and mortality.

Third are several failings regarding the crucial matter of standards. In their act of total self-creation, there could be no separate and independent (non-manmade) standard to guide the self-making or by means of which to judge it good. The men, unlike God in His creation, will be unable to see that all that they had done is good. They could, of course, see if the building as built conformed to their own blueprint, but they could not judge its goodness in any other sense.

Even more important, there could be no moral and political standards sufficient for governing civic life and for guiding the proper use of power and technique. Power and technique are ethically neutral; they can be used both justly and unjustly. The omnicompetent city lacking in justice is a menace, both to itself and to the world. Even assuming that the inhabitants wish to be just, where will the builders of Babel find any knowledge of justice or, indeed, of any moral or political principle or standard?

Perhaps they will look up to the heavens. But looking to the heavens for moral guidance cannot succeed; the heavens may, as the Psalmist says, reveal the glory of God, but they are absolutely mute on the subjects of righteousness and judgment. One can deduce absolutely nothing moral even from the fullest understanding of astronomy and cosmology. Not even the basic prohibitions against cannibalism, incest, murder, and adultery—constitutive for all decent human communities—can be supported by or deduced from the natural world. (Perhaps this is why the Bible, devoted to instruction in righteousness, begins by denying the divinity of everything we see around us, and, especially, of the heavens.) From the point of view of righteousness—indeed, for all ethical and political purposes—cosmic gods are about as useful as no gods at all.

The intelligentsia of Babel know perfectly well the moral silence of the cosmic gods, but they are not without resources. The builders can build whatever is wanted. They will, accordingly, construct their own standards of right and good; but by this device they ultimately degrade the people they mean to serve. For if right and good are themselves human creations, if they have no independent meaning, justice loses all claim upon the soul. The natural longings for the right, the noble, or the good that might arise in human beings could only be treated with contempt: the soul would be fed instead with artificial and arbitrary substitutes, cast forth by the human "makers of values." And unlike the shadows or images cast by the poets in Plato's cave, these artifacts of "the just" or "the noble" could bear no image relation to some genuine original toward which they point.

Fourth among the failings is that all speech loses its power to reveal the world. Speech can still be expressive of human intention and useful in practical affairs, as stipulated meanings, commonly agreed to, are communicated from one person to the next. One can still say, "Come, let us build," and "Pass the hammer." But speech can no longer be used for inquiry, for genuine thought, for seeking after what is. When the units of intelligibility conveyed in speech have no independent being, when words have no power to reveal the things that truly are, then speech becomes only self-referential, and finally unintelligible. Even the name one makes for oneself means nothing.

Finally, and perhaps the worst failing of all, there is no possibility in such a city of discovering all of the other failings. The much-prized fact of unity, embodied especially in a unique but created truth, believed by all, precludes the possibility of discovering that one might be in error. The one uncontested way does not even admit of the distinction between truth and error. Self-examination, no less than self-criticism, would be impossible; there could be no Socrates who knew that he did not know. With everyone given over to the one common way, there would be mass identity and mass consciousness but no private identity or true self-consciousness; there would be shoulder-to-shoulder but no real face-to-face. Unity and homogeneity in self-creation is compatible with material prosperity, but it is a prescription for mindless alienation, from the world, from one's fellows, and from one's true self.

The project for mastery and unity begins by presupposing a partial estrangement of human beings from the world, which it hopes to overcome. Yet, in the end, the project for mastery—that is, if successful—means the complete and permanent estrangement from what is real. Ironically, the proposed remedy makes the disease total and totally incurable. The self-sufficient and independent city of man means full estrangement and spiritual death for all its inhabitants.

One must thus reconsider the earlier judgment that the project of the builders could in fact succeed as planned. Over the long haul, could mutual understanding survive or cooperation flourish in the presence of spiritual, moral, and intellectual decay? Would not the meaninglessness of speech eventually foster, all by itself, the confusion that is Babel? Does God intervene only to push matters quickly to their logical conclusion, to make manifest, all at once, what was implicitly fatal and fated in the project from the start?

IV

People are often best chastened and instructed by showing them vividly the previously hidden meaning of what they thought they wanted (for example, Midas's wish for the golden touch, or Achilles' wish for glory). In the Babel story, God's intervention would serve vividly to indicate the chaos, confusion, and alienation that are the inevitable consequences—or, better, the intrinsic meaning—of any all-too-human, prideful attempt at self-creation. This is, admittedly, an unconventional way of reading the Bible, and the suggestion that God is just a workman who hastens what is necessary does not square neatly with the text. For if failure were both inevitable and desirable, why did not God just bide His time and allow the moral lesson to teach itself? And why does He speak as if the venture might succeed?

In fact, it is only God's intervention that could *prove* that failure was *inevitable,* and permanently so. Spontaneous failure, happening later in the ordinary course of things, might be perceived as an accident, avoidable by another, and better, attempt. When we remember that the story is told mainly for the edification of its readers, we who are ever-tempted by the universal city feel the power of hearing God's judgment and seeing His will behind its actual demise. We are moved to see that the highest principle of being cannot support—that is, brings down—any human project that knows it not.

God's "punishment" fits the "crime." It opposes precisely each of the failings of the city by thwarting the plan to build it. The "punishment" not only "fits" the "crime"; it is also a gift to treat and rehabilitate the "criminal." Failure is offered as cure.

Confusion of speech is the cornerstone of God's intervention. Misunderstanding and non-understanding make further cooperation on the project impossible, and the men leave off building the city. Dispersion, following upon the confounding of speech, leads to the emergence of separate nations, with separate tongues and separate ways, with the near-certain prospect of difference, opposition, and the danger of war. It is easy to see how linguistic and cultural multiplicity, contention, and the threat of destruction through war "fit," as remedies of opposition, the aspirations to unity, harmony, and prideful self-sufficiency on which the city is built. But they also serve to remedy the failings of idolatry, the denial of mortality, the lack of standards, the divorce of speech from being, the lack of self-examination, and, in sum, the full estrangement of man. In every case, it is *negativity* that fits the punishment to the crime: failure or opposition is the heart of the remedy, or at least provides its beginnings.

The emergence of multiple nations, with their divergent customs and competing interests, challenges the view of human self-sufficiency. Each nation, by its very existence, testifies against the godlike status of every other; the rivalries that spring up are, in part, both the result and the cause of the affronts to national self-esteem that such otherness necessarily implies. The prospect of war and, even more, its actual horrors prevent forgetfulness of mortality, vulnerability, and insufficiency. Such times of crisis are often times that open men most to think about the eternal and the divine.

Awareness of the multiplicity of human ways is also the necessary precondition for the active search for the better or best way. Discovering the partiality of one's own truths and standards invites the active search for truths and standards beyond one's making. Opposition is the key to the discovery of the distinction between error and truth, appearance and reality, convention and nature—between that which is said to be or which appears to be and that which truly is, independent of all saying or seeming. And, even in relations between nations, the awareness of misunderstanding is the possible beginning of the search for genuine understanding, based upon recognizing the similar aspirations of the other; such an understanding is admittedly hard to attain (in the face of mistrust and genuine conflicts of interest), but it would be an understanding much deeper than the factitious homogeneity and agreement created out of nothing. In all of these cases, failure and want—and their recognition as failure and want—are the seeds of the human aspiration to be and do better. The self-content have no aspirations and longings; the self-content are closed to the high.

After man was created and set into the Garden of Eden, God observes that it is not good for the man to be alone. Though it is common and appropriate to think that "alone" means "lonely" or "in need of assistance"—that is, that it is a badge of weakness—"alone" could also mean "self-sufficient" or "independent," a sign of apparent strength. Why might a philanthropic God find fault with such apparent human strength? Perhaps because the perfect man, because he was alone, could not know himself to be perfect, indeed, could not know himself at all. Or, more likely, perhaps the original independent man, though he dwelt in the Lord's garden, had no real awareness of the presence of God. The coming of the woman first awakens man's self-awareness, and the result of their transgression not only heightens their moral self-consciousness but brings them to their first awareness of God. Only after they discover their own insufficiency and dependence, implicit in their nakedness, do they for the first time "hear the voice of the Lord God walking in the garden." Only in discovering the distance between ourselves and the Eternal, between ourselves and the truly self-sufficient, can human beings orient themselves toward that which is genuinely highest. God's dispersion of the nations is the political analog to the creation of woman: instituting otherness and opposition, it is the necessary condition for national self-awareness and the possibility of a politics that will hear and hearken to the voice of what is eternal, true, and good.

V

The story of Babel ends abruptly with the scattering of peoples across the face of the earth. The next story, the call of Abraham, begins even more abruptly:

> And the Lord said unto Abram: "Get thee out of thy country, and from thy kindred, and from thy father's house, unto the land that I will show thee. And I will make of thee a great nation, and I will bless thee, and make thy name great; and be thou a blessing. And I will bless them that bless thee, and him that curseth thee will I curse; and in thee shall all the families of the earth be blessed. So Abram went. . . ." (Genesis 12:1–4)

Why does God choose Abram? Why does Abram go? The text is utterly silent on these matters, perhaps in order not to distract us from the overwhelming facts that God did choose him and that Abram, without a word, got up and went.

But what if the lessons of Babel have something to do with the election of Abram? Could the text, by juxtaposing the two stories, be suggesting that an understanding of the beginning of Abram is linked to an understanding of Babel? Is there a *logical* and *moral* connection, not necessarily a historical or empirical one? We are encouraged to consider this possibility because of the literary structure of the text itself. Between Babel and the call of Abram, Genesis gives the single line of descent of the ten generations leading from Shem to Abram, tying the tale of dispersion to the tale of election. With the lesson of Babel behind him, the reader is ready to hear the call of Abram. Is it also possible that, with Babel behind him, someone in the line from Shem to Abram was ready to hear the call of God?

The most obvious negative connection between Babel and the new way has already been made: The universal city of self-made men will not be a pious, moderate, just, thoughtful, or dignified home for human life, notwithstanding its ability to improve man's material conditions through technology. To have discovered the moral and political insufficiency of human artfulness opens one to the possibility of something beyond artifice, to something real and truly satisfying. Again, this is not a peculiarly biblical point but a human one. According to Plato's *Republic,* the discovery that one's life is in the grip of shadows cast by the artifacts of poets and other opinion-makers liberates the prisoners in Socrates' cave to discover and pursue a world of incredible splendor beyond the cave. But since Abram is not Socrates and biblical fear of the Lord is not philosophy, perhaps there are some specific details in the generations of Shem that help us understand the special path that Abram took, against the background of the special cave that was Babel.

The name of the head of the line, Shem, means "name," the same as the word used in the Babel story, "to make us a name." Shem has gained a name for himself, not by pursuing it proudly but rather for his leadership in the pious covering of his father Noah's nakedness. The arch-ancestor of Abram is pious, refusing to look directly upon his natural origins; he looked away from nature in the direction of the as-yet-unpromulgated law to honor father and mother. Such a one is fit for the familial task of transmission. The inviolability, not to say sanctity, of family life will be crucial to the new way.

But the lineage of Abram becomes truly interesting with Terah, Abram's father. Terah, mysteriously and on his own, leaves his family home in Ur of the Chaldees and sets forth, with Abram, Lot, and Sarai, Abram's wife, to go to the land of Canaan. Chaldees is a biblical synonym for Babylonians; Ur, though not Babylon itself, was a Babylonian city, historically a center of moon-god worship, as was Haran, the city on the way to Canaan where Terah stopped. Abram will continue and complete the migration of his father, from Babylonia to Canaan, but in obedience to God's command. Like his father, Abram, too, is a refugee from Babylonia, from the land of the worship of the heavens and the heavenly bodies. He also, therefore, becomes a man without a home, without a city, without roots, and without the gods of his place of origins. Abram is the rootless, homeless, godless son of a wanderer (or radical), one who has grown out of, but who has outgrown and rejected, the Babylonian ways and gods. Two more things we know about Abram: he is married to a beautiful woman, Sarai, and he is still childless at age seventy-five when God calls, for Sarai is barren.

In his circumstances, Abram is as far as possible from the self-satisfied and secure condition of the builders of Babel: He has no gods; he has no city; he has no children; he has no settled ways; he is discontent, yet he is not despairing; he is capable of loving a beautiful woman even though she is barren. Almost certainly a man of longing, he longs for roots, land, home, settled ways, children, for something great, and for the divine. About the divine, perhaps he has learned something important—albeit negatively—as a result of his experience of the Babylonian way: He has seen through the worship of heaven.

How this might have happened is, of course, pure speculation. But is it not conceivable that, on the basis of his *own* study of the stars, Abram intuited that the visible stars could not themselves be gods, precisely because, though they are many, they move in such an ordered whole? Could Abram have intuited that there must be an invisible, single intelligent source behind the visible, many, but silent heavenly bodies, moving dumbly yet in intelligible ways? Is this perhaps what is behind the rabbinic legends that Abram smashed his father's idols, having become persuaded of monotheism on *philosophical* grounds, even before God spoke to him directly? Could Abram have figured out that the truth cannot be one city with many gods, but many nations in search of the one God?

God calls Abram with a command and a promise. The promise answers Abram's longing for land, seed, and a great name. (God does not condemn ambition for fame but will grant it only for pious service.) Abram goes not because he knows exactly who it is that is calling him—only later does God identify himself to Abram and then only partially as almighty

God *('êl shadday)*, in chapter 17; Abram goes not only because he wants the promise but also because he has at least two reasons to believe that the speaker just might be a god indeed and one able to deliver. First of all, this speaker in fact speaks—that is, this invisible being is itself clearly intelligent. Second, the voice addresses him not only personally but knowingly and with concern: marvelously, from Abram's point of view, the speaker has seen directly into Abram's heart, for the promises that are made respond to Abram's deepest longings. Nothing revered in Babylon could speak or know what men want. Abram completes the rejection of Babel and heads off to found God's new way.

VI

Did the failure of Babel produce the cure? Has the new way succeeded? The walk that Abram took led ultimately to biblical religion, which, by anyone's account, is a major source and strength of Western civilization. Yet, standing where we stand, late in the twentieth century, it is far from clear that the proliferation of opposing nations is a boon to the race. Mankind as a whole is not obviously more reverent, just, and thoughtful. And internally, the West often seems tired; we appear to have lost our striving for what is highest. God has not spoken to us in a long time.

The causes of our malaise are numerous and complicated, but one of them is too frequently overlooked: the project of Babel has been making a comeback. Ever since the beginning of the seventeenth century, when men like Bacon and Descartes called mankind to the conquest of nature for the relief of man's estate, the cosmopolitan dream of the city of man has guided many of the best minds and hearts throughout the world. Science and technology are again on the make, defying political boundaries en route to a projected human empire over nature. God, it seems, forgot about the possibility that a new universal language could emerge, the language of *symbolic mathematics,* and its offspring, mathematical physics. It is algebra that all men understand without disagreement. It is Cartesian analytic geometry that enables the mind mentally to homogenize the entire world, to turn it into stuff for our manipulations. It is the language of Cartesian mathematics and method that have brought Babel back from oblivion. Whether we think of the heavenly city of the philosophes, or the post-historical age toward which Marxism points, or, more concretely, the imposing building of the United Nations that stands today in America's first city—we see everywhere evidence of the revived Babylonian vision.

What are we now to think? Can a new Babel succeed? And can it escape (has it escaped?) the failings of success of its ancient prototype? What, for example, will it revere? Will its makers and its beneficiaries be hospitable to procreation and child rearing? Can it find genuine principles of justice and other non-artificial standards for human conduct? Will it be conducive to inquiry and a home for serious thought? Will it be self-critical? Can it really overcome our estrangement, alienation, and despair? Anyone who reads the newspapers has grave reasons for doubt. The city is back, and so, too, is Sidom, babbling and dissipating away. Perhaps we ought to see the dream of Babel today, once again, from God's point of view.

Part III

SACRED AND PROFANE

The Assimilating of Modernity

ROBERT ROYAL

Robert Royal is Vice President and Fellow in Religion and Society at the Ethics and Public Policy Center in Washington, D.C. He is the author of *1492 and All That: Political Manipulations of History* and is currently writing books on religion and environmentalism and Dante as a spiritual guide. His essays and reviews have appeared in *First Things, Crisis, The Wilson Quarterly, Communio,* and *The Washington Post.* He is the editor of *Jacques Maritain and the Jews* and co-editor (with Virgil Nemoianu) of *The Hospitable Canon* and *Play, Literature, Religion: Essays in Cultural Intertextuality.* The essay published below was written for this reader.

Christian Humanism in a Postmodern Age

L ET US BEGIN, like Plato, with a homely example: An Englishman, a Frenchman, and a German each undertook a study of the camel. The Englishman, taking his tea basket and a good deal of camping equipment, went to set up camp in the Orient, returning after a sojourn of two or three years with a fat volume of raw, disorganized, and inconclusive facts. The Frenchman went to the Jardin des Plantes for half an hour, questioning the guard, throwing bread to the camel, and poking it with the point of his umbrella; on returning home, he wrote an article for his paper full of sharp and witty observations. And the German? Filled with disdain for the Frenchman's frivolity and the Englishman's lack of general ideas, he locked himself into his room, where he drafted a multiple-volume work entitled *The Idea of the Camel Derived from the Concept of the Ego.*[1]

The story used to end here, but I would like to add a coda: An American postmodernist became acquainted with the Camel Problematic in a graduate seminar on "Speciesism in the Bible." Uncomfortable with the Englishman's acquiescence to established social hierarchies, the Frenchman's obviously phallic probing with his umbrella, and the German's attachment to metaphysics, she started a series of self-help workshops (soon to be the subject of a PBS special hosted by Bill Moyers) entitled "Beyond the Eye of the Needle, or Getting Through the Eurocentric Reductionist Gaze of Patriarchal, Phallocentric, and Onto-Theo-logic Hegemonies to Non-Western Signs and Species."

The owl of Minerva, as we know, flies only at dusk. At our particular moment in history, the kind of humanism dominant over the past few centuries is under assault by something we vaguely call postmodernism. Yet we also easily identify and even parody the rhetoric and aims of such postmodern discourse. All of which suggests that we are really at a point that I am tempted to call (were it not for the barbarism and further confusion) post-postmodern. And it is worth noticing that despite the eccentricities and tendencies toward nihilism and skepticism evident in our moment, it also contains remarkable prospects for a new Christian humanism—whether it calls itself modern, postmodern, or by some as yet unheard-of name.

I

Christian humanism may seem a contradiction in terms for people who are accustomed to think the word *humanism* is always preceded by the specification "secular." But few periods prior to our own saw things this way. Most ancient church fathers deliberately drew on pagan wisdom, believing that revelation complemented reason, particularly where reason recognized itself as powerless. Conversely, they thought faith benefited from the human investigation of the creation carried out by the very best thinkers of pagan antiquity. It is not an accident that Plato and Aristotle, for example, have been staples of Christian thought. Saint Augustine and Thomas Aquinas are unthinkable without them, as are the humanists of the Renaissance, all distinctly Christian. The more orthodox view of faith and reason is that God created two books, nature and the Scriptures, and the faithful do well to read deeply in both of them.

For some time it has been true, however, that humanism has had a very different cast, claiming to explain all human reality in terms of a more "basic," entirely secularized and material world. Descartes starts the process for some. But it is the great modern masters of suspicion—Marx, Freud, Darwin, Nietzsche—who were supposed to have closed the door to the Christian (or religious) past forever. Today Marxism is all but dead. Freud has been discredited as a scientist, though he lingers on as a para-literary figure. Darwinism, though we have no other explanation for the obvious rise of complicated life forms on Earth, is beset by theoretical problems and gaps in the fossil records that call for, if not abandonment, at least a serious modification in theory.[2] And Nietzsche, though the darling of most postmodern academics, seems a good battering ram to bring down established structures, but is virtually useless for anything constructive. Our moment is one in which the central doubters have been subjected to doubt, and no definite replacements have emerged.

Some figures in the movements known as postmodernism and poststructuralism have tried to step into the breach. It is important to keep these two terms distinct, even though they are related. *Poststructuralism,* as I would use the term, refers to a family of theories about language, truth, identity, and organizing "master narratives" of various kinds. For the most part, these theories basically take their origins from a group of French followers of the German philosopher Martin Heidegger who dominate much academic thought. Luc Ferry and Alain Renaut have formulated this neatly: the social critic Michel Foucault equals Heidegger plus Nietzsche; the psychiatrist Jacques Lacan equals Heidegger plus Freud; the French political theorist Pierre Bourdieu equals Heidegger plus Marx; and the father of deconstruction Jacques Derrida equals Heidegger plus the style of Derrida. Whatever the justice of this formula, it shows how the old modern binary cleavages such as rational and irrational in Nietzsche, unconscious and ego in Freud, and bourgeoisie and proletariat in Marx have themselves been deconstructed. Sophisticated people once thought they had the key to explaining the behavior and beliefs of the unsophisticated with these substitutions of one, supposedly deeper reality for another. Today, those presumptions have been undermined and rendered problematic by French Heideggerians.

Postmodernism, as I use the term, is broader than these specific changes both in its conceptualization and (I believe) in staying power. Outside of formal philosophy, postmodernism reflects a curious perception already present in the nineteenth century. There is no better formulation than Matthew Arnold's in "Stanzas from the Grande Chartreuse," where he speaks of our age as "Wandering between two worlds, one dead/The other powerless to be born." For Arnold, the dead world was the old modern world—including, we can now see, its Christian vestiges. The world powerless to be born is partly modern and partly something hard to specify. Its very essence is to remain in a zone of unresolvable ambivalence, hence its name faces in two directions at once: postmodern.

Clearly, such an epochal shift is a serious affair. Nietzsche and Heidegger recognized as much; Derrida, too, to a less serious extent. And this makes the often-silly politicization of postmodern and poststructuralist thought (as in our camel parable) all the more distressing. Arnold's notion of powerlessness, impotence, and incapacity to issue in a live birth results precisely from something that postmodern thinking either has not done or can never do, at least as it is currently practiced.

Take Jean-François Lyotard, the most influential French theorist of postmodernism. Lyotard, in a typically combative formula, called philosophy "the mental illness of the West."[3] Many people who come upon phrases like that in postmodern theory understandably get the impression that postmodernism is itself a mental illness and that it portends the decline of the West. In fairness to what is good in postmodernism, I would like to draw a distinction that may prevent unnecessary conflict. During the existence of the late, unlamented Soviet Union, sophisticated Marxists (mostly in the West) defended themselves by denouncing "vulgar Marxists"—that is, people who crudely used a few notions out of Marx to score debating points. I would argue that there is a fairly large cadre of vulgar postmodernists, mostly situated on campuses and in editorial offices and in television and film studios, who know little of Heidegger or Nietzsche and operate in a spirit far different from the figures they invoke. They give ample reason to fear that we are in the throes of a barbarian invasion in which all human structures and civilization shall be undermined and "problematized" in the name of we know not what.

Yet knowing a bit about Lyotard's work, when I first read the statement about philosophy as mental illness, it reminded me not of Oswald Spengler or other theorists of Western decline, but of G. K. Chesterton, who included a famous chapter in his *Autobiography* titled "How to Be a Lunatic." Chesterton recounts how as a young man the passion to be absolutely rational, in the modern sense, drove him back to questioning the very wellsprings of thought—and also almost drove him mad. In *Heretics* and *Orthodoxy* he describes the "narrow infinity" of a certain kind of reason, which presumes it can specify all of reality, as the maddest use of our minds. The postmodern talk about the problems of Descartes and a certain Enlightenment view of human beings is helpful here. It takes an effort of imagination to break out of this iron circle. Imagination in these conditions is not mere fantasy or poetry, in the bad sense of the term. Properly understood and under Christian humanist auspices, it could become a vehicle of a true liberation.

Chesterton is often regarded as a humorous Christian essayist whose thought moves within well-known boundaries of English tradition. But as is clear in the above remarks, perhaps he should not be read with a priori assumptions. Chesterton, in spite of his nonphilosophical method, puts into question whether postmodernism is quite as unprecedented as we suppose. He and some other Christian writers of this century were premoderns who, precisely because they were also Christians, anticipated both where modernism was headed and what some postmodern reactions would be to that course. Paradox plays a large role in Chesterton, for example, precisely because he knows that any simple discursive use of language at the end of the modern age must appear either as a reductivist objectivity bordering on scientism, or as impressionism threatening to fall into mere subjectivism. Thus he has to use language playfully to suggest something beyond the usual categories of thought, to approach what is absent by what is present—a difficult artistic task postmodern writers have claimed as their own.

If you think this overstates Chesterton's literary strategies, re-read the conclusion of *The Man Who Was Thursday*, where the very breakdown of all explanation and the appearance of an entire menagerie of animals to suggest the identity of the character Sunday (who is God or something like Being) anticipates postmodern fiction. Chesterton, who never heard of Heidegger, often sounds like him. For example, who wrote this?

> There is at the back of all our lives an abyss of light, more blinding and un-
> fathomable than any abyss of darkness; and it is the abyss of actuality, of
> existence, of the fact that things truly are incredibly and sometimes almost
> incredulously real. It is the fundamental fact of being, as against not being;
> it is unthinkable, yet we cannot unthink it, though we may sometimes be
> unthinking about it; unthinking and especially unthanking. For he who has
> realized this reality knows that it does outweigh, literally to infinity, all
> lesser regrets or arguments for negation, and that under all our grumblings
> there is a substance of gratitude.[4]

Or this? "All our heart's courage is the/echoing response to the/first call of Being which/gathers our thinking into the/play of the world."[5] The first was Chesterton, the second, Heidegger.

The literary critic George Steiner emphasizes a dimension of Heidegger, little-noticed among the fruitier postmodern literary theorists but not lost on pure philosophers and theologians: "I have come to believe that Heidegger's use and exploration of the seventeenth-century Pietist tag *Denken ist Danken,* 'To think is to thank', may well be indispensable if we are to carry on as articulate and moral beings."[6] Contrary to much that we see all around us, at least some kinds of postmodern thought find a kind of piety toward the universe as constitutive of proper thought itself. That basic gratitude and piety—"a piety of thinking" toward Being, as Heidegger put it—is lacking in many of what I have called the vulgar postmodernists. It is no wonder that many people think therefore that postmodernism makes it impossible for us to carry on as fully human beings. But that is far from being everything that can be found in postmodernism.

Following Steiner's lead, we might look at how the postmodern might be made to open out onto some older concepts related to the Christian humanist tradition. And as a comprehensive set of pegs on which to hang some reflections, let us examine in turn the three transcendentals: the good, the true, and the beautiful.

II

First, the good. Postmodernism is most vulnerable in its apparent inability to state an ethic. Insofar as it has ethical interests, it tends toward the mere deconstruction of "master narratives," the reversals of margin and center, and the questioning of identities. The reason for this, put very simply, is that existing religion, metaphysics, politics, and domestic life are regarded as without foundations. Both in theory and practice they can be oppressive—or even terroristic. But contrary to postmodern assumptions, merely undermining such institutions does not guarantee greater freedom and justice. Most American inner cities today contain large numbers of young people who have been freed from the old Western master narratives of patriarchy, religion, and enlightenment democracy. The result of that liberation, it would seem, is that (to borrow a well-known formula of Heidegger's) "only a god can save us now." Also, in a world where ethnic cleansing, political uses of famine, and totalitarian regimes still exist, ironic undermining is a very weak weapon with which to pursue justice. At the absurd limit, we find figures like the American philosopher Richard Rorty saying that, yes, democracies are nice, but we should not look for any deep reasons in religion or philosophy to defend them because there are no such reasons. Or he argues that because liberal societies lack universal foundations, a "liberal ironist" like himself, faced with an Adolf Hitler, could only try to "josh him out of" his anti-Semitic obsessions.[7]

In addition, I think we have to say that the real-life histories of the central postmodern figures present us with a cautionary tale. Nietzsche and Heidegger both display strong signs of what philosopher Philippa Foote has called simple "immoralism."[8] The Nazi appropriation of Nietzsche, of course, falsified his work somewhat. And Heidegger's adherence to Nazism (an adherence he never entirely renounced) must be thought through in non-Heideggerian terms. In a famous interview in *Der Spiegel,* he describes the inner greatness of Nazism as its participation in the global struggle with technology. If you get the proportions of existing nazism wrong on such a scale, you might do better to sit down and remind yourself of some simple notions of good and evil before you venture to say any more about the complex relations of history and technology.

I cannot go here into the intricacies of the argument, but let me state baldly that both Nietzsche and Heidegger fail—and cannot help but fail—as moral thinkers because, whatever their other accomplishments, they have no place for absolute moral truths or universal principles of justice. To put an end to slavery, for instance, as happened primarily through the agency of British Christianity in the nineteenth century, requires a deep belief in and willingness to sacrifice for the truth that slavery is wrong. Would Nietzsche, looking at the pitiful condition of the "last men" ravaged by Christian "slave morality" and by the depredations of the modern world feel such a burning need? Nietzscheans will no doubt object that his revolt against that decadence was spurred precisely by the will to free those poor creatures. But in the meantime, it is clear, he feels—and shows—a good deal of contempt for the slaves.

A related set of problems persists in Jacques Derrida in spite of his own worries about Nietzsche and Heidegger's connections to Nazism. In particular, Derrida worries that any "proper of man," as Heidegger put it in his "Letter on Humanism," is the root of all Nazisms.[9] Astonishingly, however, Derrida says in a more recent book that universal principles of justice must be maintained in human societies, or disasters will follow.[10] As Europe goes about unifying itself, he continues, it must also deconstruct the old hegemonic view of itself as the exemplary culture. Europe must see itself as defined both by its past and by its openness and recognition of the Other. I agree with all of this, after a fashion. But I don't understand where in Derrida's thought these universals could possibly find a place, let alone a grounding. Deconstruction is almost by definition the enemy of identity, "henophobic." For the vulgar postmodernists, at least, we have no self on the Cartesian model who could be the subject of rights or obliged to observe universal principles. Paradoxically, for the same vulgar postmodernists (along with many other people), this insubstantial self still has an ever-expanding set of desires conceived of as rights.

I would propose a different starting point. We must ask ourselves: By what principles do we judge good and bad behavior in Western and non-Western societies?[11] I am prepared to say that we do so on the basis of Western natural-law notions that emerged in the reflection of a group of theologians shortly after the discovery of the Americas, especially Francisco de Vitoria.[12] These theologians had to decide how Christians should treat the newly discovered peoples in the Americas—peoples who clearly had had no significant previous contact with Europe, could not have known the Old or New Testaments, and lived in societies that partly observed but also grossly violated the natural law.

The answers of Vitoria, Cano, and later Suarez set us on the road toward Locke, the U.S. Constitution, the Declaration of the Rights of Man, modern international law, and the U.N. Universal Declaration of Human Rights, which reads in many places as if it had been lifted from Vitoria. I am well aware that these later developments—particularly the ever-growing notions of rights—are not without their own philosophical difficulties. Furthermore, Vitoria and his colleagues were powerless to stop the atrocities Europeans committed against native peoples. To go back to Vitoria, however, might enable us to make a fresh start at thinking about rights again. If we all value modern rights and liberties, at least to some extent, we might do well to recall from what soil they sprang. It was not from the soil of postmodern bows to the Other, or from the undermining and unmasking of our own discourses of power, but from a religiously based philosophy confronting a wholly new human situation in the Americas.

We may see the importance of universal principles in a more recent and notorious case. Salman Rushdie has written what I consider to be one of the most remarkable postmodern fictions, *The Satanic Verses*. Despite his quarrels with Islam and his often-silly denigration of Margaret Thatcher and the United States, Rushdie paints a remarkably funny, rich, and imaginative portrait of the strange disorientations of self, society, and reality currently under way throughout the world as various cultures meet and mingle. That said, though, Rushdie's real-life adventures do not lead us to put much confidence in his novel's postmodern discourse on multiculturalism and non-Eurocentric categories.

Margaret Thatcher used to be called the Iron Lady. But had she been a postmodern Ironist Lady and not been supremely confident in the justice of using the British Special Forces to protect Rushdie from the Other (namely, the Ayatollah Khomeini), Rushdie's doubts about the truth of Islam and the existence of the world to come would have been settled, one way or another, long ago. No amount of talk about multiculturalism, anticolonialism, perspectivism, relativism, or antifoundationalism can get around disputes of this kind. We have to decide what we think good and right, and be able to give reasons that can have cash value, as William James used to say, in the world.

For me, the best place to begin thinking about that ethical question is in Christian humanism, not in Heidegger or any of his followers. And if we begin to pay careful attention again to what we think right and why, we will be led back to a living and fruitful tradition.

III

What about the second transcendental, the true? In spite of vulgar postmodernism's posturings and play with the "abyss," it seems to me that one of the strongest claims of postmodernism is its greater truth compared with the old modernism, even if postmodernists would probably not put the relationship quite that way. The reductive visions of modernism and technological scientism are so obviously false that almost any movement which reopens forgotten regions cannot help but appeal to anyone sensitive to the riches and mysteries of the world. When all is said and done, even Heidegger has a vision of the world that is a recognizably more human place than the old modernity. Death means something there besides extinction; things are both themselves and part of something larger and more significant.

Postmodern literature is the place to observe some of the most lush effects of those insights. On the whole, the Latin American and Central European postmodernists do better when they turn to these subjects than do the North Americans. North American postmodernist writers, like North American postmodernist theorists, tend to run riot in subvertings and decentering of so-called hegemonies and proclaiming their own daring in doing so. But compared to most times and places in human history, the "hegemonies" in developed societies are not very powerful or oppressive in the first place. Some critics have argued that the first-world postmodern fiction is really hypermodern fiction and therefore not a contribution to solving the old modern problems.[13] There is unfortunately no terminological police force or justice system to which we can appeal on these issues.

So it is useful to keep in mind that there are several forms of sensibility that have been given the name postmodern.

But the kind of postmodern fiction that has appeared in Latin America and Central Europe sometimes has unusual truths to tell. Milan Kundera, for example, exhibits something that rises beyond the mere destruction, *mise en abîme,* and shaking of foundations that characterizes much American and French postmodernism. At the end of the *Book of Laughter and Forgetting,* we find this remarkable scene at—of all places—a Czechoslovakian nude beach:

> A man with an extraordinary paunch began developing the theory that Western civilization was on its way out and we would soon be freed once and for all from the bonds of Judeo-Christian thought—statements Jan had heard ten, twenty, thirty, a hundred, five hundred, a thousand times before—and for the time being those few feet of beach felt like a university auditorium. On and on the man talked. The others listened with interest, their naked genitals staring dully, sadly, listlessly at the yellow sand.

Could any American, with the exception perhaps of the late Walker Percy, have written that moving statement of the impotence of postmodern sexual aspirations and, at the same time, the clear postmodern or post-postmodern insight that all this points only to dust and death?

Kundera has quarreled with another Czech postmodernist, Václav Havel (the current president of the Czech Republic), in ways relevant to our subject. Tomás, a character in *The Unbearable Lightness of Being,* chooses to make his wife happy by staying with her instead of participating in a public protest on the grounds that the resistance to a totalitarian regime "can't do any good anyway." Havel, of course, has spent much of his life trying to "live in truth," which had become a slogan among the Eastern European thinkers influenced by Husserl and Heidegger. Living in truth meant not compromising with the system and believing that seemingly hopeless acts of resistance were "useless" only if you lost genuine hope.

Havel and Kundera have each done solid work, but in light of the second transcendental, the true, I think we can begin to see the problem with some of the postmodern attempts to subvert all large-scale theories of meaning, whether pre-modern or modern. The postmodern strategy usually denies

those "master narratives" in favor of the *petites histoires,* that is, personal stories as the only places where rich meaning opens to us. In this view, all the
old *grands récits*—Christianity, Hegelianism, Marxism, even liberalism—are
dangerous totalizing and potentially terroristic illusions.

We should probably not identify Kundera's character, Tomás, with Kundera himself. But can Havel's "living in truth" be accommodated in postmodernism? Perhaps the most powerful attempt to derive that sort of
commitment is Edith Wyschogrod's *Saints and Postmodernism.*[14] For
Wyschogrod, saints are not models in the traditional fashion whose selfless
action we imitate, but people who teach us how to go beyond traditional
categories to unprecedented postmodern types of freedom from all previous systems and models. It may be that someone, somewhere, someday,
will be moved by people of that sort. It is much more likely, however, that
heroism and saintliness will continue to come from where they have always
come, from "living in truth" in the sense of concrete imitation and following in the path that others have demonstrated is simply good.

The contemporary Christian humanist, faced with continuing political
and spiritual struggles, has a much better starting place than do most of his
contemporaries for considering how hope and living in truth may be justified in spite of all postmodern challenges. After all, if the *petites histoires*
were everything—and there were no Václav Havels or Lech Walesas willing to die for a vision of the human good—much of the world might still
be enslaved, and more of it would be threatened. Alexander Solzhenitsyn
prophetically concluded his Nobel Prize lecture with the old Russian peas-
ant aphorism: "One word of truth outweighs the whole world." If we admire the results of such heroism, we may find that some older ways are
better than newer ones to account for the unlooked-for triumph of freedom and truth.

IV

This brings us to our third transcendental, the beautiful, and the question
of aesthetics. Art has become more important in the postmodern world, it
seems to me, because the truth claims of philosophy, theology, ethics, and
even nature seem weak. The argument on many campuses over the literary

canon has taken on added heat precisely because, where truth is assumed a priori not to exist, images and atmosphere will shape how most people think. Literature in particular is one of the few places where we still come upon whispers of transcendence. Sensing that postmodern theory and practice threaten to close off even that escape hatch, George Steiner has defended some older views of works of art under the intentionally religious title *Real Presences.*[15] At the outset, he disputes all the current postmodern theories that claim language can refer only to other uses of language. Instead, he argues that the "capacity of human speech to communicate meaning and feeling is underwritten by the assumption of God's presence."[16]

In the inquiring spirit of Christian humanism, however, we have to approach the bizarre, complicated, and at times self-contradictory forms of postmodern art and aesthetics for what they tell us about current ways of being human in the world. Lyotard has formulated the task of postmodern art as "presenting the unpresentable in presentation itself"—an almost religious aspiration. And under postmodern conditions, this means denying ourselves what Lyotard calls the "consolation of beautiful forms." At the other extreme, Susan Shell has explained the difference between the old modern existentialism and postmodern art as follows:

> The dizzying horror of the abyss is replaced by the virtuosity of performance—a kind of perpetual mid-air tap dance, in which the ground isn't needed—not as in the land of [car]toons, because its absence isn't noticed, but because the ground itself is no longer sought.[17]

These two formulations show the ambivalent, even contradictory aspirations of postmodern aesthetics. In part, with Heidegger, it points toward what exceeds the concept in the direction of Being and of the Kantian sublime. For the much larger part, however, it looks to the superficial deconstruction of everything familiar—especially in performance art, because performance "artists" are always still available to us when all that is solid melts into air.

Sometimes the two tendencies appear in the same work, as in the American Paul Auster's anti-detective novel *City of Glass.* An anti-detective novel, if you have not read Auster or Robbe-Grillet's *Les Gommes,* turns the usual story line upside down: the detective starts out with the familiar in-vestigation of a crime, but then identities, meanings, and characters gradu-ally become confused and slip into an abyss of mysteries. Sometimes the real-life author shows up by name as a troubled and troubling character. It's as if Kafka were called in to do a rewrite of Raymond Chandler. There is a destruction of the usual frameworks of life on the way toward a transcen-dence that never comes—a kind of tap dancing in mid air.

The two different postmodern aesthetics, the sublime and the perfor-mative, seem opposed but stem, I think, from a common source, a turning away from existing beings. For example, there is little discussion of natural beauty in postmodern theory largely because postmodern belief in the constructedness of all reality has occluded nature itself, even though na-ture is talked about a great deal. This does not bode well, by the way, for those trying to think through the question of technology and, more broadly, questions about the environment.

When pre-modern people looked at nature they saw both change and, more rarely, permanence. Whatever order and reason could be introduced into the environment by pre-modern man was seen as an achievement that perfected untutored and often-threatening nature. Attempts to reproduce the cosmological order in political systems and even within the human spirit (microcosm answering to macrocosm) sought to rise above the in-evitable processes of generation and corruption. In his poem "Sailing to Byzantium," W. B. Yeats shows a similar impulse in protesting against his own old age:

> O sages dancing in God's Holy fire
> As in the gold mosaic of a wall
> Come from the fire, perne in a gyre
> And be the dancing masters of my soul.
> Sick with desire and fastened to a dying animal
> It knows not what it is. And gather me
> Into the artifice of eternity.

Note the connection here: eternity is, for man, the product of a wisdom, almost a craft, that enables him to step outside even his own most intense desires. Yeats is a modernist, but his existential situation, his realization of being-toward-death, leads him back to an old solution for our ever-new sense of impermanence and mortality.

A much different mood emerged as modern technologies began their dominance over the world. Since at least the eighteenth century, for most artists regular mechanism and artifice have become "mechanical and artificial." The romantic revolt against artificiality and dead social and moral forms is more than an emotional outburst. Mechanism, more than at any time in human history, is perceived as threatening human particularity and spontaneity. In a world of mechanism, all that seems left for the authentically human is the uncanny, the unassimilable, perhaps even the monstrous. Much of the postmodern talk about transgressing boundaries, open or fragmentary art forms, draws on this sentiment.

Those postmodern currents that took their start from a one-sided desire to free the human person from all mechanism and "closed" social systems have now worked out their own logic. They wind up denying the existence of the person, the intelligibility of the world, and the possibility of a just order. Given the vacuum they have created, it is no wonder that nature has rushed in to fill the void and we find quite authoritarian forms of feminism, gay rights, and anti-European *tercermundista* ideologies speaking, quite incongruously, a uniform language of deconstruction in several fields. Iris Murdoch has astutely explained this phenomenon:

> Philosophy, anthropology, history, [and] literature have different procedures and methods of verification. It is only when the idea of truth as relation to separate reality is removed that they can seem in this odd hallucinatory light to be similar. With the idea of truth, the idea of value also vanishes. Here the deep affinity, the holding hands under the table, between structuralism and Marxism becomes intelligible.[18]

Theology must be theology, philosophy must be philosophy, not poetry; but in spite of imagination's dangers, of which Plato was already aware, imagination (even postmodern imagination) may be a powerful tool for finding truth. While no one with any sense expects a novelist, poet, painter, or composer to render the whole truth about the human condition, forms of the imagination are an important testimony of the modes of being and truth in any period. But there is something more to the best art than a portrait of one historical moment. Some forms of art, far from being merely fantasies, point toward transcendent truths and realities. As Simone Weil has said repeatedly, art may also be a form of attention, the first faint flickering of a light that can lead us out of the Platonic cave.

The particular difficulty in dealing with postmodern art forms is that they combine the potentially transcendent and the trivial in ways that leave you dissatisfied with both—sometimes unsure which is which. The power of true imagination, which Coleridge was the first to distinguish from mere fantasy, is thereby darkened. Postmodern philosophy has allowed various forms of fantasy, not imagination, to present themselves as profoundly philosophical art works. Any image that can claim vague relationship with the subverting of identities in Heidegger or Derrida is automatically granted a certain profundity before we have even looked at the real aesthetic value of the product.

True imagination will emerge where and in whatever forms it wishes. A Christian humanism that desires to be faithful to reality can only try to understand it clearly when it does. But that very faithfulness demands we also remember that many postmodern themes were not entirely unknown to pre-modern thinkers and artists. We thus need a kind of philosophical border patrol that will undertake to show, without a clumsy crushing of exploratory imagination, that some postmodern work may bear quite different meanings and artistic resolutions than currently thought.

V

Let me conclude with a plea that contemporary Christian humanists, like their predecessors, begin to reconstruct a language that is philosophically potent enough to allow the new, powerless world (first discerned by Matthew Arnold), finally to be born. That language must not talk solely of difference and absence; it must be able to affirm in some fashion, especially for non-philosophers, identity and presence. At the limit it must of course be able to defend not only presence but—for some of us—the identity of the Real Presence. To do so does not require, I think, a school of vulgar Christian humanists to meet the vulgar postmodernists point for point. Rather, we need a whole generation of thinkers who better understand their obligations not only to Being but to beings, including human beings.

The conclusion of Chesterton's *Heretics* sounds the battle charge for the kind of struggle I envision. I regard this passage as a kind of post-post-modern ideal that both tap dances over the void as lightly as any postmodern Fred Astaire, yet never forgets where the real ground lies:

> Truths turn into dogmas the instant they are disputed. Thus every man who utters a doubt defines a religion. And the skepticism of our time does not really destroy the beliefs, rather it creates them; gives them their limits and their plain and defiant shape. We who are Liberals once held Liberalism lightly as a truism. Now it has been disputed, and we hold it fiercely as a faith. We who believe in patriotism once thought patriotism to be reasonable, and thought little more about it. Now we know it to be unreasonable, and know it to be right. We who are Christians never knew the great philosophic common sense which inheres in that mystery until the anti-Christian writers pointed it out to us. The great march of mental destruction will go on. Everything will be denied. Everything will become a creed. It is a reasonable position to deny the stones in the street; fires will be kindled to testify that two and two make four. Swords will be drawn to prove that leaves are green in summer. We shall be left defending, not only the incredible virtues and sanities of human life, but something more incredible still, this huge impossible universe which stares us in the face. We shall fight for visible prodigies as if they were invisible. We shall look on the impossible grass and the skies with a strange courage. We shall be of those who have seen and yet have believed.[19]

ROBERT COLES

Robert Coles is widely known as one of the most humane voices in American intellectual life. An M.D. and a psychiatrist, Coles won the Pulitzer Prize for his *Children of Crisis* series. The author of more than fifty books, Coles has written on literary and religious figures such as Walker Percy, Flannery O'Connor, Dorothy Day, and Simone Weil. Among his other books are *The Spiritual Life of Children* and *The Call of Stories*. This essay was originally published in *The Virginia Quarterly Review* and was reprinted in *The Mind's Fate: A Psychiatrist Looks at His Profession*.

Freud and God

RELATIVELY UNKNOWN, and resident of a strongly Catholic city, Freud dared take on belief in God at a meeting in early March 1907 of the Vienna Psychoanalytical Society. He presented a paper with the title "Obsessive Actions and Religious Practices." Most of the observations were clinical—the work of a brilliant physician connecting instances from his practice into a narrative presentation meant to convey a theoretical point of view. But at the end, when Freud mentions "the sphere of religious life," a morally argumentative strain begins to appear. The reader is told that "complete backslidings into Sin are more common among pious people than among neurotics," an incautious generalization even then (despite the inhibitions Freud had noticed among "his" neurotics) and a quaintly unsupportable one now.

When Freud approaches "religious practices," he is intelligent and helpful to the kind of scholar who is not interested in debunking, but rather in understanding man's churchgoing history. The "petty ceremonials" of a given religion can, he points out, become tyrannical; they manage to "push aside the underlying thoughts." He suggests that historically various "reforms" have been intended to redress "the original balance"—rescue beliefs from arid pietism. But in his concluding paragraphs Freud again makes a sweeping generalization, tries to join an analysis of psychopathology to social criticism: "One might venture to regard obsessional neurosis as a pathological formation of a religion, and to describe that neurosis as an individual religiosity and religion as a universal obsessional neurosis."

This is a kind of naïve and gratuitous reductionism we have seen relentlessly pursued, these days, in the name of psychoanalysis. Freud himself was often more careful. In the well-known essay "Dostoievski and Patricide" he acknowledged the futility of a psychoanalytic "explanation" of a writer's talent, as opposed to any psychological difficulties he or she may happen to share with millions of other human beings. When he risked social and political speculation (in the exchange of letters with Einstein or in *The New Introductory Lectures*), he could be guarded about using his ideas to interpret culture. Sometimes, even when writing about religious matters, as in *Totem and Taboo* or *Moses and Monotheism,* he was frank about being conjectural. In his first draft, completed in 1934, a book on the origins of monotheism was titled *The Man Moses, a Historical Novel.*

But religion clearly excited him to truculence, nowhere more evidently than in *The Future of an Illusion* (1927). He starts out warning himself to be objective, to summon a long-range historical view, to be modest, restrained. Yet he quickly connects religious ideas to man's obvious helplessness in the face of life's mysteries. He then connects *that* condition to the child's predicament—"an infantile prototype." After pointing out that there is no conclusive "proof," in the word's modern scientific sense, of God's existence, he refers to "the fairy tales of religion" and indicates with a rising vehemence that religion is a mere illusion "derived from human wishes." His tone here is distinctly different from his other sociological writing. He contrasts his line of argument ("correct thinking") to another ("lame excuse"). "Ignorance is ignorance," he reminds us, and adds immediately, "no right to believe anything can be derived from it." And then:

"In other matters [than religion] no sensible person will behave so irresponsibly or rest content with such feeble grounds for his opinions." He declares that "the effect of religious thinking may be likened to that of a narcotic," and that religion, "like the obsessional neurosis" he had described so vividly years earlier, "arose out of the Oedipus complex, out of the relation to the father."

To his great credit, he then pulls back, and acknowledges that "the pathology of the individual" does not provide a fully accurate analogy to the nature of religious faith, but he is soon referring to faith as "the consolation of religious illusion" and expressing the hope that in some future, when human beings have been "sensibly brought up," they will not have this "neurosis"—will "need no intoxicant to deaden it." Then, at the end, he embraces "our God, Logos," insists yet again that "religion is comparable to a childhood neurosis," and makes an invidious distinction between his stoic adherence to science and those who look with faith to God: "My illusions are not, like religious ones, incapable of correction. They have not the character of delusion."

Philip Rieff, whose essays and books have been among the most learned and suggestive responses to Freud's writings, has been harsh about *The Future of an Illusion* and the kindred writing that preceded it. Rieff refers to Freud's "genetic disparagements of the religious spirit" and finds his reasoning tautological: "He will admit as religious only feelings of submission and dependence; others are dismissed as intellectual dilutions or displacements of the primary infantile sentiment." It is, Rieff says, "scientific name-calling," though in the service of a sincerely held modern rationalism.

Freudian psychologists have seldom challenged Freud's views as Rieff has done. But in 1979 Ana-Maria Rizzuto, who teaches at the Psychoanalytic Institute of New England, published a major study of the relation between psychiatry and faith, *The Birth of the Living God.* "The cultural stance of contemporary psychoanalysis," she begins, "is that of Freud: religion is a neurosis based on wishes. Freud has been quoted over and over again without considering his statements in a critical light." Examining her own experience as a psychoanalyst, she finds herself rejecting Freud's assertion that "God really *is* the father"; she also rejects his insistence that religion is a kind of oedipal offshoot—a "sublimation," a means by which erotic and aggressive feelings toward a particular man, the father, are given expression. Such an explanation, she argues, takes an extremely complicated and still-continuing emotional and intellectual process and "reduces it to a representational fossil, freezing it at one exclusive level of development." And it incidentally denies mothers, grandparents, brothers, and sisters any substantial involvement in the emotional events that affect religious belief. Extremely preoccupied with "the father-son relationship" in his analysis of the psychology of religion, "Freud does not concern himself with religion or God in women."

The English psychoanalysts D. W. Winnicott, Charles Rycroft, and Harry Guntrip have obviously influenced this American psychoanalyst. Like them, she puts strong emphasis on the texture of "object relations": the mind as constantly responding to and reflecting involvements with a range of human beings, rather than the mind as a battlefield in which certain "agencies" fight things out with various maneuvers—in the hands of some psychoanalytic theorists, a kind of solipsism.

She seems especially influenced by Winnicott's revisions of Freud as a result of his work as a pediatrician and child psychoanalyst. He emphasized the significance of early months and years, when babies begin to distinguish *themselves* (the mother is there, and I am here) and to show the distinctively human characteristic of symbolization. The first instance of that lifelong habit is known to all parents—those so-called "transitional objects" which mean so much to young children: a part of a blanket, a teddy bear, a doll, a spoon, an article of clothing, and later on, a certain song or story or scene. To be sure, even in the nursery, history, culture, class, and caste determine what "materials" are available; but Winnicott's work with infants casts a new light on their mental complexity and variability. Anywhere, any time, infants discover their very own world of word and thought, symbol and memory.

Winnicott did not find that adult ideas or inclinations were similar to a baby's mental stratagems. His point is that, early on, all children learn to carry with themselves ideas and feelings connected to persons, places, things—and these mental "representations" attest to nothing less or more than powerful human capacities. It would be foolish to *equate* a baby's attachment to a part of a blanket with a poet's use of synecdoche or a supplicant's attachment to Rosary beads, but there *is* a connection—as in that between incipient and full-fledged humanity rather than early and later psychopathology. What analysts such as Winnicott or Rizzuto aim to document is a beginning effort at self-definition—through our thoughts and interests, likes and dislikes, fantasies and dreams, affections and involvements.

Dr. Rizzuto calls *one* of these efforts "God representation," referring to the notion about God that most of us in the West acquire early in life from what we hear at home, at school, in church, in the neighborhood playing lots. Even agnostics or atheists, she finds, have had ideas about God, given Him some private form—a mental picture, some words, a sound. In the lives of children, as parents know in one way, child psychiatrists in another, God joins company with all sorts of kings, generals, superheroes, witches, monsters, demons, friends, brothers and sisters, parents, teachers, policemen, firemen, and on and on. Dr. Rizzuto offers histories of His presence in the minds of people who firmly call themselves nonbelievers. She points out that God may be someone rejected, denied, ridiculed as well as embraced, relied upon constantly—and that each of those psychological attitudes can be connected to the constraints and opportunities (and good and bad luck) of a given life. Her interests, in this regard, are not clinical or categorically judgmental. She is writing as a phenomenological psychologist.

II

Freud continually returned to the idea of God; he wrote about His origin in the minds of others, devoted numerous articles and three books to Him. Why? Not necessarily to work out a "problem." As did Winnicott, Rizzuto sees religious ideas as part of our cultural life—like music, art, literature, or for that matter, formal intellectual reasoning and scientific speculation. They are all connected to our endless effort to place ourselves in space and time, to figure out where we come from and what we are and where we're going. In a touching statement at the end of her book, she arrives at the point where her "departure from Freud is inevitable." Great as her daily professional loyalty and obligation are to him, she writes:

Freud considers God and religion a wishful childish illusion. He wrote asking mankind to renounce it. I must disagree. Reality and illusion are not contradictory terms. Psychic reality—whose depth Freud so brilliantly unveiled—cannot occur without that specifically human transitional space for play and illusions. . . . Asking a mature, functioning individual to renounce his God would be like asking Freud to renounce his own creation, psychoanalysis, and the "illusory" promise of what scientific knowledge can do. This is, in fact, the point. Men cannot be men without illusions. The type of illusion we select—science, religion, or something else—reveals our personal history—the transitional space each of us has created between his objects and himself to find a "resting place" to live in.

In her view it is in the nature of human beings, from early childhood until the last breath, to sift and sort, and to play, first with toys and games and teddy bears and animals, then with ideas and words and images and sounds and notions. We never stop trying to touch base with significant others, to settle upon some satisfying idea of who and what we ourselves are, to build a world that is ours—with blocks or bricks or iron, with money and signatures of ownership, with acts of affirmation and loyalty and affiliation, with outbursts of meanness and rancor, with mental images, and not least with theories saying the life we live should go one way or another.[1] Dr. Rizzuto should be clearer about how we ought to analyze and evaluate the different "illusions" she refers to. The history of science is in large part the demonstration of illusion; and if "reality and illusion are not contradictory terms," they are not the same, either. And, of course, some of us are willing and able to be more skeptical of the beliefs in which we've invested our hopes and wishes. With respect to the activities or beliefs in which we invest hope or feeling, we differ in the degree of skeptical scrutiny we may be willing or able to apply to them. Nevertheless, this book, one assumes, will not be smugly classified as evidence of someone's "psychopathology," a practice that has been all too much a part of the contemporary, bourgeois Western world, for which psychoanalysis itself has been so useful in establishing, interestingly enough, a version of the saved and the damned.

A psychoanalyst has wanted to demonstrate the universality of an element of mental function. She need not at all have summoned the polarity of "reality" as against "illusion"; she did so, actually, because Freud had repeatedly thrown that either/or gauntlet down to his readers and followers. What she means she states better when she refers to a "capacity" each of us has and indulges—"to symbolize, fantasize and create super-human beings"—or when she describes the role that fantasy has in the lives of people: a means by which they (meaning, again, every single one of us) "moderate their longings for objects, their fears, their poignant disappointment with their limitations." A baby uses its eyes with the "longings" Dr. Rizzuto mentions, and we adults, babes in the woods of a universe whose enormity and mystery and frustrations are only too obvious, do likewise. The word *theory* is derived from *Oewpía*, which refers to the act of looking and seeing—as in the spectator at a religious ceremonial, or as in examining portents, or as in scanning the sky to figure out what is going on, what will happen next. Theorists assemble facts to help us look with a little less anguish at enigmas often enough impenetrable. Not because we are sick, or uneducated, or naïve, but in response to our nature as human beings, we elaborate upon factuality: "The objects we so indispensably need are never themselves alone, they combine the mystery of their reality and our fantasy."

What does Dr. Rizzuto mean by that crucial statement? She is saying, in the tradition of Winnicott and others, that facts may be stated independently, as in a chemical equation, a physics formula, a finding by a psychologist about rat behavior on a maze, an observation by a psychoanalyst that people who do X have had, to a significant degree, a Y kind of childhood—but the matter doesn't rest there. Skinner takes his behaviorist laboratory findings and constructs of them stories, recommendations on child rearing, utopian suggestions—notions of how to live a life. And Steven Weinberg, in a lovely book, *The First Three Minutes,* uses his work in theoretical physics to give us "a modern view of the origin of the universe." Wonderfully, he starts with an old Norse myth about that "origin," yet ends up with his own candid surmise, his own effort to deal with the "uncertainties" he keeps on mentioning. "It is almost irresistible," he tells us, "for humans to believe that we have some special relation to the universe, that human life is not just a more-or-less farcical outcome of a chain of accidents reaching back to the first three minutes" [when this universe may have begun, so his *facts* have prompted him to *speculate* or *fantasize,* the latter verb used nonpejoratively]. A little later on, he observes that "the more the universe seems comprehensible, the more it also seems pointless."

Dr. Rizzuto knows, from her work with children, that they, too, struggle with just such a sense of things—and can be heard saying so again and again. Witches emerge from the desire of boys and girls to understand life's cruel arbitrariness. Witches are discarded for Satan—and, yes, for notions such as a "drive" called "aggression," or what Freud called Thanatos. It is not necessarily "neurotic" for a child to talk of witches, nor is it necessarily "immature" or, again, "neurotic" for an adult religious person to summon Satan, or for Freud to talk of a "primal horde" or a "totem" or of Thanatos—examples of *his* move from fact-finding to the kind of rumination Dr. Rizzuto refers to: an exploratory play of the mind characteristic of all of us, though of course it varies in symbolic complexity and content, or in clarity or pretentiousness. (Freud himself once referred to his "mythological theory of instincts.") From Plato's *Timaeus* to Professor Weinberg's essay, from Egyptian stories to the modern-day notion of "black holes," man's cosmological yearnings have found in various facts, or in ancient geometry or contemporary physics, a means for—what? Not illusion maybe, strictly defined, but a little help in knowing what this life is about, or as Winnicott and Rizzuto would have it, a little help in gaining a sense of greater proximity to the heart of the matter, namely, the particular "objects," or symbols of them, which we have learned to regard, with good reason, as literally life-giving, then life-supporting. The issue is not, though, a "regressive" tendency; the issue is the nature of our human predicament, no matter our age—*and* the way our mind deals with that predicament, from the earliest years (as child analysts have observed) to the final breath.

That is why it is particularly ironic and dismaying to find both Freudian and Marxist thought so arrogantly abusive when the subject of religion comes up. True, religious thought, like everything else, has lent itself to tyranny and exploitation. But so has Marxist thought, Freudian thought. The clarity of Marx the economist and historian (the facts, or speculations tied closely to them) become the futurist "fantasies" of a supposedly (one day) "withering" entity called "the dictatorship of the proletariat." Talk about opium—and ingested not by gullible peasants but by all-too-theoretical advocates of "dialectical materialism." The clarity of Freud the clinician and historian of lives became the "movement" called psychoanalysis, with special rings given to a few anointed ones, with sectarian argument, with "schools" and splits and expulsions, with references by analysts themselves to "punitive orthodoxy." A century that has seen Lenin's mausoleum, pictures of Karl Marx waved before the leaders of the gulag, Freud fainting in the arms of Jung and postponing for years a trip to Rome, even as he immersed himself in accounts of Hannibal's life and turned heatedly on this, then that colleague, cannot be considered a stranger to what Dr. Rizzuto has described: among the most brilliant and decent of individuals, those most determined to explore "reality," one or another fantasy, if not illusion, will take deep root, often getting worked into something called a theory.

III

Dr. Rizzuto's understanding of Freud's battle with religion is not quite that of the contemporary Catholic theologian Hans Kung. In his recent Terry lectures at Yale, published as *Freud and the Problem of God* (1979), Father Kung deals with Freud's religious preoccupations rather more gingerly than Dr. Rizzuto has done. He takes pains to acknowledge the Catholic anti-Semitism Freud had to contend with, and he spells out what he calls "ecclesiogenic neuroses"—the result of a prudish, overbearing church. "Over the centuries," he acknowledges, "the churches have acted like a superego: dominating souls in the name of God, exploiting the dependence and immaturity of poor sinners, requiring submission to the taboos of untested authority, continually repressing sexuality and displaying contempt for women (in the law of celibacy, in excluding women from church ministries)." His is a sweeping denunciation of Catholic rigidity rendered in the name of a late 20th-century (second Vatican Council) Catholic humanism. (This part of his book recalls his *On Being a Christian*, in which some of the same points were made at substantially greater length.)

At times Kung sounds like Freud. He describes the religion of many people as "a return to infantile structure," or "a regression to childish wishing"; further, he calls attention to "the churches' misuse of power." As a social and cultural critic, Freud was often right, Kung says: "How abundant are the examples of arrogance or power and misuse of power in the history of the churches: intolerance and cruelty toward deviationists, crusades, inquisition, extermination of heretics, obsession with witches, struggle against theological research, oppression of their own theologians—right up to the present time."

Such thoughts are sweet music to the ear of many critics of the church, and they are not often heard from Catholic theologians. He thanks Freud for the very real help psychoanalysis offers ministers and priests in their daily work; is grateful to Jung, who deigned to grant us a "religious need" and who generously declared God "psychologically existent"; and to Adler, who, seeing God as a handy ally in a theoretical battle with Freud, wrote:

> The idea of God and its immense significance for mankind can be understood and appreciated from the viewpoint of Individual Psychology as concretization and interpretation of the human recognition of greatness and perfection, and as commitment of the individual as well as of society to a goal which rests in man's future and which in the present heightens the driving force by enhancing the feelings and emotions.

The fuzzy and inspirational tone here—the opposite of Freud's scientific pessimism—is shared by other psychologists. Kung summons as witness Erich Fromm, for instance, who reassures us that "the attitude—religious in the widest sense of the term—of wonder, of rapture, and of becoming one with the universe, is found also in psychoanalysis." The psychoanalytic process, Fromm writes, is one "of breaking through the barriers of the conscious ego and of contact with the hitherto-excluded unconscious, advancing toward a surrender to a framework of orientation which transcends the individual, to an unconditional assent to life."

We not only have a "religious need"; we have, again, a "need" to invest our observations, as did Jung his, with our various hopes and fears, with our mind's associative and symbolic nature, its daily insistence upon our moment-by-moment trains of thought—and by night, our dreams. Kung calls upon psychoanalysis to help him criticize Catholic history, Catholic religious reality—forgetting that much of what he finds unacceptable in Rome was to be found not only in Freud's Viennese world but Jung's Zurich world: rigidity, arrogance, pettiness, or legalistic fractiousness. And when Kung starts using normative judgments ("maturity" or "childish wishing"), he is on dangerously thin ice. For just the reasons Dr. Rizzuto has made clear, it is sadly inappropriate for a Catholic theologian to use psychoanalysis as a means of name-calling. And we may have a clue, here, about what is now going on between Rome and Kung. He doesn't like some of the meditative fantasies (again, absolutely no pejorative implication intended) that the Pope, the cardinals, and millions of Catholics find congenial, and they don't like his way of seeing things—regarding what they believe. In all such shared reveries or "beliefs" (political, scientific, religious) there are felt limits by those involved. At a certain point, for instance, it is possible for a psychoanalyst to shift thinking to such a degree (from, say, notions of "id" or "super-ego" to those of "drive" and "conditioning and learning"), to the point that colleagues, as well as men of power in professional societies, begin to wonder about a particular intellectual commitment, and *especially* if a newly embraced terminology gets used invidiously—as in the phrase Kung uses, "childish wishing." Needless to say, the point is not that Kung or anyone else ought to abstain from taking a tough critical look at the Vatican, its past and present shortcomings, its moral vulnerability—as well documented, actually, in this century by such grave Catholic writers as Georges Bernanos and François Mauriac. But Kung is so busy criticizing the psychological development of his religious brethren, he seems to have lost sight of the feisty, theoretical possessiveness, narrowness, or truculence that Marxists or Freudians, in *their* humanity, have demonstrated.

From Fromm, Kung learned that there are two kinds of psychoanalysts—some "adjustment advisors," but also another kind: "for them the primary goal is the 'cure of the soul,' that is, the optimal development of a person's potentialities, the realization of his individuality and of his moral and intellectual integrity in the unfolding of a fruitful affirmation of life and of love." Such talk is not, alas, meant (by Fromm or Kung) in any sardonic or even ironic sense. One can sense the glee in the Curia—*this* is what we have to gain from these secular liberal movements! Nor is Kung more convincing when he describes how "an authentic regression," supposedly to "infantile" behavior or thinking, can be facilitated by faith. "A regression rightly understood, with the aid of certain religious practices (prayer, worship, examination of conscience, confession), can be supremely helpful for a healthy person and can smooth the path to progression and maturity, inasmuch, that is, as he reexperiences, positively assimilates, and reintegrates into his self-identification what has been forgotten or repressed."

Kung is offering what Flannery O'Connor called a "stomach full of liberal religion." Dr. Rizzuto, in contrast, wants to make it clear that hers "is not a book on religion." The sociologist Peter Berger in his recent book *The Social Reality of Religion* similarly excludes "questions of the ultimate truth or illusion of religious propositions about the world." They seem to be saying that psychological and sociological analyses are not meant to tell us whether God exists; are not meant to serve as arbiters on the nature of faith, grace, and transcendence. Everyone's ideas and beliefs have a psychological and sociological history: the liberal's, the conservative's, the radical's, the agnostic's, the atheist's, the convinced mystic's, the half-believing, half-doubting churchgoer's. To explore that history is one thing; to use the exploration as a means of insisting on philosophical, theological, or moral conclusions is quite another matter. Every psychoanalyst would presumably accept that there is a psychological explanation of his or her choice of vocation (voyeurism, narcissism, and on and on), as well as sociological ones—membership in one or another family, class, ethnic group. But what analyst would allow such explanations wholly to determine a judgment on the essential nature, meaning, and worth of his or her work?

Both Winnicott and Rizzuto connect our religious thinking to the kind of thinking we do, from the time of childhood to the time of old age, as the aware creature who hungers for an answer to the well-known question: What is the meaning of life? The history of philosophy and theology is, to a significant degree, the history of proposed answers to that question— even as psychoanalysts observe the nature of one person's, then another person's fantasies, connected to the "objects" that were once "incorporated" as enduring "representations" to which, directly or indirectly (symbolically), we continually appeal for reassurance.

IV

In a recent book, *The God of the Philosophers* (1979), Anthony Kenny shows how certain ideas "propounded by scholastic theologians and rationalist philosophers" don't fit the demands of logic—omniscience and omnipotence, for instance:

> If God is to be omniscient, I have argued, then he cannot be immutable. If God is to have infallible knowledge of future human actions, then determinism must be true. If God is to escape responsibility for human wickedness, then determinism must be false. Hence in the notion of a God who foresees all sins but is the author of none, there lurks a contradiction. Omnipotence may perhaps be capable in isolation, of receiving a coherent formulation; but omnipotence, while capable of accounting for some historic doctrines of predestination, is inadequate as a foundation for divine foreknowledge of undetermined human conduct. There cannot, if our argument has been sound, be a timeless, immutable, omniscient, omnipotent, all-good being.

But no matter what other religious philosophers would say in reply, Dr. Rizzuto would simply point out that the attribution of those qualities (omniscience and omnipotence) is, obviously, something human beings have always done in order to gain just the kind of mental and physical mastery those two words *omniscience* and *omnipotence* suggest. But we do so not necessarily because we are "superstitious" or in need of a psychiatrist. We do so as Steven Weinberg did, as Freud did, and, yes, as plenty of ordinary human beings do all the time: "I'll be standing there on that assembly line, and my mind will wander, and I'll be asking myself why, a thousand whys, about the reason things happen, and what the future has in store, and just about everything. I remember asking my mother and father how we got here in the first place, and damn if my kids don't ask me, and I don't know—but I still ask myself. I even picture my mother and dad sitting near our old Philco radio, and I'm talking with them; and then I'll be out in our yard with my kids, and we're talking—and meanwhile I keep up with that conveyer belt! I add my 25¢ to the Ford Motor Company!"

Ultimately (even for theoretical physicists or psychoanalysts or proponents of dialectical materialism), what Kenny and others before him have called "The God of Reason" merges, in one way or another, with an imaginative, symbolic, fantasying life that becomes a kind of upheld "faith"; and the "reason" for that outcome is connected, as Kenny states, to our situation rather than our personal "problems":

> There is no reason why someone who is in doubt about the existence of God should not pray for help and guidance on this topic as in other matters. Some find something comic in the idea of an agnostic praying to a God whose existence he doubts. It is surely no more unreasonable than the act of a man adrift in the ocean, trapped in a cave, or stranded on a mountainside, who cries for help though he may never be heard or fires a signal which may never be seen.
>
> Such prayer seems rational whether or not there is a God; whether, if there is a God, it is pleasing to him or conducive to salvation is quite another question.

To which Winnicott and Rizzuto, not to mention the philosophical novelist Walker Percy, would add something like this: we are the creatures who recognize ourselves as "adrift" or as "trapped" or as "stranded," or as in some precarious relationship to this world; and as users of language, we are the ones who not only take in the world's "objects" but build them up in our mind, and use them (through thoughts and fantasies) to keep from feeling alone, and to use Kenny's imagery, to gain for ourselves a sense of where we came from and where we are and where we're going, lest we feel rudderless, at a dead end, or hopelessly out of touch.[2]

Kung deplores "Protestant biblicism and Catholic traditionalism" for their attitudes toward science. He admires Freud's "critical rationality." He wants "dialogic cooperation" with twentieth-century empirical minds. In case we want specific warnings, he offers this broadside:

> For we can see in connection with Pascal, Jansenism, Kierkegaard, and Barth how often Christians and theologians have been in danger of devaluing the conclusions of reason, in order to revalue faith—a specific form of hostility to reason which does not seem in any way to be required by Christian faith. Must we cease to be philosophers and scholars in order truly to

believe in God? Did not Pascal, Kierkegaard, and Barth allow faith to over-whelm reason in this way?

It is something of an irony that Dr. Rizzuto, a psychoanalyst who for the most part protests loyalty to Freud, has understood better how to criticize Freud's view of religion than a theologian who expresses great admiration for what various psychoanalytic theorists insist on telling us about God. As for Kierkegaard, one could wish that Kung would confront his reasoning in the electrifying essay on "The Difference Between a Genius and an Apostle." It is a "difference" that Dr. Rizzuto and Professors Berger and Kenny know well. It is a difference that has to do with the use and limita-tions of the intellect.

Kierkegaard says that a genius and an apostle are "qualitatively differ-ent." The former is pursuing an intellectual or aesthetic inquiry with the greatest of distinction. The latter is on an errand: "No genius has an *in order that:* the Apostle has, absolutely and paradoxically, an *in order that.*" Those last words of the essay (italics Kierkegaard's) have to do with faith of the kind Kenny describes—faith connected to a perceived situation or predicament, whether localized at sea, in a cave, up a mountain. In mat-ters of the meaning of life and death, some gather the best facts avail-able—if with the imaginative elaborations mentioned earlier; others turn explicitly to prayer and stop talking about ideas or theories. Here is Kierkegaard saying it his way:

> That is how the errors of science and learning have confused Christianity. The confusion has spread from learning to the religious discourse, with the result that one not infrequently hears priests, bona fide, in all learned sim-plicity, prostituting Christianity. They talk in exalted terms of St. Paul's bril-liance and profundity, of his beautiful similes and so on—that is mere aestheticism. If St. Paul is to be regarded as a genius, then things look black for him, and only clerical ignorance would ever dream of praising him in terms of aesthetics, because it has no standard, but argues that all is well so long as one says something good about him.

For Kierkegaard, the God of Faith is not available to us through factual analysis or presentation, however gifted the genius making the attempt.

For Rizzuto, the "difference" Kierkegaard mentions is not so absolute; we successfully see larger and larger elements of the world (by means of rationality, logic, the work of various "geniuses"); but we also embark on quite other (subjective, existential, teleologically or cosmologically speculative) lines of mental activity. In any event, speaking of "aestheticism," one can imagine the contempt Kierkegaard would feel for some of the stupid talk, the dreary banalities that have become the proud property of twentieth-century "psychological man"—a contempt, one imagines, not unlike Philip Rieff's, and perhaps a contempt Freud himself would feel, were he to be given a chance to take a look at what has happened in his name.

Barth, also, was not one to need a defense. Like Kung, he visited America to give university lectures (in 1962), and thereafter put them into a book, *Evangelical Theology,* at the beginning of which he made the following observation—not to dethrone reason, but simply to describe what happens time and again, and may even happen to the work of Hans Kung:

> Ever since the fading of its illusory splendor as a leading academic power during the Middle Ages, theology has taken too many pains to justify its own existence. It has tried too hard, especially in the nineteenth century, to secure for itself at least a small but honorable place in the throne room of general science. This attempt at self-justification has been no help to its own work. The fact is that it has made theology, to a great extent, hesitant and halfhearted; moreover, this uncertainty has earned theology no more respect for its achievements than a very modest tip of the hat.

Pascal, the physicist and mathematician, struggled hard and knowingly with the issue of science and religion. Freud's *The Future of an Illusion* can be read as a footnote to Pascal's *Pensées* and *Provincial Letters,* and it is a scandal that Kung doesn't choose to recognize the power of Pascal's analysis of religious faith. What Kierkegaard and Barth knew, what Pascal before them made preeminently clear, is the difference between a consideration of man and nature (scientific inquiry) and a consideration of God; intellectually through theology, but also through the various mental motions of a life—not just the awareness of prayers or the commitment of energy to rituals of church attendance, but a day-to-day attentiveness (including the fantasies and reveries, the symbolic work Rizzuto and Winnicott describe) that touches all spheres of activity and is best characterized, with regard to its nature, by the Latin phrase *sub specie aeternitatis.* Pascal puts it in this matter-of-fact way: "Therefore, those to whom God has imparted religion by intuition are very fortunate, and justly convinced. But to those who do not have it, we can give it only by reasoning, waiting for God to give them spiritual insight, without which faith is only human, and useless for salvation."

Such a comment, part of the 282nd *pensée,* is a recognition that for some men and women there comes a point at which the issue is not knowledge, not even asserted and analyzed belief, but really, what Pascal calls "spiritual insight," a quite distinct kind of psychology, put in the service of a particular exertion of love; maybe in Dr. Rizzuto's words, a love for "a living God"—for, that is, a particular "representation" which (Who) rescues us, so we fervently hope and pray, from our otherwise absurd condition. For Hans Kung, one assumes, that God was the one who entered history, Jesus of Nazareth. For Hans Kung, one assumes, the earthly institution, for all its flaws, entrusted to give that love a continuing setting, so to speak, is the Holy Roman Catholic Church. It is a church for whose thousands of priests and nuns it comes surely as no great surprise that we all work facts into our imaginative constructions; that reason can turn to faith, be it religious or secular; and that part of our love life is a cosmological passion connected to no small measure of felt (existential) desperation. Dr. Rizzuto, one suspects, would find Pascal's *Pensées* more congenial than Kung seems to; they would be, for her, yet additional examples of the kind of rapt and suggestive contemplation she has seen so repeatedly in the lives she has studied—lives that belong to particular boys and girls, men and women, who are all on a decidedly perplexing journey, and who, as they plunge on, are trying to figure and sort out, the way Pascal tried to do, the various requirements of the head and heart.

VIRGINIA STEM OWENS

Virginia Stem Owens is the director of the Milton Center at Kansas Newman College, a "center of excellence" dedicated to fostering outstanding imaginative writing by Christians. Her books include *Assault On Eden: A Memoir of Communal Life in the Early '70s, Wind River Winter, Daughters of Eve,* and *If You Do Love Old Men,* which won the Texas Institute of Letters Nonfiction Prize for 1990. She is also the author of several novels, including *Generations of Women.* This excerpt is taken from her book on the relationship between religion and science, *And the Trees Clap Their Hands: Faith, Perception, and the New Physics* (1983).

Faith, Perception, and the New Physics

I KNOW A MAN who had a tumor and, along with it, a sizable chunk of the right hemisphere of his cerebral cortex excised from his brain. He survived the surgery with no complications, woke up, functioned well, even talked to the doctors and nurses. There was only one problem: he was convinced he was dreaming. Nothing could persuade him that he was actually awake and aware. Descartes would have been proud of him. Perhaps he would have gone on in this dream world forever if it hadn't been for television. He finally decided that his own mind could not possibly produce the meager and unsatisfying scenarios he found on the screen. If he had been dreaming, he would have made a better job of it.

All sorts of centers for specialized functions have been located in the brain: areas controlling vision, speech, hearing, muscular reactions. But the search for the residence of will, decision, and belief has yielded nothing.

There is no place where the brain can be jarred by charged electrodes into believing or deciding. Slices of cerebral cortex may be extracted by surgery; brains may be battered in automobile accidents so that thinking is greatly impaired. Still, consciousness goes on. Thinking—the taking in, sorting, and interpreting of stimuli—is indeed localized in that slick, meandering gray matter we call brain. But where do we decide what to think about? And behind that, who directs the brain in its harvesting of sensory impressions that provide the material for thinking?

Our minds do not work in the haphazard way of a scavenger on the sea bottom. Obviously, not all the storm of stimuli bombarding our nerve endings at every moment gets stored in the brain as food for thought. Consciousness has already made up a shopping list before the brain ever begins its daily marketing. From all the photons, sound waves, sensations of heat and pressure, it filters the information it has been instructed to attend to. Wilder Penfield, the pioneer of experimenting neurosurgeons, has pointed out that no one ever learned a skill or remembered an experience unless he had attended to it, focused his brain on it. A mere random sampling of stimuli leaves no mark on the mind. And my friend with the carved-up cortex could have gone on dreaming his life away if he had not come to believe in his own consciousness.

We say we must pay attention, and the verb in the idiom is well chosen, because the cost of consciousness is immense. Focusing requires a fine grinding of the lens. The distortions must be discovered and, with utmost care, ground out. We sand down our sensibilities by a constant friction against the world, flaying our eyeballs with sights that can sear like the sun, rounding the curvature of the cornea with the glaze of alkaline tears. Pain is the price of paying attention. Even the pleasures we perceive are fleeting, and cause us the greatest grief of all. We are constantly saying good-bye to good.

Honing is a hazardous process. Scraped to the bone, we set ourselves up like lightning rods to catch the finest disturbance in the atmosphere. No wonder the demission rate is so high. Who wants to risk incineration, a brain burnt to a frazzle like an overloaded filament? Rimbaud, the French poet, had by twenty-one charred his cortex by trying to raise to the level of consciousness every single stimuli his senses were capable of assimilating. Even so, he said it was worth it.

But it is only brain most of us want, not consciousness. And in itself, the organ seems marvelous enough. Its endless compartments hold codes for the way to get to work, the way home again, what we like to eat, the names and faces of friends. Even when consciousness is suspended, the brain continues to function, although it may miss a few red lights on the way to the office. An epileptic suffering a *petit mal* seizure will continue to breathe, walk, open the door, and sit down, though no memory remains of those actions. And most of us live our lives in a constant state of *petit mal* seizures. The difference is that epileptics have their brains blown about by unsought electrical storms whereas we decide to detach consciousness through a failure of nerve.

Memory itself seems to be in an intermediary position between brain and consciousness. What consciousness decides to pay attention to is coded in chemical structures called engrams. But they are not stored in any particular cell or area of the brain; they are diffused throughout the brain. Dispersed, non-local, they wash the cortex like an inland sea. And like sea water, any single cup can hold the clue to the composition of the whole. Karl Pribram's work on the structure of the brain gives evidence that memory is generally recorded all over the brain. Structure, in fact, implies too rigid a picture, at least for memory, which seems a fluid sort of phenomenon. For any single memory merges with other memories from different times, forms associations with present sensory excitations, changes the perceptual patterns, flows in what we call a "stream" of consciousness.

Our skull is like a cup holding this heady decoction of mingled memories, saved from decaying into chaos by the preservative of reason and kept brimming by continually new distillations from the senses. Few, I think, choose to bear such a cup, to stand under such a load.

For the load is just this: the creation, the fabrication of phenomena. Without perception, not only is there no crash as the tree falls in the forest, but there is no tree, no forest, no sound of any kind. Not the clicking of chitin-shelled insects in the quivering summer heat, not the call of birds stitching through the branches, not the tensile creak of the tree's raised column of water and minerals sprouting like a fountain in the wind. Not even silence.

Not that I doubt the world or think I'm dreaming. This is no Descartes who confides only in consciousness, who would cut the carnal cords that bind him to the earth and float free of phenomena. However one digs at the roots of the world—with quantum bundles of energy, with molecular galactic systems, with undulating fields of electromagnetism—the world is still out there waiting—pure movement, pure being. But in here, and only in here, sucked up by the senses into the nervous system and delivered crackling and popping to consciousness, it takes shape as tree, leaf, resin, root.

We tramped on the Blue Lake Trail in the Cache la Poudre Valley the day after Christmas, following the narrow bands of ice compressed by cross-country skis. The land, elaborate with underbrush and firs, rose and fell away, forcing us down diagonals and up along edges. Thirsty for the righteousness of rocks and what grows there, we could only sponge up so much stimuli before the overload built up, the cup we balanced brimmed and spilled. We unburdened ourselves by knocking the snow off a stump in a spray of infinite crystals and speaking. "Look," my companion says, "at all the trees God made."

And I reply in my own electrical storm, "You help him make them trees." You. And you are lifting the ink from this page, and alchemizing it into trees you've never even seen. You. The truest name for consciousness. Truer than Descartes' "I" because it reciprocates its own image, recognizes itself in reflection. This is how we most often address it. You.

One makes the woods he walks in. He takes the raw materials of reality spread before his senses, chomps out a bit here, a bite there, chews them up with the saliva of memory, swallows, and spits out "Tree!"—all in a split second, and while simultaneously taking a nip from what he will name "sky" and "snow."

Humankind is an organism for transmuting raw, undifferentiated energy into phenomena. Just as plants, on a theoretically less conscious level, transmute light into leaf. Plants make a properly slow, leisurely activity of it, although an elm at six million leaves per summer is no slouch. But a human, voracious and swift, images and caches a store of summers, inviolate in engrams in his brain. The various creatures of the universe move at different tempos but to the same music. In the harmonic spheres of the cosmos, we are at the nucleus of knowing, oscillating at incredible speeds.

We are the world's philosophers' stones, its means of making meaning. Without us, however hard the elm root sucks the soil, no single serrate leaf will be brought to light. Mere molecules may spin, faithful to their pattern, obedient to the order given them, unerring electricity. But no light-filtering mist of green appears, no wind of Newtonian mechanics lifts them lightly. They neither rustle in spring nor rattle in fall. They exist, but only in what we may best call undifferentiated being, I suppose, unless we prefer the words physicists make up and discard periodically to describe the farthest-back thing that matter is. But being, pure and undifferentiated, or atomic particles or energy fields are colorless, tasteless, and mute. Unless or until they have an instrument to play upon. An Aeolian harp of human consciousness.

It is easy enough to imagine the world without us, scrubbed of cities, clean of our creations, clear of consciousness. In fact, it is often pleasant to do so: a pristine Eden, still uninfected by man. But it is impossible to imagine without a mind. We are able to shape a sphere, marbled and miracled, ourselves erased. But even that image lives only in our mind. Take away the mind and the bubble bursts, dissolves, drifts into inarticulate arrangements.

There are no phenomena without perception, no perception without attention, no attention without desire. Beauty is in the eye of the beholder, says the cynic. Precisely. But he says more than he knows. More elusive than engrams is a code in our consciousness that recognizes beauty when it sees it, that builds it out of molecular movement. But an even more elemental code desires, searches for, insists upon beauty.

Why do we seek out trails over rocks and through snow-drifts that do not accommodate for comfort? Why do we, at great difficulty and expense, search out experiences that provide totally intangible satisfaction? Because beauty is in our eye, itching like a curious conjunctivitis that refuses to be soothed until proper material is supplied it to sort, arrange, pattern, proportion.

Perception, especially visual perception, has been counted as one of the most passive occupations of human intelligence. Supposedly one simply opens his eyes and takes it all in. But the research of physiologists has shown the whole process to be one of continual interaction with the environment. The eyeball itself is undergoing small, steady, rapid vibrations, shifting the image received on the retina by the microscopic distance that lies between its adjacent cells. Added to that rapid oscillation is a slow drift of the image across the retina, continually corrected by a flick, like a typewriter carriage being flung back to its starting point. When these normal movements of vision are impeded in an experiment using a series of mirrors, sight first becomes distorted and finally fails altogether. The researchers discovered that the nerves must constantly participate in an interchange with light, must probe and feel the image presented to it. If the stimulus supplied to each retinal cell is kept constant, the nerves learn to accommodate the stimulus, and it soon falls below the level of perception. The eye, in other words, must toss light about as if it were winnowing wheat from chaff, sifting, sliding, and flicking it in order to garner shape, distinction, color, form.

Nor is perception merely a matter of present stimuli assaulting the senses. Put on a pair of distorting spectacles that make straight lines look curved and walk into a strange room. At first the result is utter sensory confusion. What you see isn't what you're getting. But before long you will be able to move about accurately, undeceived by the images actually being recorded on your retinas. Indeed, you will cease to "see" the curves at all; they will straighten themselves out in your mind, even though the data taken in by the optic nerve remain curved. The same thing happens with people given spectacles that invert images: they quickly learn to "see" right side up again.

Part of the ability to adjust for distortion is a product of memory. It is partially achieved by the interplay of kinesthetic and visual senses. The point here is that the optic nerve does not simply transmit a copy of the image to the retina. It selects, emphasizes, even discounts data. Sometimes it "sees" what is not even there on the retina at a particular moment.

We are not mere blank tablets being written upon, scored and splotched by stimuli. Perception is not a simple matter of taking sense impressions the way film emulsion takes pictures inside a camera. We do not see only what is right before our eyes; there are much more accurate analogies for describing perception. In one of them we are likened to directors constantly casting parts for the theater of our minds, what Bohm calls the "inner show" that the brain presents to consciousness as reality.

The retina scouts about for likely actors. They are put on stage probationally, asked to turn this way and that to show what sort of stuff they're made of. And consciousness, sitting back in the darkened director's corner of the theater, decides. Some of the parts are found to be discordant and demand a reconciling adaptation. Others are discovered to be false entirely, unsuited to the overall drama.

Or perception is like a dance. We engage our surroundings in a spinning, drifting matrix of matter and mind. Shall we dance? The elm lifts its leafed arms and we fall into them, clicking our retinal heels, arabesquing among the branches.

Perception demands participation, not detachment. We've fooled ourselves for several centuries now, thinking our proper place was one step removed, on the sidelines, observing like a wallflower. We thought that clear-headed perception of phenomena required that we not be swept off our feet, that we stand aside, even outside. And art, too, invented a mechanism to match this detached ideal of science. We called it perspective because we believed we had finally seen through everything, seen through the world's ruse of meaning.

"There was a time," H. G. Wells once remarked, "when my little soul shone and was uplifted by the starry enigma of the sky. That has now disappeared. I go out and look at the stars in the same way I look at wallpaper." This is the extreme disengagement from physical reality that began simultaneously in the arts and in science. Looking at stars as wallpaper was incipient in Francis Bacon's pronouncement in *Novum Organum* that "nothing really exists except individual bodies, which produce real motion according to law; in science it is just that law, and the inquiry, discovery, and explanation of it, which are the fundamental requisite, both for the knowledge and for the control of Nature."

Perspective is the visual representation of that mental trick of disengagement from the world. It recreates a way of seeing that places the eyes of the individual viewer at the center of a spatial sphere. It is a device not, as we usually assume, for imitating or reproducing reality, but rather for underscoring depth and separation in space. During the Renaissance, the point from which the world was viewed wavered, swerved, and finally staggered outside the picture frame. Bacon's individual bodies viewed other isolated bodies with detachment. The space that lay between them became only a void; space was defined as merely the absence of phenomena. With perspective there was no participation, no engagement of the world, only the rigid rails of geometry disappearing at the horizon, carrying off the cosmos into oblivion.

Had no one ever noticed perspective before? Had centuries of artists been so blind, so witless as to ignore the way the world *really* looks? Or was perspective simply a visual convention that did not fit what they found to be significant about reality? To Bacon and his inheritors, separation was significant. For the millennia of artists, both pagan and Christian, that went before, participation in and identification with reality was significant. In the Middle Ages, says Owen Barfield, paintings were done "as if the observers were themselves in the picture. Compared with us, they felt themselves and the objects around them and the words that expressed those objects, immersed together in something like a clear lake of—what shall we say—of 'meaning,' if you choose."

Space as a mindless, lifeless void had no place in any of man's cosmologies before the scientific revolution. Before that, not only did the bushes burn, the serpent speak, and the trees clap their hands, but the ether, that vast, ineffable ocean in which we were all submerged, trembled with intelligence. Then came the drought, the four hundred years' temptation in the desert. We became accustomed to living in a wasteland where life receded steadily from being, and being receded from space. In our collective mind's eye, subject shrank from object. Our feet faltered, the music stopped, we fell out of the tree, the dance was over. The image of Bacon's individual bodies, reduced to external relationships, ruled our imagination. Empires broke into nation-states, matter into atoms, psyches into compartments of consciousness, the body into systems.

Nowadays we look back and see even the past in perspective. We feel acutely our separation from that primitive perception of the world. Unlike our animistic forebears, we are not at home in the world nor in the picture. And we diagnose the case to favor our own symptoms: they were the victims of a delusion that projected a consciousness upon a dumb, drooling cretin of a cosmos, and God was only a melancholy, wish-fulfilling reflection of themselves. But was God an anthropomorphic fantasy, or have we become mechanomorphic nightmares? Without our paying much attention to how we got here, we have come to the point of talking about our bodies as marvelous machines, our minds as computers, our behavior as mechanisms.

Theory and *theater,* however, are sibling words stemming from the same parent. At root they both mean "seeing place." And theoretical scientists are those who stage possibilities for the "inner show," who crawl back through the proscenium arch to put their imaginations into the picture again.

Joshua Lederberg, a Nobel prize-winning biochemist, describes how he went about making his laboratory discoveries, which were as much a function of the imagination as of rationality:

> One needs the ability to strip to the essential attributes of some actor in a process, the ability to imagine oneself inside a biological situation; I literally had to be able to think, for example, "What would it be like if I were one of the chemical pieces in a bacterial chromosome?"—and to try to understand what my environment was, try to know *where* I was.

Now that is hardly looking at stars as wallpaper. Such diving inside among the twining ropes of chromosomes through the agency of consciousness is an act of phenomenal participation in reality.

And lest we leave consciousness to the waking hours only, consider the testimony of Friedrich Kekulé. He discovered the molecular structure of organic compounds while dreaming. How did they appear to him in this dream? He saw the atoms "dancing."

It seems the question of whether one clump of matter can observe another clump of matter is moot after all. That's not an adequate description of what's going on here. We're not *observing,* Heisenberg, we're *dancing.* Locked in an embrace with the world, our retinal cells quivering at the approach of the pulsating photons like any giddy girl at the prom, we are ourselves phenomena dancing with phenomena. No more looking at things in perspective, artfully abstracting ourselves from the situation as though we feared rejection, feared finding no partner. We are a little clumsy, it's true, and have forgotten most of the steps. We're inhibited and more than a little embarrassed at throwing ourselves into the arms of the universe with such abandon. Other peoples seem to have mastered the necessary inter-penetrations of the movements more successfully than we of the West, who are understandably rusty after so many centuries of trying to act like machines. Many of us rush off to find foreign dance masters at the expense of losing our own long-neglected lore.

Still, the great thing is to say yes to the invitation.

David Bohm defines science as "basically a mode of extending our *perception* of the world, and not mainly a mode of obtaining *knowledge* about it." What we have in the past taken for knowledge about the world is merely an abstracting of a single configuration in the pattern of the dance, and calling that the last word on reality. We're only just discovering the impoverishment of the kind of vision that mistakes stars for wallpaper. "For in science too the totality of the universe is too much to be grasped definitively in any form of knowledge," Bohm concludes, "not because it is so vast and immeasurable, but even more because in many levels, domains, and aspects it contains an inexhaustible variety of structures which escape any conceptual 'net' we may use in trying to express their order and pattern."

My dog died the other morning on the floor beside the bed. As the last of his mortal breath rattled his throat and his eyes glazed over like tough gelatin, I knew that what he had been wasn't there any more. A corpse lay beside the bed, something that once had been a dog but now was only short-hand, an abbreviation, a sign with "dog" printed on it, growing stiff as a cipher. My dog was—is—more than I know, more than all the coded engrams for him my brain has collected over ten years' time. There were, for example, all those hours—days, even—when I was not particularly conscious of him, when I did not, could not pay attention. He caught my wandering awareness from time to time with a deep, disgusted sigh and a desultory flop of his tail. Did my attention call him into being, or at least into more being? Is that why he so often demanded it? Was he nonexistent when I wasn't looking? These are precisely the questions physicists ask themselves today about bits of matter smaller than a medium-sized mammalian. And the answer has something to do with C. S. Lewis' contention that our dogs will be "raised" in us as we are raised in Christ.

Certainly my dog had being as molecular movement, just as I do. But as another writer has pointed out,

> molecular movement is not sound; molecular movement is not light. The vibrational effects—or whatever we wish to call them—are interpreted by us as sound and light. Could we see the waves or vibrations, per se, we would not see redness or blueness, loudness or music. Yet when cells in our brains begin to be shaken up in certain ways light and sound enter our minds.

It is at this point that phenomena are conceived. Or, as Ruskin put it, " 'let there be light' is as much, when you understand it, ordering of intelligence as the ordering of vision."

So the answer is yes. As a phenomenal dog, he did depend on my attention. Or on the attention of the cat that was always pestering his ears and tail. Or perhaps, in some dim way, he depended on himself. Dogs are surely not as self-conscious as we, but they know enough to stage a little drama of their own to distract us from time to time.

Still, it is ourselves—alert, aware, attentive—who are the universe knowing itself, perceiving the patterns, imagining ourselves bacterial chromosomes or organic compounds, building the steely structures of Bach, finding the suburbs rasping the shape of beauty in our eye. And we are the ones who perceive the evaporation of consciousness in death and yet decide, in some place undiscoverable by spatial coordinates, to believe beyond the brain in the implication of consciousness.

Saint Paul, in that uncanny way saints as well as scientists have of staging possibilities before us, promised an interpenetration of consciousness, a participation in divine life. We live in Christ; he lives in us. The consciousness that upholds us in being, that attends us into being, that conceptualizes all the "levels, domains, and aspects" of the universe simultaneously, will expand, open its arms, and ask us to dance.

Part IV

HEAVEN AND EARTH

The Church in the World

ROBERT W. JENSON

Robert W. Jenson is professor of religion at St. Olaf College in Northfield, Minnesota. He is the cofounder and editor of two publications, *Dialog* and *Pro Ecclesia,* and serves as associate director of the Center for Catholic and Evangelical Theology. He is the author of *Essays in the Theology of Culture,* and the editor of *Either/Or: The Gospel or Neopaganism* and *Reclaiming the Bible for the Church.* This essay was originally published in *First Things.*

How the World Lost Its Story

I

IT IS THE WHOLE mission of the church to speak the gospel. As to what sort of thing "the gospel" may be, too many years ago I tried to explain that in a book with the title *Story and Promise,* and I still regard these two concepts as the best analytical characterization of the church's message. It is the church's constitutive task to tell the biblical *narrative* to the world in proclamation and to God in worship, and to do so in a fashion appropriate to the content of that narrative, that is, as a *promise* claimed from God and proclaimed to the world. It is the church's mission to tell all who will listen, God included, that the God of Israel has raised his servant Jesus from the dead, and to unpack the soteriological and doxological import of that fact.

That book, however, was directed to the *modern* world, a world in which it was presumed that stories and promises make sense. What if

135

these presumptions are losing hold? I will in this essay follow the fashion of referring to the present historical moment as the advent of a "*post*modern" world, because, as I am increasingly persuaded, the slogan does point to something real, a world that has no story and so cannot entertain promises. Two preliminary clarifications are, however, needed.

The first of these is that while the Western world is now "post"-modern in the sense that modernity is dying around us, it is not "post"-modern in the sense that any new thing is yet replacing it. Most of those who talk of postmodernism are belated disciples of Friedrich Nietzsche. Specifically, we must learn from Nietzsche about *nihilism,* about a historical reality defined purely by negations. But only half of Nietzsche's prophecy shows any sign of being fulfilled. In Nietzsche's vision, the nihilism in which Western civilization ends was to be at once a collapse into decadence and the fulfillment of an absolute freedom. There would at once appear the hollow "last man" and the glorious "superman." The "last man" is plainly on the scene, but superman is so far missing. In my use of *postmodern,* "post-" has purely apophatic force.

The second clarification is terminological. When general or theological historians refer to the "modern world" or "modernity," they mean the Western era dominated by the strategies and organizations of instrumental and critical reason. Whether they then date the beginning of modernity with the first appearances of the Enlightenment or earlier depends on their interpretation of Reformation and Renaissance.

But the term *postmodernism* became current outside this general discourse, within artistic and literary criticism, and in this other more specialized discourse, the "modernism" to which "post-" was prefixed has meant the sensibility that emerged in the arts around the turn of the present century, in deliberate *rejection* of the world shaped by Enlightenment and Romanticism—that is, of the world otherwise called "modern." "Postmodern-ism" in its original use merely named a variant of that "modernist" sensibility itself, insofar as the avant-garde was perceived to have somehow survived itself.

When participants in and historians of the more general intellectual and spiritual culture outside the arts have subsequently come to speak of "postmodernism" in larger application, the "modern" to which something is said be "post-" is modernity in its more general historical sense. Thus *postmodernism* in this use denotes the penetration into the wider spiritual and cultural life of that sensibility which appeared earlier in the arts and there was called precisely "modernism." That is, "postmodernism" *outside* the arts is the same thing as "modernism"—including "postmodernism" as there spoken of—*in* the arts. That a "postmodernist" turn is seen in the general culture all these years after modernism/postmodernism appeared in the arts simply marks the usual historical lag between developments in the arts and analogous developments in politics and philosophy and theology and daily life.

II

The modern world, the world that instrumental and critical reason built, is falling about us. Modernity, it now becomes evident, has been all along eroding its own foundations; its projects and comforts have depended on an inheritance to which it has itself been inimical. Walter Lippmann spoke of "the acids of modernity"; as it turns out, the stones attacked by this acid have been those on which the modern world was itself erected. Analysts from all relevant disciplines converge on one insight: modernity has lived on a moral and intellectual capital that it has not renewed, and indeed could not have renewed without denying itself. They moreover agree that this intellectual and moral capital was that built up by the Christian church's long establishment in the West, also if they themselves do not share the church's faith or even admire it.

Perhaps the fall of modernity will be complete in our lifetimes; perhaps it will occupy another century. However long it takes, any successor society is still too distant—or perhaps too precluded—to discern. It is the collapse itself amidst which the church must for the foreseeable future live and speak the gospel, it is modernity's time of ending as such that constitutes the Western church's postmodern mission field. As the church once lived and conducted her mission in the precisely post-Hellenistic and post-Roman-imperial world, remembering what had vanished but not knowing what if anything could come next, so the church must now live and conduct her mission in the precisely "post"-modern world.

The self-destruction of modernism can be described basically under two rubrics: story and promise. The question is what the church is now required to do with respect to each. First, story.

III

The modern world's typical way of knowing human life was what Hans Frei has taught theologians to call "realistic narrative." The novels of Jane Austen and James Baldwin are "realistic narratives"; so are the histories of Gibbon or your local newspaper; so are soap operas. "Realistic narrative" is a particular way of telling a sequence of events which is distinguished from other possible forms by two characteristics.

First, the sequential events are understood jointly to make a certain kind of sense—a dramatic kind of sense. Aristotle provided the classic specification of dramatically coherent narrative. In a dramatically good story, he said, each decisive event is unpredictable until it happens, but immediately upon taking place is seen to be exactly what "had" to happen. So, to take the example of Aristotle's own favorite good story, we could not know in advance that Oedipus would blind himself but once he has done it instantly see that the whole story must lead to and flow from just this act.

Second, the sequential dramatic coherence is of a sort that could "really" happen—that is, happen in a presumed factual world "out there," external to the text. Thus Len Deighton's story of the Winter family did not in fact occupy time and space in pre-Nazi and Nazi Germany, but there is nothing in the story itself to say that it might not have. With this kind of narrative the question of whether the story depicts something beyond itself, and if it does, how accurately, are therefore subsequent and independent questions.

But now notice two things supposed by this way of reporting our lives to ourselves. First and obviously, it is supposed that stories dramatically coherent à la Aristotle are the *appropriate* way to understand our human task and possibility. The modern West has supposed that living on the patterns of King Lear or Horatio Alger is appropriate to beings of the sort we are, and living on the patterns of a schizophrenic or Till Eulenspiegel is not. We have supposed that we somehow "ought" to be able to make dramatic sense of our lives. (We should note that humankind does not universally share the supposition: neither shamanist cultures nor Confucian or Taoist China nor the high Indian religions suppose any such thing.)

And it is further supposed that some stories dramatically coherent à la Aristotle are "realistic"—that is, that they may be fitted to the "real" world, the world as it is in itself prior to our storytelling. The use of realistic narrative as the normal way of understanding human existence supposes that reality out there, "the world" itself, makes dramatic sense à la Aristotle, into which narrative the stories we tell about ourselves can and sometimes do fit. Put it this way: The way in which the modern West has talked about human life supposes that an omniscient historian could write a *universal* history, and that this is so because the universe with the inclusion of our lives is in fact a story written by a sort of omnipotent novelist.

That is to say, modernity has supposed we inhabit what I will call a "narratable world." Modernity has supposed that the world "out there" is such that stories can be told that are true *to it*. And modernity has supposed that the reason narratives can be true to the world is that the world somehow "has" its own true story, antecedent to, and enabling of, the stories we tell about ourselves in it.

There is no mystery about how Western modernity came by this supposition. The supposition is straightforwardly a secularization of Jewish and Christian practice—as indeed these are the source of most key suppositions of Western intellectual and moral life. The archetypical body of realistic narrative is precisely the Bible; and the realistic narratives of Western modernity have every one been composed in, typically quite conscious, imitation of biblical narrative. Aristotle's definition found its future through a strange channel.

Postmodernism is characterized by the loss of this supposition in all of its aspects. We can see this most vividly in literature. The paradigmatic fictional works of the twentieth century either present accounts that make dramatic sense in themselves, but tell of events or sequences that could not occur in the world outside the storytelling; or they meticulously describe events that could occur or perhaps actually have occurred in "the real world," but in such fashion as to display precisely their lack of dramatic coherence. Gunter Grass's *The Tin Drum* may serve as an example of the first mode, Sartre's *Nausea* as an example of the second, and Joyce's *Ulysses* of both at once.

The same modes appear in the visual arts. The classical visual art of the modern West was at once realistic and narrative; it portrayed the world beyond itself, and constrained within itself some portion of a narrative possible in that world. Thus one of Velásquez's royal family portraits depicts both a set of actual and recognizable human individuals, and relationships between them that can be described only by narrative.

Modernist/postmodernist art is in most of its modes defined precisely by a passion to avoid any such portrayal. Most usually this is done by elevating the formal or expressive aspects of the act or product of art to be themselves the subject matter of the work. I have long remembered the remark of a notable art critic—though I have forgotten which one—that many modernist paintings could be understood as *fragments* of classical painting blown up for their own sake, displaying the formal and technical elements by which painting is accomplished but eschewing the narrative depiction within which such patches of paint on canvas would earlier have had their place.

But there is also a meticulously realistic modernism that carefully reproduces pieces of the world out there, but in such fashion as either to tell a story that is impossible in the world, as in surrealism, or to alienate the depicted reality altogether from our quest for coherence. So every item in a painting by Magritte is an item of our accustomed world, and yet nothing hangs together in the way we expect: we cannot make out what story has been, or will be going on with the persons and objects depicted. And precisely to induce this schizophrenic apprehension in us was the stated purpose for which Magritte and other surrealists and modernist realists have made their works.

If there is little mystery about where the West got its faith in a narratable world, neither is there much mystery about how the West has lost this faith. The entire project of the Enlightenment was to maintain realist faith while declaring disallegiance from the God who was that faith's object. The story the Bible tells is asserted to be the story of God with His creatures; that is, it is both assumed and explicitly asserted that there is a true story about the universe because there is a universal novelist historian. Modernity was defined by the attempt to live in a universal story without a universal storyteller.

The experiment has failed. It is, after the fact, obvious that it had to: if there is no universal storyteller, then the universe can have no story line. Neither you nor I nor all of us together can so shape the world that it can make narrative sense; if God does not invent the world's story, then it has none, then the world has no narrative that is its own. If there is no God, or indeed if there is some other God than the God of the Bible, there is no narratable world.

Moreover, if there is not the biblical God, then realistic narrative is not a plausible means for our human self-understanding. Human consciousness is too obscure a mystery to itself for us to script our own lives. Modernity has added a new genre of theater to the classic tragedy and comedy: the absurdist drama that displays precisely an absence of dramatic coherence. Sometimes such drama depicts a long sequence of events with no turning points or denouement: sometimes it displays the absence of any events at all. Samuel Beckett has, of course, written the arch-examples of both, with *Waiting for Godot* and *Krapp's Last Tape*. If we would be instructed in the postmodern world, we should seek out a performance of Beckett—the postmodern world *is* the world according to Beckett.

The arts are good for diagnosis, both because they offer a controlled experience and because they always anticipate what will come later in the general culture. But the general culture has now caught up with postmodernism, and for experience of the *fact,* we should turn from elite art to the streets of our cities and the classrooms of our suburbs, to our congregations and churchly institutions, and to the culture gaps that rend them.

There we will find folk who simply do not apprehend or inhabit a narratable world. Indeed, many do not know that anyone ever did. The reason so many now cannot "find their place" is that they are unaware of the possibility of a kind of world or society that could have such things as places, though they may recite, as a sort of mantra, memorized phrases about "getting my life together" and the like. There are now many who do not and cannot understand their lives as realistic narrative. John Cage or Frank Stella; one of my suburban Minnesota students whose reality is rock music, his penis, and at the very fringes some awareness that in order to support both of these medical school might be nice; a New York street dude; the pillar of her congregation who one day casually reveals that of course she *believes* none of it, that her Christianity is a relativistic game that could easily be replaced altogether by some other, religion or yoga— all inhabit a world of which no stories can be true.

IV

So how, with respect to "story," must the church's mission now be conducted? The prescription itself is obvious and simple, carrying it out hard and in some situations perhaps impossible.

Throughout modernity, the church has presumed that its mission was directed to persons who *already* understood themselves as inhabitants of a narratable world. Moreover, since the God of a narratable world is the God of Scripture, the church was also able to presume that the narrative sense people had antecedently tried to make of their lives had somehow to cohere with the particular story, "the gospel," that the church had to communicate. Somebody who could read Rex Stout or the morning paper with pleasure and increase of self-understanding was for that very reason taken as already situated to grasp the church's message (which did not of course mean that he or she would necessarily believe it). In effect, the church could say to her hearers: "You know that story that you think you must be living out in the real world? We are here to tell you about its turning point and outcome."

But this is precisely what the postmodern church cannot presume. What then? The obvious answer is that if the church does not *find* her hearers antecedently inhabiting a narratable world, then the church must herself *be* that world.

The church has in fact had great experience of just this role. One of many analogics between postmodernity and dying antiquity—in which the church lived for her most creative period—is that the late antique world also insisted on being a meaningless chaos, and that the church had to save her converts by offering herself as the narratable world within which life could be lived with dramatic coherence. Israel had been the nation that lived a realistic narrative amid nations that lived otherwise: the church offered herself to the gentiles as their Israel. The church so constituted herself in her *liturgy*.

For the ancient church, the walls of the place of Eucharist, whether these were the walls of a basement or of Hagia Sophia or of an imaginary circle in the desert, enclosed a world. And the great drama of the Eucharist was the narrative life of that world. Nor was this a fictive world, for its drama is precisely the "real" presence of all reality's true author, elsewhere denied. The classic liturgical action of the church was not about anything else at all; it was itself the reality about which truth could be told.

In the postmodern world, if a congregation or churchly agency wants to be "relevant," here is the first step: it must recover the classic liturgy of the church in all its dramatic density, sensual actuality, and brutal realism, and make this the one exclusive center of its life. In the postmodern world, all else must at best be decoration and more likely distraction.

Out there—and that is exactly how we must again begin to speak of the society in which the church finds itself—there is no narratable world. But absent a narratable world, the church's hearers cannot believe or even understand the gospel story—or any other momentous story. If the church is not herself a real, substantial, living world to which the gospel can be true, faith is quite simply impossible.

Protestantism has been modernity's specific form of Christianity. Protestantism supposed that addressees of the gospel already inhabited the narratable world in which stories like the gospel could be believed, and that we therefore could dismantle the gospel's own liturgical world, which earlier times of the church had created. Protestantism has from the beginning supposed that the real action is in the world, and that what happens "in church" can only be preparation to get back out into reality. This was always a wrong judgment—indeed a remarkable piece of naiveté—but the blunder is understandable and in the modern world Protestantism could, just barely, get away with it. In a postmodern world, those days are gone forever.

Of course ritual as such is not the point: the point is the church's reality as herself a specific real narrated world. Which leads to a further matter.

To be a real world for her members, and not just a ritual illusion, the church must pay the closest attention to the substance of her liturgical gatherings and to their constitutive language. If the church's interior drama is not fiction, this is because the subject of that drama is a particular God, the Creator God who authors all reality. If liturgy is not to be sickly pretense, if it is to be real presence of reality's God, everything must enact the specific story Scripture actually tells about that particular God. Two polemical points here insist on hearing, and come together in a third.

Polemical point one: The story is not your story or my story or "his-story" or "her-story" or some neat story someone read or made up. The story of the sermon and of the hymns and of the processions and of the sacramental acts and of the readings is to be God's story, the story of the Bible. Preachers are the greatest sinners here: the text already is and belongs to the one true story, it does need to be helped out in this respect. What is said and enacted in the church must be with the greatest exactitude and faithfulness and exclusivity the story of creation and redemption by the God of Israel and Father of the risen Christ. As we used to say: Period.

Polemical point two: Modern Christianity (i.e., Protestantism) has regularly substituted slogans for narrative, both in teaching and in liturgy. It has supposed that hearers already knew they had a story and even already knew its basic plot, so that all that needed to be done was to point up certain features of the story—that it is "justifying," or "liberating," or whatever. The supposition was always misguided, but sometimes the church got away with it. In the postmodern world, this sort of preaching and teaching and liturgical composition merely expresses the desperation of those who in their meaningless world can believe nothing but vaguely wish they could.

Now the synthetic polemical point: There is one slogan-like phrase that is precisely a maximally compressed version of the one God's particular story. This is the revealed name, "Father, Son, and Holy Spirit." It is thus no accident at all that in our postmodern situation, the struggle between realistic faith and religious wool-gathering settles into a struggle over this name. The triune name evokes God as the three actors of His one story, and places the three in their actual narrative relation. Substitutes do not and cannot do this; "Creator, Redeemer, and Sanctifier," for example, neither narrates nor specifically names, for creating, redeeming, and sanctifying are timelessly actual aspects of the biblical God's activity, and are moreover things that *all* putative gods somehow do. In the postmodern situation, we will easily recognize congregations and agencies that know what world they inhabit by their love and fidelity to the triune name; and we will recognize antiquated Protestantism by its uneasiness with the triune name.

V

So much for story. Now for *promise.* Here too modernity was constituted by secularization of an aspect of Christian faith. The gospel is ineradicably an eschatological message; it tells its story as the story of created time's end and fulfillment. Modernity's secularized version of eschatological faith was its notorious confidence in progress, and was constitutive for modernity's whole practice and self-understanding. In its liberal version, confidence in progress shaped Europe and founded the United States. In its Marxist and pre-Marxist versions, confidence in progress fueled the great modern revolutions.

In a world that was progressing, or thought it was, Protestantism supposed the church's role was to provide motivation and direction for movement that was occurring anyway. In the most recent and already rather quaint version of this supposition, it was said to be the church's role to look around the world to see where God was at work, and then jump in to help. This—again—was always a remarkable piece of naiveté, but occasionally someone got away with it.

The First World War terminated Western Europe's liberal faith in progress, and disastrous experiment has now terminated the Marxist version. America escaped the worst devastations of the wars and has always been more exclusively shaped by modernity than other nations, and so held on a couple of generations longer: now America too seems slowly to be accepting the evidence.

Modernity's hope was in progress: the model of this hope was biblical hope in God as the Coming One, the Eschatos. Modernity cannot hope in the biblical God, founded as it is in a declaration of independence from him. Therefore, when hope in progress has been discredited, modernity has no resource either for renewing it or for acquiring any other sort of hope. The mere negation of faith in progress is sheer lack of hope; and hopelessness is the very definition of postmodernism.

Much modernist/postmodernist literature and art is directly and thematically either lamentation about, or defiant proclamation of, hopelessness: promises, our artists tell us in drumbeat monotony, should not be made, because they cannot be kept. Promises, in the postmodern world, are inauthentic simply because they are promises, because they commit a future that is not ours to commit. Where the impossibility of promise appears less thematically and more formally, it runs together with the renunciation of plotted narrative instanced earlier: promises can be made only if reality is getting someplace, that is, if it has a plotted story.

And again, while the arts are diagnostic, the condition they reveal is the condition of our streets and institutions. The impossibility of promises is there our daily experience. And in this matter, we have a paradigm case, in which the whole situation is instantly manifest and which I need only name. There is a human promise that is the closest possible creaturely approach to unconditional divine promise, and that is therefore throughout Scripture the chosen analog of divine promise: the marital promise of faithfulness unto death. Among us, that promise has become a near impossibility, socially, morally, and even legally.

VI

So again, how, in a world that entertains no promises, is the church to speak her eschatological hope with any public plausibility? There is one line here that obviously must be followed: The church must herself be a communal world in which promises are made and kept. But this line has already been pursued with enormous energy by Stanley Hauerwas, whose work deserves its own study. Let me take the question in a different direction.

It is the whole vision of an Eschaton that is now missing outside the church. The assembly of believers must therefore itself be the event in which we may behold what is to come. Nor is this necessity new in the life of the church. For what purpose, after all, do we think John the Seer recorded his visions?

If, in the *post*-modern world, a congregation or whatever wants to be "relevant," its assemblies must be unabashedly events of shared apocalyptic vision. "Going to church" must be a journey to the place where we will behold our destiny, where we will see what is to come of us. Modernity's version of Christianity—that is, Protestantism—has been shy of vision and apocalypse alike. Just so, its day is over. As before, I can see two aspects of the new mandate.

First and most obviously, preaching and teaching and hymns and prayers and processions and sacramental texts must no longer be shy about describing just what the gospel promises, what the Lord has in store. Will the City's streets be paved with gold? Modernity's preaching and teaching—and even its hymnody and sacramental texts—hastened to say, "Well, no, not really." And having said that, it had no more to say. In modern Christianity's discourse, the gospel's eschatology died the death of a few quick qualifications.

The truly necessary qualification is not that the City's streets will not be paved with real gold, but that gold as we know it is not real gold, such as the City will be paved with. What is the matter with gold anyway? Will goldsmiths who gain the Kingdom have nothing to do there? To stay with this one little piece of the vision, our discourse must learn again to revel in the beauty and flexibility and integrity of gold, of the City's true gold, and to say exactly why the world the risen Jesus will make must of course be golden, must be and will be beautiful and flexible and integral as is no earthly city. And so on and on.

Because Jesus lives to triumph, there will be the real Community, with its real Banquet in its real City amid its real Splendor, as no penultimate community or banquet or city or splendor is really just and loving or tasty or civilized or golden. The church has to rehearse that sentence in all her assemblings, explicitly and in detail.

Second, the church's assemblies must again become occasions of *seeing*. We are told by Scripture that in the Kingdom this world's dimness of sight will be replaced by, as the old theology said it, "beatific vision." It is a right biblical insight that God first of all *speaks* and that our community with him and each other is first of all that we *hear* him and speak to him. It does not, however, follow, as Protestantism has made it follow, that to listen and speak we must blind ourselves. In this age, accurate hearing is paired with dimmed vision: it is precisely a promised chief mark of the Eschaton that accurate hearing will then be accompanied by glorious sight. And in this age, the church must be the place where beatific vision is anticipated and trained.

Late antiquity suffered and lamented the same blindness with which postmodernity is afflicted, the same inability to see any Fulfillment up there before us. Gradually, as the church worked out the theology, the church made herself a place of such seeing. She did this with the icons of the East and the windows and statues of the West. Protestantism supposed that folk in the civil society already envisioned glorious Fulfillment, and needed no specific churchly envisioning, and therefore Protestantism for the most part eliminated the images and even where it retained them forgot how to use them. Protestantism's reliance on the world was here too an illusion, but here too an illusion it got away with for modernity's time. That time is over.

If we are in our time rightly to apprehend the eschatological reality of the gospel promise, we have to hear it with Christ the risen Lord visibly looming over our heads and with His living and dead saints visibly gathered around us. Above all, the church must celebrate the Eucharist as the dramatic depiction, and as the succession of tableaux, that it intrinsically is. How can we point our lives to the Kingdom's great Banquet, if its foretaste is spread before us with all the beauty of a McDonald's counter?

VII

A necessary afterword, lest all the above be misunderstood. It was modernity's great contribution to Christian history to have recognized the church's mandated preferential options for the poor and oppressed with a clarity previously cultivated only in the monastic orders. It was perhaps the real substance of Protestantism that it demanded that all believers live with the attention to justice and charity which had for centuries been demanded only of those under special vows. We must maintain modernity's insight. The church must indeed pursue God's action in the world.

But modernity's contribution will be lost if the church fails to notice that modernity is dying, and to face the new necessities mandated in that death. And *those* necessities—which I surely have not exhausted—are necessities of concretion and density and vision laid upon the life of the church within herself.

GLENN TINDER

Glenn Tinder is emeritus professor of political science at the University of Massachusetts, Boston campus. He is the author of *Political Thinking: The Perennial Questions, The Political Meaning of Christianity, Tolerance and Community,* and *Community: Reflections On A Tragic Ideal.* This essay was first published in *The Atlantic Monthly.*

Can We Be Good Without God?

WE ARE SO used to thinking of spirituality as withdrawal from the world and human affairs that it is hard to think of it as political. Spirituality is personal and private, we assume, while politics is public. But such a dichotomy drastically diminishes spirituality, construing it as a relationship to God without implications for one's relationship to the surrounding world. The God of Christian faith (I shall focus on Christianity, although the God of the New Testament is also the God of the Old Testament) created the world and is deeply engaged in the affairs of the world. The notion that we can be related to God and not to the world—that we can practice a spirituality that is not political—is in conflict with the Christian understanding of God.

And if spirituality is properly political, the converse also is true, however distant it may be from prevailing assumptions: politics is properly spiritual. The spirituality of politics was affirmed by Plato at the very beginnings of Western political philosophy and was a commonplace of medieval political thought. Only in modern times has it come to be taken for granted that politics is entirely secular. The inevitable result is the demoralization of politics. Politics loses its moral structure and purpose, and turns into an affair of group interest and personal ambition. Government comes to the aid of only the well organized and influential, and it is limited only where it is checked by countervailing forces. Politics ceases to be understood as a preeminently human activity and is left to those who find it profitable, pleasurable, or in some other way useful to themselves. Political action thus comes to be carried out purely for the sake of power and privilege.

It will be my purpose in this essay to try to connect the severed realms of the spiritual and the political. In view of the fervent secularism of many Americans today, some will assume this to be the opening salvo of a fundamentalist attack on "pluralism." Ironically, as I will argue, many of the undoubted virtues of pluralism—respect for the individual and a belief in the essential equality of all human beings, to cite just two—have strong roots in the union of the spiritual and the political achieved in the vision of Christianity. The question that secularists have to answer is whether these values can survive without these particular roots. In short, can we be good without God? Can we affirm the dignity and equality of individual persons—values we ordinarily regard as secular—without giving them transcendental backing? Today these values are honored more in the breach than in the observance; Manhattan Island alone, with its extremes of sybaritic wealth on the one hand and Calcuttan poverty on the other, is testimony to how little equality really counts for in contemporary America. To renew these indispensable values, I shall argue, we must rediscover their primal spiritual grounds.

Many will disagree with my argument, and I cannot pretend there are no respectable reasons for doing so. Some may disagree, however, because of misunderstandings. A few words at the outset may help to prevent this. First, although I dwell on Christianity, I do not mean thus to slight Judaism or its contribution to Western values. It is arguable that every major value affirmed in Christianity originated with the ancient Hebrews. Jewish sensitivities on this matter are understandable. Christians sometimes speak as though unaware of the elemental facts that Jesus was a Jew, that he died before even the earliest parts of the New Testament were written, and that his scriptural matrix was not Paul's letter to the Romans or the Gospel of John but the Old Testament. Christianity diverged from Judaism in answering one question: Who was Jesus? For Christians, he was the anticipated Messiah, whereas for traditional Jews (Paul and the first Christians were, of course, also Jews), he was not. This divergence has given Christianity its own distinctive character, even though it remains in a sense a Jewish faith.

The most adamant opposition to my argument is likely to come from protagonists of secular reason—a cause represented preeminently by the Enlightenment. Locke and Jefferson, it will be asserted, not Jesus and Paul, created our moral universe. Here I cannot be as disarming as I hope I was in the paragraph above, for underlying my argument is the conviction that Enlightenment rationalism is not nearly so constructive as is often supposed. Granted, it has sometimes played a constructive role. It has translated certain Christian values into secular terms and, in an age becoming increasingly secular, has given them political force. It is doubtful, however, that it could have created those values or that it can provide them with adequate metaphysical foundations. Hence if Christianity declines and dies in coming decades, our moral universe and also the relatively humane political universe that it supports will be in peril. But I recognize that if secular rationalism is far more dependent on Christianity than its protagonists realize, the converse also is in some sense true. The Enlightenment carried into action political ideals that Christians, in contravention of their own basic faith, often shamefully neglected or denied. Further, when I acknowledged that there are respectable grounds for disagreeing with my argument, I had secular rationalism particularly in mind. The foundations of political decency are an issue I wish to raise, not settle.

Christian Love

Love seems as distant as spirituality from politics, yet any discussion of the political meaning of Christianity must begin by considering (or at least making assumptions about) love. Love is for Christians the highest standard of human relationships, and therefore governs those relationships that make up politics. Not that political relationships are expected to exhibit pure love. But their place in the whole structure of human relationships can be understood only by using the measure that love provides.

The Christian concept of love requires attention not only because it underlies Christian political ideas but also because it is unique. Love as Christians understand it is distinctly different from what most people think of as love. In order to dramatize the Christian faith in an incarnate and crucified God, Paul spoke ironically of "the folly of what we preach," and it may be said that Christian love is as foolish as Christian faith. Marking its uniqueness, Christian love has a distinctive name, *agape,* which sets it apart from other kinds of love, such as *philia,* or friendship, and *eros,* or erotic passion.

When John wrote that "God so loved the world, that he gave his only Son," he illuminated the sacrificial character of divine love. This is the mark of *agape.* It is entirely selfless. If one could love others without judging them, asking anything of them, or thinking of one's own needs, one would meet the Christian standard. Obviously, no one can. Many of us can meet the requirements of friendship or erotic love, but *agape* is beyond us all. It is not a love toward which we are naturally inclined or for which we have natural capacities. Yet it is not something exclusively divine, like omnipotence, which human beings would be presumptuous to emulate. In fact, it is demanded of us. *Agape* is the core of Christian morality. Moreover, as we shall see, it is a source of political standards that are widely accepted and even widely, if imperfectly, realized.

The nature of *agape* stands out sharply against the background of ordinary social existence. The life of every society is a harsh process of mutual appraisal. People are ceaselessly judged and ranked, and they in turn ceaselessly judge and rank others. This is partly a necessity of social and political order; no groups whatever—clubs, corporations, universities, or nations—can survive without allocating responsibilities and powers with a degree of realism. It is partly also a struggle for self-esteem; we judge ourselves for the most part as others judge us. Hence outer and inner pressures alike impel us to enter the struggle.

The process is harsh because all of us are vulnerable. All of us manifest deficiencies of natural endowment—of intelligence, temperament, appearance, and so forth. And all personal lives reveal moral deficiencies as well—blamable failures in the past, and vanity, greed, and other such qualities in the present. The process is harsh also because it is unjust. Not only are those who are judged always imperfect and vulnerable, but the judges are imperfect, too. They are always fallible and often cruel. Thus few are rated exactly, or even approximately, as they deserve.

There is no judgment so final nor rank so high that one can finally attain security. Many are ranked high; they are regarded as able, or wise, or courageous. But such appraisals are never unanimous or stable. A few reach summits of power and honor where it seems for a moment that their victory is definitive. It transpires, however, that they are more fully exposed to judgment than anyone else, and often they have to endure torrents of derision.

Agape means refusing to take part in this process. It lifts the one who is loved above the level of reality on which a human being can be equated with a set of observable characteristics. The *agape* of God, according to Christian faith, does this with redemptive power; God "crucifies" the observable, and always deficient, individual, and "raises up" that individual to new life. The *agape* of human beings bestows new life in turn by accepting the work of God. The power of *agape* extends in two directions. Not only is the one who is loved exalted but so is the one who loves. To lift someone else above the process of mutual scrutiny is to stand above that process oneself. To act on the faith that every human being is a beneficiary of the honor that only God can bestow is to place oneself in a position to receive that honor. (That is not the aim, of course; if it were, *agape* would be a way of serving oneself and would thus be nullified.) *Agape* raises all touched by it into the community brought by Christ, the Kingdom of God. Everyone is glorified. No one is judged, and no one judges.

Here we come to the major premise (in the logic of faith, if not invariably in the history of Western political philosophy) of all Christian social and political thinking—the concept of the exalted individual. Arising from *agape,* this concept more authoritatively than any other shapes not only Christian perceptions of social reality but also Christian delineations of political goals.

The Exalted Individual

To grasp fully the idea of the exalted individual is not easy, but this is not because it rests on a technical or complex theory. The difficulty of grasping the concept is due to its being beyond the whole realm of theory. It refers to something intrinsically mysterious, a reality that one cannot see by having someone else point to it or describe it. It is often spoken of, but the words we use—"the dignity of the individual," "the infinite value of a human being," and so forth—have become banal and no longer evoke the mystery that called them forth. Hence we must try to understand what such phrases mean. In what way, from a Christian standpoint, are individuals exalted? In trying to answer this question, the concept of destiny may provide some help.

In the act of creation God grants a human being glory, or participation in the goodness of all that has been created. The glory of a human being, however, is not like that of a star or a mountain. It is not objectively established but must be freely affirmed by the one to whom it belongs. In this sense the glory of a human being is placed in the future. It is not a mere possibility however, nor does it seem quite sufficient to say that it is a moral norm. It is a fundamental imperative, even though all of us, in our sinfulness, to some degree refuse it. This fusion of human freedom and divine necessity may be summarily characterized by saying that the glory of an individual, rather than being immediately given, is destined.

Destiny is not the same as fate. The word refers not to anything terrible or even to anything inevitable, in the usual sense of the word, but to the temporal and free unfolding of a person's essential being. A destiny is a spiritual drama.

A destiny is never completely fulfilled in time, in the Christian vision, but leads onto the plane of eternity. It must be worked out in time, however, and everything that happens to a person in time enters into eternal selfhood and is there given meaning and justification. My destiny is what has often been referred to as my soul.

Realizing a destiny is not a matter of acquiescing in some form of relentless causality. If it were, there would be no sin. A destiny can be failed or refused. That is why it is not a fate. True, the very word *destiny* is indicative of necessity, but the necessity of a destiny is not like the necessity that makes an object fall when it is dropped. Rather, it is the kind I recognize when I face a duty I am tempted to evade and say to myself, "This I must do." Yet my destiny has a weight unlike that of any particular duty, since it is the life given to me by God. As is recognized in words like *salvation* and *damnation,* the call of destiny has a peculiar finality.

The *agape* of God consists in the bestowal of a destiny, and that of human beings in its recognition through faith. Since a destiny is not a matter of empirical observation, a person with a destiny is, so to speak, invisible. But every person has a destiny. Hence the process of mutual scrutiny is in vain, and even the most objective judgments of other people are fundamentally false. *Agape* arises from a realization of this and is therefore expressed in a refusal to judge.

The Lord of all time and existence has taken a personal interest in every human being, an interest that is compassionate and unwearying. The Christian universe is peopled exclusively with royalty. What does this mean for society?

To speak cautiously, the concept of the exalted individual implies that governments—indeed, all persons who wield power—must treat individuals with care. This can mean various things—for example, that individuals are to be fed and sheltered when they are destitute, listened to when they speak, or merely left alone so long as they do not break the law and fairly tried if they do. But however variously care may be defined, it always means that human beings are not to be treated like the things we use and discard or just leave lying about. They deserve attention. This spare standard has of course been frequently and grossly violated by people who call themselves Christians. It has not been without force, however. Even in our own secularized times people who are useless or burdensome, hopelessly ill or guilty of terrible crimes, are sometimes treated with extraordinary consideration and patience.

The modest standard of care implies other, more demanding standards. Equality is one of these; no one is to be casually sacrificed. No natural, social, or even moral differences justify exceptions to this rule. Of course, destinies make people not equal but, rather, incomparable; equality is a measurement and dignity is immeasurable. But according to Christian claims, every person has been immeasurably dignified. Faith discerns no grounds for making distinctions, and the distinctions made by custom and ambition are precarious before God. "Many that are first will be last, and the last first." Not only love but humility as well—the humility of not anticipating the judgments of God—impels us toward the standard of equality.

No one, then, belongs at the bottom, enslaved, irremediably poor, consigned to silence; this is equality. This points to another standard: that no one should be left outside, an alien and a barbarian. *Agape* implies universality. Greeks and Hebrews in ancient times were often candidly contemptuous of most of the human race. Even Jesus, although not contemptuous of Gentiles, conceived of his mission as primarily to Israel. However, Jesus no doubt saw the saving of Israel as the saving of all humankind, and his implicit universalism became explicit, and decisive for the history of the world, in the writings and missionary activity of Paul. Christian universalism (as well as Christian egalitarianism) was powerfully expressed by Paul when he wrote that "there is neither Jew nor Greek, there is neither slave nor free, there is neither male nor female, for you are all one in Christ Jesus."

Christian universalism was reinforced by the universalism of the later Stoics, who created the ideal of an all-embracing city of reason—*cosmopolis.* Medieval Christians couched their universalist outlook in Hellenic terms. Thus two streams of thought, from Israel and Greece, flowed together. As a result the world today, although divided among nations often ferociously self-righteous and jealous, is haunted by the vision of a global community. War and national rivalry seem unavoidable, but they burden the human conscience. Searing poverty prevails in much of the world, as it always has, but no longer is it unthinkingly accepted in either the rich nations or the poor. There is a shadowy but widespread awareness, which Christianity has had much to do with creating, that one person cannot be indifferent to the destiny of another person anywhere on earth. It is hardly too much to say that the idea of the exalted individual is the spiritual center of Western politics. Although this idea is often forgotten and betrayed, were it erased from our minds our politics would probably become altogether what it is at present only in part—an affair of expediency and self-interest.

The exalted individual is not an exclusively Christian principle. There are two ways in which, without making any religious assumptions, we may sense the infinite worth of an individual. One way is love. Through personal love, or through the sympathy by which personal love is extended (although at the same time weakened), we sense the measureless worth of a few, and are able to surmise that what we sense in a few may be present in all. In short, to love some (it is, as Dostoevsky suggested, humanly impossible to love everyone) may give rise to the idea that all are worthy of love. Further, the idea of the exalted individual may become a secular value through reason, as it did for the Stoics. Reason tells me that each person is one and not more than one. Hence my claims upon others are rightfully matched by their claims upon me. Simple fairness, which even a child can understand, is implicitly egalitarian and universal; and it is reasonable.

Can love and reason, though, undergird our politics if faith suffers a further decline? That is doubtful. Love and reason are suggestive, but they lack definite political implications. Greeks of the Periclean Age, living at the summit of the most brilliant period of Western civilization, showed little consciousness of the notion that every individual bears an indefeasible and incomparable dignity. Today why should those who assume that God is dead entertain such a notion? This question is particularly compelling in view of a human characteristic very unlike exaltation.

The Fallen Individual

The fallen individual is not someone other than the exalted individual. Every human being is fallen and exalted both. This paradox is familiar to all informed Christians. Yet it is continually forgotten—partly, perhaps, because it so greatly complicates the task of dealing with evil in the world, and no doubt partly because we hate to apply it to ourselves; although glad to recall our exaltation, we are reluctant to remember our fallenness. It is vital to political understanding, however, to do both. If the concept of the exalted individual defines the highest value under God, the concept of the fallen individual defines the situation in which that value must be sought and defended.

The principle that a human being is sacred yet morally degraded is hard for common sense to grasp. It is apparent to most of us that some people are morally degraded. It is ordinarily assumed, however, that other people are morally upright and that these alone possess dignity. From this point of view all is simple and logical. The human race is divided roughly between good people, who possess the infinite worth we attribute to individuals, and bad people, who do not. The basic problem of life is for the good people to gain supremacy over, and perhaps eradicate, the bad people. This view appears in varied forms: in Marxism, where the human race is divided between a world-redeeming class and a class that is exploitative and condemned; in some expressions of American nationalism, where the division—at least, until recently—has been between "the free world" and demonic communism; in Western films, where virtuous heroes kill bandits and lawless Indians.

This common model of life's meaning is drastically irreligious, because it places reliance on good human beings and not on God. It has no room for the double insight that the evil are not beyond the reach of divine mercy nor the good beyond the need for it. It is thus antithetical to Christianity which maintains that human beings are justified by God alone, and that all are sacred and none are good.

The proposition that none are good does not mean merely that none are perfect. It means that all are persistently and deeply inclined toward evil. All are sinful. In a few sin is so effectively suppressed that it seems to have been destroyed. But this is owing to God's grace, Christian principles imply, not to human goodness, and those in whom it has happened testify emphatically that this is so. Saints claim little credit for themselves.

Nothing in Christian doctrine so offends people today as the stress on sin. It is morbid and self-destructive, supposedly, to depreciate ourselves in this way. Yet the Christian view is not implausible. The twentieth century, not to speak of earlier ages (often assumed to be more barbaric), has displayed human evil in extravagant forms. Wars and massacres, systematic torture and internment in concentration camps, have become everyday occurrences in the decades since 1914. Even in the most civilized societies subtle forms of callousness and cruelty prevail through capitalist and bureaucratic institutions. Thus our own experience indicates that we should not casually dismiss the Christian concept of sin.

According to that concept, the inclination toward evil is primarily an inclination to exalt ourselves rather than allowing ourselves to be exalted by God. We exalt ourselves in a variety of ways: for examples, by power, trying to control all the things and people around us; by greed, accumulating an inequitable portion of the material goods of the world; by self-righteousness, claiming to be wholly virtuous; and so forth. Self exaltation is carried out sometimes by individuals, sometimes by groups. It is often referred to, in all of its various forms, as "pride."

The Christian concept of sin is not adequately described, however, merely by saying that people frequently engage in evil actions. Our predisposition toward such actions is so powerful and so unyielding that it holds us captive. As Paul said, "I do not do what I want, but I do the very thing I hate." This does not imply, of course, that I am entirely depraved. If I disapprove of my evil acts, then I am partly good. However, if I persist in evil in the face of my own disapproval, then I am not only partly evil but also incapable of destroying the evil in my nature and enthroning the good. I am, that is to say, a prisoner of evil, even if I am not wholly evil. This imprisonment is sometimes called "original sin," and the phrase is useful, not because one must take the story of Adam's disobedience literally but because it points to the mysterious truth that our captivity by evil originates in a primal and iniquitous choice on the part of every person. I persistently fail to attain goodness because I have turned away from goodness and set my face toward evil.

The political value of the doctrine of original sin lies in its recognition that our evil tendencies are not in the nature of a problem that we can rationally comprehend and deliberately solve. To say that the source of sin is sin is to say that sin is underivable and inexplicable. A sinful society is not like a malfunctioning machine, something to be checked and quickly repaired.

Sin is ironic. Its intention is self-exaltation, its result is self-debasement. In trying to ascend, we fall. The reason for this is not hard to understand. We are exalted by God; in declaring our independence from God, we cast ourselves down. In other words, sin concerns not just our actions and our nature but also the setting of our lives. By sin we cast ourselves into a degraded sphere of existence, a sphere Christians often call "the world." Human beings belong to the world through sin. They look at one another as objects; they manipulate, mutilate, and kill one another. In diverse ways, some subtle and some shocking, some relatively innocuous and some devastating, they continually depersonalize themselves and others. They behave as inhabitants of the world they have sinfully formed rather than of the earth created by God. Original sin is the quiet determination, deep in everyone, to stay inside the world. Every sinful act is a violation of the personal being that continually, in freedom, vision, and love, threatens the world. The archetype of sin is the reduction of a person to the thing we call a corpse.

The Man-God Versus the God-Man

When the paradox of simultaneous exaltation and fallenness collapses, it is replaced by either cynicism or (to use a term that is accurate but masks the destructive character of the attitude it refers to) idealism.

Cynicism measures the value of human beings by their manifest qualities and thus esteems them very slightly. It concludes, in effect, that individuals are not exalted, because they are fallen. Idealism refuses this conclusion. It insists that the value of human beings, or of some of them, is very great. It is not so simplistic, however, as to deny the incongruity of their essential value and their manifest qualities. Rather, it asserts that this incongruity can be resolved by human beings on their own, perhaps through political revolution or psychotherapy. Human beings can exalt themselves.

We shall dwell in this discussion on idealism, partly because idealism is much more tempting and therefore much more common than cynicism. Idealism is exhilarating, whereas cynicism, as anything more than a youthful experiment, is grim and discouraging. We shall dwell on idealism also because it is so much more dangerous than it looks. The dangers of cynicism are evident; that a general contempt for human beings is apt to be socially and politically destructive scarcely needs to be argued. But idealism looks benign. It is important to understand why its appearance is misleading.

Idealism in our time is commonly a form of collective pride. Human beings exalt themselves by exalting a group. Each one, of course, exalts the singular and separate self in some manner. In most people, however, personal pride needs reinforcement through a common ideal or emotion, such as nationalism. Hence the rise of collective pride. To exalt ourselves, we exalt a nation, a class, or even the whole of humanity in some particular manifestation like science. Such pride is alluring. It assumes grandiose and enthralling proportions yet it seems selfless, because not one person alone but a class or nation or some other collectivity is exalted. It can be at once more extreme and less offensive than personal pride.

To represent the uncompromising and worldly character of modern idealism we may appropriately use the image of the man-god. This image is a reversal of the Christian concept of the God-man, Christ. The order of the terms obviously is crucial. In the case of the God-man, it indicates the source of Christ's divinity as understood in Christian faith. God took the initiative. To reverse the order of the terms and affirm the man-god is to say that human beings become divine on their own initiative. Here pride reaches its most extreme development. The dignity bestowed on human beings by God, in Christian faith, is now claimed as a quality that human beings can acquire through their own self-creating acts.

In using the concept of the man-god, I do not mean to suggest that divinity is explicitly attributed to certain human beings. Even propagandists, to say nothing of philosophers, are more subtle than that. What happens is simply that qualities traditionally attributed to God are shifted to a human group or type. The qualities thus assigned are various—perfect understanding, perhaps, or unfailing fairness. Illustrative are the views of three great intellectual figures, familiar to everyone, yet so diversely interpreted that the fundamental character of their thought—and their deep similarity—is sometimes forgotten.

Friedrich Nietzsche set forth the ideal of the man-god more literally and dramatically than any other writer. Nietzsche's thinking was grounded in a bitter repudiation of Christianity, and he devoted much of his life to scouring human consciousness in order to cleanse it of every Christian idea and emotion. In this way his philosophy became a comprehensive critique of Western civilization, as well as a foreshadowing of an alternative civilization. It is, as practically everyone now recognizes, remarkable in its range, subtlety, and complexity; Nietzsche is not easily classified or epitomized. It can nevertheless be argued that the dramatic center of his life-work lay in the effort to overthrow the standard of Christian love and to wipe out the idea that every human being deserves respect—leading Nietzsche to attack such norms in the field of politics as equality and democracy. If Christian faith is spurned, Nietzsche held, with the courage that was one of the sources of his philosophical greatness, then Christian morality must also be spurned. *Agape* has no rightful claim on our allegiance. And not only does *agape* lack all moral authority but it has a destructive effect on society and culture. It inhibits the rise of superior human beings to the heights of glory, which, we realize at last, are not inhabited by God. By exalting the common person, who is entirely lacking in visible distinction and glory, *agape* subverts the true order of civilization. The divine quality that Nietzsche claimed for humanity was power—the power not only of great political leaders like Julius Caesar and Napoleon but also of philosophers, writers, and artists, who impose intricate and original forms of order on chaotic material. Such power, in the nature of things, can belong only to a few. These few are human gods. Their intrinsic splendor overcomes the absurdity that erupted with the death of the Christian God, and justifies human existence.

Karl Marx is perhaps not only as well known among Christian intellectuals as even the most celebrated theologians but also as influential. The familiar saying "We are all Marxists now" dramatizes the fact that Marx's views on such matters as class and capitalism are part of the furniture of the modern mind. Christian writers are not exceptions; spontaneously they think in some measure in Marxist terms. A considerable number of them can even be called Marxist Christians—an appellation fully justified in the case of most liberation theologians. Marx has in that sense become a familiar member of the Christian household. When he is thus domesticated, however, we tend to forget what he really thought. We may forget that he was as apocalyptically secular and humanistic as Nietzsche, even though he disdained the kind of elevated and poetic rhetoric that abounds in Nietzsche's writings. He called for the entire transformation of human life by human beings, and this, in Marx's mind, included the transformation of nature. The universe was to become radically—in its roots, in its sources and standards—human. True, like the Christians he scorned, and unlike Nietzsche, Marx was egalitarian. The transformation of humanity and being was envisioned as the work of multitudes, the proletariat, and not of exceptional individuals, and ahead lay justice and community rather than glorious solitude, as in Nietzsche. Nevertheless, Marx tacitly claimed for the proletariat qualities much like those attributed in the Old Testament to God—omniscience, righteousness, and historical sovereignty, all devoted to avenging past wrongs and transfiguring human existence.

Sigmund Freud, of course, avoided both the rhetoric of redemption and the thought; he regarded any great change in the character of human beings or the conditions of human life as unlikely, and by intention was a scientist, not a prophet or a revolutionary. He belongs among the heralds of the man-god, however, because of the conviction that underlay all his psychological investigations. Disorders of the soul, which for Christians derive in one way or another from sin, and hence in their ultimate origins are mysterious, Freud believed to be scientifically explicable. From this conviction it followed that the healing work Christians believe to be dependent on divine grace Freud could assign altogether to human therapy. The soul was thus severed from God (for Freud a childish illusion) and placed in the province of human understanding and action. Not that psychoanalysis and Christianity are in all ways mutually exclusive; the many Christians who have learned from Freud testify to the contrary. But for Freud and his major followers, psychoanalysis is a comprehensive faith, not merely a set of useful hypotheses and techniques. As a faith, it attributes to humanity alone powers and responsibilities that Christians regard as divine. Human beings are exalted by virtue of purely human faculties. Freud's attitude of resignation was a matter mainly of temperament; his methods, theories, and basic assumptions have reinforced the efforts of human beings to seize the universal sovereignty that Christians assign exclusively to God.

Nietzsche, Marx, and Freud represent a movement by no means restricted to those who consciously follow any one of them or even to those familiar with their writings. Not only are we all Marxists now; it could be said with nearly equal justification that we are all Nietzscheans and Freudians. Most of us have come to assume that we ourselves are the authors of human destiny. The term *man-god* may seem extreme, but I believe that our situation is extreme. Christianity poses sweeping alternatives—destiny and fate, redemption and eternal loss, the Kingdom of God and the void of Hell. From centuries of Christian culture and education we have come habitually to think of life as structured by such extremes. Hence Christian faith may fade, but we still want to live a destiny rather than a mere life, to transform the conditions of human existence and not merely to effect improvements, to establish a perfect community and not simply a better society. Losing faith in the God-man, we inevitably begin to dream of the man-god, even though we often think of the object of our new faith as something impersonal and innocuous, like science, thus concealing from ourselves the radical nature of our dreams.

Political Idolatry

The political repercussions are profound. Most important is that all logical grounds for attributing an ultimate and immeasurable dignity to every person, regardless of outward character, disappear. Some people may gain dignity from their achievements in art, literature, or politics, but the notion that all people without exception—the most base, the most destructive, the most repellent—have equal claims on our respect becomes as absurd as would be the claim that all automobiles or all horses are of equal excellence. The standard of *agape* collapses. It becomes explicable only on Nietzsche's terms: as a device by which the weak and failing exact from the strong and distinguished a deference they do not deserve. Thus the spiritual center of Western politics fades and vanishes. If the principle of personal dignity disappears, the kind of political order we are used to— one structured by standards such as liberty for all human beings and equality under the law—becomes indefensible.

Nietzsche's stature is owing to the courage and profundity that enabled him to make this all unmistakably clear. He delineated with overpowering eloquence the consequences of giving up Christianity and every like view of the universe and humanity. His approval of those consequences and his hatred of Christianity give force to his argument. Many would like to think that there are no consequences—that we can continue treasuring the life and welfare, the civil rights and political authority, of every person without believing in a God who renders such attitudes and conduct compelling. Nietzsche shows that we cannot. We cannot give up the Christian God— and the transcendence given other names in other faiths—and go on as before. We must give up Christian morality, too. If the God-man is nothing more than an illusion, the same thing is true of the idea that every individual possesses incalculable worth.

It is true, as we have seen, that love and reason provide intimations of such worth—but intimations alone provide little basis for overruling the conclusions of our senses. The denial of the God-man and of God's merciful love of sinful humanity is a denial of destiny, and without destiny there is simply life. But life calls forth respect only in proportion to its intensity and quality. Except in the case of infants and children, we ordinarily look on those lacking in purposeful vitality with pity or disgust. Respect we spontaneously reserve for the strong and creative. If it is life we prize, then institutions that protect and care for people whose lives are faltering are worse than senseless. It is hard to think of anyone else, with the single exception of Dostoevsky, who has understood all of this as profoundly as did Nietzsche.

Marx certainly did not. His mind was on matters of a different kind, matters less philosophical. The result was an illogical humanitarianism. Marx was incensed by the squalor in which the common people of his time were forced to live and by the harsh conditions and endless hours of their work. Marx sympathized deeply with the downtrodden and disinherited. But this expressed his personal qualities, not his philosophy or faith. His philosophy was a materialism that can be interpreted in differing ways but that implied, at the very least, that reality was not created by and is not governed by God; his faith was in science and human will. He provided no philosophical or religious grounds whatever for the idea that every person must be treated with care. In spite of Marx's humanitarianism, therefore, there is a link between Marxist thought and the despotic regimes that have ruled in his name. It is perfectly true, as his defenders aver, that Marx adhered to political principles quite unlike those manifest in the purges and prison camps of the Soviet Union. That such practices should claim the authority of his name is thus outrageous in a sense. Nonetheless, the connection between Marx himself and modern Marxist despots is not entirely accidental. They share the principle that a single individual does not necessarily matter.

If the denial of the God-man has destructive logical implications, it also has dangerous emotional consequences. Dostoevsky wrote that a person "cannot live without worshipping something." Anyone who denies God must worship an idol—which is not necessarily a wooden or metal figure. In our time we have seen ideologies, groups, and leaders receive divine honors. People proud of their critical and discerning spirit have rejected Christ and bowed down before Hitler, Stalin, Mao, or some other secular savior.

When disrespect for individuals is combined with political idolatry, the results can be atrocious. Both the logical and the emotional foundations of political decency are destroyed. Equality becomes nonsensical and breaks down under attack from one or another human god. Consider Lenin: as a Marxist, and like Marx an exponent of equality, under the pressures of revolution he denied equality in principle (except as an ultimate goal) and so systematically nullified it in practice as to become the founder of modern totalitarianism. When equality falls, universality is likely also to fall. Nationalism or some other form of collective pride becomes virulent, and war unrestrained. Liberty, too, is likely to vanish; it becomes a heavy personal and social burden when no God justifies and sanctifies the individual in spite of all personal deficiencies and failures.

The idealism of the man-god does not, of course, bring as an immediate and obvious consequence a collapse into unrestrained nihilism. We all know many people who do not believe in God and yet are decent and admirable. Western societies, as highly secularized as they are, retain many humane features. Not even tacitly has our sole governing maxim become the one Dostoevsky thought was bound to follow the denial of the God-man: "Everything is permitted."

This may be, however, because customs and habits formed during Christian ages keep people from professing and acting on such a maxim even though it would be logical for them to do so. If that is the case, our position is precarious, for good customs and habits need spiritual grounds, and if those are lacking, they will gradually, or perhaps suddenly in some crisis, crumble.

To what extent are we now living on moral savings accumulated over many centuries but no longer being replenished? To what extent are those savings already severely depleted? Again and again we are told by advertisers, counselors, and other purveyors of popular wisdom that we have a right to buy the things we want and to live as we please. We should be prudent and farsighted, perhaps (although even those modest virtues are not greatly emphasized), but we are subject ultimately to no standard but self-interest.

If nihilism is most obvious in the lives of wanton destroyers like Hitler, it is nevertheless present also in the lives of people who live purely as pleasure and convenience dictate.

And aside from intentions, there is a question concerning consequences. Even idealists whose good intentions for the human race are pure and strong are still vulnerable to fate because of the pride that causes them to act ambitiously and recklessly in history. Initiating chains of unforeseen and destructive consequences, they are often overwhelmed by results drastically at variance with their humane intentions. Modern revolutionaries have willed liberty and equality for everyone, not the terror and despotism they have actually created. Social reformers in the United States were never aiming at the great federal bureaucracy or at the pervasive dedication to entertainment and pleasure that characterizes the welfare state they brought into existence. There must always be a gap between intentions and results, but for those who forget that they are finite and morally flawed the gap may become a chasm. Not only Christians but almost everyone today feels the fear that we live under the sway of forces that we have set in motion—perhaps in the very process of industrialization, perhaps only at certain stages of that process, as in the creation of nuclear power—and that threaten our lives and are beyond our control.

There is much room for argument about these matters. But there is no greater error in the modern mind than the assumption that the God-man can be repudiated with impunity. The man-god may take his place and become the author of deeds wholly unintended and the victim of terrors starkly in contrast with the benign intentions lying at their source. The irony of sin is in this way reproduced in the irony of idealism: exalting human beings in their supposed virtues and powers, idealism undermines them. Exciting fervent expectations, it leads toward despair.

Ideology and Ambiguity

Practically everyone today agrees that "being good," in a political sense, depends on recognizing the measureless worth of the human being. When this recognition is translated into ideological terms such as liberalism and conservatism, however, agreement vanishes. The main moral assumption underlying the discussion above becomes controversial. Nevertheless, we have to ask what the ideological implications of Christianity are, for this is simply to inquire about the practical meaning of the ideas that we have been discussing and thus to carry the argument to its logical conclusion.

In asking about ideology, however, we immediately encounter something that seemingly undermines any ideological commitment. This is an implicit political ambiguity. This ambiguity is deeply rooted in Christian principles, and must at the outset be taken into account.

In the Christian view, while every individual is exalted, society is not. On the contrary, every society is placed in question, for a society is a mere worldly order and a mere human creation and can never do justice to the glory of the human beings within it. The exaltation of the individual reveals the baseness of society. It follows that our political obligations are indeterminate and equivocal. If we recognize what God has done—so Christian principles imply—we shall be limitlessly respectful of human beings but wary of society. Yet human beings live in society, and we meet them there or not at all. Hence we cannot stand wholly apart from society without failing in our responsibilities to the human beings whom God has exalted. So far as we are responsive to God, we must live within human kingdoms as creatures destined to be fellow citizens in God's Kingdom. This obligation gives rise to a political stance that is ambiguous and, in a world of devastatingly unambiguous ideologies, unique: humane and engaged, but also hesitant and critical.

Christianity implies skepticism concerning political ideals and plans. For Christianity to be wedded indissolubly to any of them (as it often has been, "Christian socialism" and Christian celebrations of "the spirit of democratic capitalism" being examples) is idolatrous and thus subversive of Christian faith.

Trying to take into account both the profound evil in human nature and the immense hope in the human situation, as Christians must, leads inevitably to what reformers and radicals—particularly those of the Third World, surrounded as they are by impoverished multitudes—are apt to regard as fatal equivocations. It leads, as I have already indicated, to a critical spirit and to qualified commitments. It would be easy to charge that such a posture reflects the self-interest and complacency of those who do not suffer from the injustice characterizing existing structures. Equivocation, it may be said, is one of the luxuries of bourgeois life in the industrial world.

Still, a Christian in the United States, without being particularly discerning or morally sensitive, can see at least two things not so clearly visible to Third World Christian writers, particularly those liberation theologians who long for immediate social transformation. One of these is the universal disaster of revolution. There is perhaps not a single example in our time of a determined effort to produce swift and sweeping change which has not ended in tyranny; such efforts have often also ended in abominations, such as those witnessed in recent times in Cambodia, incalculably worse than those perpetrated by the old social order.

The second thing a Christian in a prosperous industrial nation can see is visible because it is near at hand: that life can be culturally vulgar, morally degraded, and spiritually vacuous even under conditions of substantial justice. Not that justice has been fully achieved in the United States. But it has been approximated closely enough for us to begin to gauge its significance. We can begin to see that justice does not necessarily mean an entirely good society. The great masses of people in the United States enjoy historically unprecedented prosperity, in stark contrast with conditions in the Third World. Accompanying this prosperity, however, are signs—too numerous and flagrant to need mentioning—of moral cynicism, spiritual frivolity, and despair. If revolutions make plain the power of sin—its ability to captivate idealistic reformers—mass society displays the ingenuity of sin. Human beings in their passion for justice have not devised institutions that they cannot in their pride and selfishness outwit.

It may seem that the ideological meaning of Christianity is becoming clear: Christianity is solidly, if covertly, on the side of the status quo. It is conservative. There are good reasons for arguing, however, that Christianity cannot logically be conservative but is rather—in its own distinctive fashion—radical.

A Hesitant Radicalism

The Christian record in the annals of reform, it must be granted, is not impressive. Christians have accepted, and sometimes actively supported, slavery, poverty, and almost every other common social evil. They have often condemned such evils in principle but failed to oppose them in practice. Faith does not necessarily conquer selfishness and is particularly unlikely to do so when connected with an established religion and thus with privileged groups. That Christianity has in various times and places, and in various ways, been an established religion is perhaps the major reason why it has been implicated in injustices such as slavery, serfdom, and the oppressive wage labor of early capitalism.

Nevertheless, Christianity in essence is not conservative. The notion that it is (the historical record aside) probably stems mainly from the fact that Christians share with conservatives a consciousness of the fallibility of human beings. The two camps occupy common anthropological ground. But the consciousness of human fallibility is far keener among Christians than among conservatives, for Christians are skeptical of human arrangements that typically command deep respect in conservatives. Thus, Christians cannot logically assume that the antiquity of institutions provides any assurance of their justice or efficacy. They realize, if they consult Christian principles, that long-standing customs and traditions embody not only the wisdom of generations but also the wickedness—in particular, the determination of dominant groups to preserve their powers and privileges.

Christians are also mistrustful of aristocracies and elites. Conservatives typically commend the rule of long-ascendant minorities, those certified by the established order as wise and noble. But Paul, addressing early Christians in Corinth, noted that "not many of you were wise according to worldly standards, not many were powerful, not many were of noble birth." New Testament passages indicate that Christ had a special concern for the despised and disinherited, the ignorant and unsophisticated: "God chose what is foolish in the world to shame the wise." The attitude expressed in such a passage is remote from the topical conservative reverence for minorities of inherited rank and traditional learning.

Conservatives (like non-Christian radicals) commonly assume that sin can be circumvented by human skill. In the conservative view, allowing only those institutional changes that are gradual and protracted, and according authority to traditional elites, will accomplish this.

For Christians, sin is circumvented only by grace. It is certainly not circumvented by society, the form that sinful men and women give to the fallen world.

In America, conservatives believe that sin is effectively redirected to the common good through the market. The alchemy of capitalist competition transmutes sin into virtue. But it is difficult to see how any Christian who fully grasps Christian principles can be an unqualified supporter of capitalism. Insofar as the market governs social relations, people are forced into acquisitive rivalry; to count in any way on a gift of "daily bread" rather than on money in the bank would be the mark of a fool. Acquisitive success is candidly equated with virtue, and personal worth naively measured in material terms. Charity is often bestowed on the needy, but it is a matter of personal generosity, not of justice or community; and it is unsanctioned in capitalist theory. No principles could be more thoroughly anticommunal than those of capitalism. Indeed, capitalism is probably more anticommunal in theory than in practice, for human beings cannot be as consistently selfish and calculating as capitalist doctrine calls on them to be. Capitalism has one bond with Christianity—the premise that human beings are ordinarily selfish. A system that enables an industrial society to achieve a degree of order and efficiency without depending on either human goodness or governmental coercion cannot be entirely despised. Nevertheless, even if capitalism worked as well as its supporters claim, it would by Christian standards fail morally and spiritually.

But if Christians are more pessimistic about human beings and about social devices like the market than are conservatives, how can they act on the side of serious social change? How can they do anything but cling to all institutions, however unjust, that counteract the chaotic potentialities of human beings and achieve some sort of order? There are three answers to these questions.

First of all, Christian ideas place one in a radical—that is, critical and adverse—relationship to established institutions. The Kingdom of God is a judgment on existing society and a symbol of its impermanence. Jesus was crucified because his presence and preaching were profoundly unsettling to reigning religious and political groups. Jesus did not seek the violent overthrow of these groups, but neither did he show much concern for their stability.

Further, these attitudes have to be acted on. This is a matter of spiritual integrity. To anticipate the coming of the Kingdom of God is merely sentimental, a private frivolity, unless one tries to reshape society according to the form of the imminent community, a form defined by equality and universality and requiring particular attention to the disinherited and oppressed.

Finally, however, to take it for granted that all attempted reforms will fail would be as presumptuous as to assume that they will succeed. It is not only sinful human beings who are at work in history, Christians believe, but God as well. *Agape* is not merely a standard of personal conduct, powerless over events. In exalting individuals, it discloses the inner meaning of history. To practice love is to be allied with the deepest currents of life. From a Christian standpoint, a frightened refusal of all social change would be highly inappropriate.

Clearly the immediate political aims of Christians are not necessarily different from those of secular radicals and reformers. Their underlying attitudes are different, however. The Christian sense of the depth and stubbornness of evil in human beings, along with the faith that the universe under the impetus of grace is moving toward radical re-creation, gives a distinctive cast to the Christian conception of political action and social progress.

Secular conceptions of reform are apt to be characterized by optimistic oversimplifications and distortions. American reformers, for example, typically assume that human beings are both reasonable and just and that beneficent social change is therefore easy. The main thing necessary, after identifying a problem, is to devise and propagate a rational solution. Poverty, crime, class conflict, war, and all other great social evils can gradually but surely be eliminated. Good will and intelligence, well organized and fully informed (through the studies of social scientists), will suffice. Such illusions stem from a dilemma noted above. It is difficult for secular reformers to reconcile their sense of the dignity of individuals with a recognition of the selfishness and perversity of individuals. They are thus led persistently to exaggerate human goodness. Trying to match their view of human nature with their belief in human dignity, they fail to see how human beings actually behave or to understand the difficulties and complexities of reform.

Tocqueville suggested, approvingly, that Christianity tends to make a people "circumspect and undecided" with "its impulses . . . checked and its works unfinished." This expresses well the spirit of reform inherent in Christian faith. Christianity is radical, but it is also hesitant. This is partly, of course, because Christianity restrains our self-assurance. Efforts at social transformation must always encounter unforeseen complexities, difficulties, limits, and tragedies. Caution is in order. But Christian hesitancy has deeper grounds than prudence and more compelling motives than wariness of practical blunders. Hesitation expresses a consciousness of the mystery of being and the dignity of every person. It provides a moment for consulting destiny. Recent decades have seen heroic political commitments in behalf of social reform, but hesitation has been evident mainly in the service of self-interest. Christian faith, however, suggests that hesitation should have a part in our most conscientious deeds. It is a formality that is fitting when we cross the frontier between meditation and action. And like all significant formalities, it is a mark of respect—for God and for the creatures with whom we share the earth.

Some will dislike the implication that "being good" consists in being radical; others will think it strange to link radicalism with hesitation or religious faith. I suggest, however, that the main task facing political goodness in our time is that of maintaining responsible hope. Responsible hope is hesitant because it is cognizant of the discouraging actualities of collective life; it is radical because it measures those actualities against the highest standards of imagination and faith. Whether so paradoxical a stance can be sustained without transcendental connections—without God—is doubtful.

We live in a disheartening century—"the worst so far," as someone has said. There have never before been wars so destructive as the series of conflicts that erupted in 1914; never have tyrannies been so frenzied and all-consuming as those established by Nazism and communism. All great political causes have failed. Socialism has eventuated in the rule either of privileged ideological bureaucrats or of comfortable, listless masses; liberal reform in America has at least for a time passed away, leaving stubborn injustices and widespread cynicism; conservatism has come to stand for an illogical combination of market economics and truculent nationalism. Most of the human race lives in crushing poverty, and the privileged minority in societies where industrial abundance undergirds a preoccupation with material comfort and an atmosphere of spiritual inanity.

It is not just that hope itself is difficult to maintain in our situation. One is forced, so to speak, to hope alone. After all that has happened, in what party or cause or movement can one find a hope that can be unreservedly shared? Inherent in the disheartenment of our century is the impossibility of believing any longer in political commitment. And to draw back from commitment is to face political solitude. The individual must find a way of standing for authentic values with little or no human support. A radicalism that is hesitant must also be solitary.

If the great causes and movements all have failed, and unqualified political commitments have become impossible, why not, as Paul asked, eat and drink, since tomorrow we die? This is a question that secular reason should take far more seriously than it ever has.

It is a question to which all of us need an answer. The need is partly political; there can be no decent polities unless many people can resist the historical discouragement so natural in our times. Consumerism and fascism exemplify possible outcomes when nations are populated predominantly by people incapable of the hesitation in which reality needs to be faced or the hope in which it must be judged and reshaped.

The need is also personal. In its depths, the life of an individual is historical and political because it is one with the lives of all human beings. To despair of history is to despair of one's own humanity. Today we are strongly tempted to split the individual and history, the personal and the political. When this occurs, personal being is truncated and impoverished. People in earlier times of bewilderment and disillusionment, such as the era of the downfall of the ancient city-state system, were similarly tempted, and a standard of life first clearly enunciated by Epicurus in the aftermath of the Macedonian conquest of the city-states is still attractive in the twentieth century. Epicurus called for withdrawal from public life and political activity; he argued that everything essential to one's humanity, such as friendship, can be found in the private sphere. Personal life thus is salvaged from the raging torrent of history. But it is also mutilated, for it is severed from the human situation in its global scope and its political contours.

The absorption of Americans in the pleasures of buying and consuming, of mass entertainment and sports, suggests an Epicurean response to our historical trials. The dangers—erosion of the grounds of political health and impairment of personal being—are evident.

Being good politically means not only valuing the things that are truly valuable but also having the strength to defend those things when they are everywhere being attacked and abandoned. Such strength is exemplified by Dietrich Bonhoeffer, the great German pastor and theologian, who uncompromisingly opposed the Nazi regime from the beginning, even to the extent of returning to Germany from a guaranteed haven in America to join the anti-Hitler resistance. Arrested by the Gestapo, he was killed at the end of the war. One of Bonhoeffer's prayers, composed in prison, was "Give me the hope that will deliver me from fear and faintheartedness." Much that I have tried to say in the preceding pages might be summarized simply in this question: If we turn away from transcendence, from God, what will deliver us from a politically fatal fear and faintheartedness?

OS GUINNESS

Os Guinness was born in China but raised and educated in England. A resident of the United States since 1984, he has served as executive director of the Williamsburg Charter Foundation, which seeks to promote a deeper understanding of the nature of religious liberty in a pluralistic society. Well known in evangelical circles for his books on religious themes, including *The Dust of Death,* Guinness has also held fellowships at such organizations as the Brookings Institution and the Woodrow Wilson International Center for Scholars. This excerpt is taken from his book *The American Hour: A Time of Reckoning and the Once and Future Role of Faith* (1993).

Tribespeople, Idiots, or Citizens?

GEORGE WASHINGTON'S HOME, Mount Vernon, is among America's most visited sites. But one of the most fascinating things at Mount Vernon is one of the least noticed—the key to the Bastille, the forbidding Paris fortress whose fall on July 14, 1789, became the symbol of the French Revolution. The key hangs in the hall at Mount Vernon, oversized for its classically proportioned surroundings and often overlooked. But it once spoke eloquently for the highest hopes in both nations. Six weeks after the ratification of the U.S. Constitution in September 1787, Jefferson rejoiced at the meeting of the Estates General and the prospect of applying revolutionary American principles to France. In that same spirit, the Marquis de Lafayette took the key of the Bastille in 1789 and sent it to his good friend Washington as a symbol of their common vision of the future.

Jefferson's and Lafayette's hopes were to be dashed. Sobered by the reign of terror and the revolutionary ugliness from Robespierre and Danton to Napoleon, both Americans and French supporters of the United States revised their views. Gouverneur Morris, for example, the U.S. ambassador to France, wrote home in disgust: "They want an American Constitution with the exception of a king instead of a President, without reflecting that they have no American citizens to uphold that constitution."[1]

Two hundred years later, that discussion sounded astonishingly fresh as the stirring events of 1989 unfolded. Old hopes and fears that the framers' generation would have understood were alive again. Issues that echo those discussed by Washington and Jefferson were in the air—how realistic is it to view democracy as a model set of political arrangements to be exported? What is the role of technology as a force for freedom and democratic change? For democracy to prosper, does a nation have to have certain ideals and assumptions, or is it enough to copy institutions and political arrangements, such as free, recurrent elections, separation of the executive and judiciary branches, and respect for civil liberties?

Opinions differ sharply over the answers to these questions. But what seems odd in a century clouded by state repression and sectarian violence is that no part of the American experiment stands out more clearly yet is less appreciated or copied as a key to modern troubles than the religious liberty clauses of the First Amendment. The tensions and challenges now surrounding the clauses are some of the deepest and most significant issues of our time. Above all, there is the simple but vital question: How do we, in an age of expanding worldwide pluralism, live with our deepest— that is, our religiously and ideologically intense—differences? In short, what is the relationship of religious liberty and American democracy today?

This chapter examines a key task of rebuilding a civil society—reforging the public philosophy. It moves from the negative side of reappraising the controversies and repudiating civil religion to something constructive. Again, the overall purpose is reconstitution—the genuine reappropriation of the constitutional heritage through citizens engaging in a new debate reordered in accord with constitutional first principles and considerations of the common good.

Behind this proposal lie four judgments about the relationship of religion and American public life today. First, it is evident that a period of recurring conflict has left the nation with the urgent need to clarify the role of religion in public life. Second, it is recognized that this clarification is vitally significant not only for the American republic but as a foundational ordering principle of the new *pax moderna*. Third, the best way to clarify this relationship lies in reaffirming the place of religious liberty in the American public philosophy in accord with the notion of covenantalism, or chartered pluralism, that is outlined here. Fourth, the present situation confronts Americans directly with a threefold choice first stated by supporters of democracy in Greece and restated by John Courtney Murray in the early sixties.

The choice is as follows: As the crisis of the public philosophy deepens and controversies over religion and public life continue to arise, will Americans respond as "tribespeople," in the sense of those who seek security in a form of tribal solidarity and are intolerant of everything alien to themselves (a problem that grows from a distortion of communitarianism and an exaggerated view of group sensitivities, whether religious, racial, sexual, or ethnic)? Or will they respond as "idiots," in the original Greek sense of the totally private person who does not subscribe to the public philosophy and is oblivious to the importance of "civility" (a problem that grows from a distortion of libertarianism and an exaggerated view of individual and personal rights)? Or will they respond as "citizens," in the sense of those who stand for their own interests but who also recognize their membership in a "commonwealth" and who appreciate the knowledge and skills that underlie the public life of a civilized community?[2]

Agreement over the place of religious liberty in a civil society is only one component of the wider public philosophy, but a vital one. Because of the personal importance of faiths to individuals and to communities of faith in America, and the public importance of both to American national life, a common vision of religious liberty in public life is critical to both citizens and the nation. It affects personal and communal liberty, civic vitality, and social harmony directly. Far from lessening the need for a public philosophy today, expanding pluralism increases it. For anyone who has reflected on the last generation of conflict over religion and public life, few questions in

America are more urgent than a fresh agreement on how we are to deal with each others' deepest differences in the public sphere.

America's First Liberty

The first step in reforging the public philosophy is to show why the notion of religious liberty remains important to the public philosophy today. For, to underscore the point once more, to many Americans, especially the thought leaders, the question of religion in public life has become unimportant. It is viewed as a nonissue or a nuisance factor—something that should be purely a private issue, which inevitably becomes messy and controversial when it does not stay so, and which should therefore revert to being private as quickly as possible.

A more helpful view is to see that the swirling controversies that surround religion and public life create a sort of sound barrier effect: At one level, the issue appears all passions, problems, prejudices. But break through to a higher level, and it touches on several of the deepest questions of human life in the modern world. Once these are appreciated, it clearly becomes in the highest interest of the common good to resolve the problems rather than ban the topic out of personal disdain or fear.

There are at least five reasons why religious liberty remains a vital part of America's public philosophy. First, religious liberty, or freedom of conscience, is a precious, fundamental, and inalienable human right—the freedom to reach, hold, freely exercise, or change one's beliefs, subject solely to the dictates of consciences and independent of all outside, especially governmental, control. Prior to and existing quite apart from the Bill of Rights that protects it, religious liberty is not a luxury, a second-class right, a constitutional redundancy or a subcategory of free speech. Since it does not finally depend on the discoveries of science, the favors of the state and its officials, or the vagaries of tyrants or majorities, it is a right that may not be submitted to any vote nor encroached upon by the expansion of the bureaucratic state. Since it is a free-standing right, it is integrally linked to other basic rights, such as freedom of speech, but it does not need them to supplement its legitimacy. There is no more searching test of the health of the public philosophy than this nonmajoritarian standard set forth in the Williamsburg Charter: "A society is only as just and free as it is respectful of this right for its smallest minorities and least popular communities."[3] Religious liberty as a political right guaranteed by a legal institution is barely two hundred years old in the world. But considering why and how it was formulated, it has correctly been called America's "first liberty."

Unless America's public philosophy respects and protects this right for all Americans, the American promise of individual freedom and justice is breached.

Second, the religious liberty clauses of the First Amendment are the democratic world's most distinctive answer to one of the entire world's most pressing questions: How do we live with our deepest—that is, our religiously intense—differences?

Some regions of the world (for example, in Western Europe) exhibit a strong political civility that is directly linked to their weak religious commitments; and others (for example, in the Middle East) exhibit a strong religious commitment directly linked to their weak political civility. Owing to the manner of the First Amendment's ordering of religious liberty and public life, American democracy has afforded the fullest opportunity for strong religious commitment and strong political civility to complement, rather than threaten, each other.

Unless America's public philosophy respects and protects this distinctive American achievement, the American promise of democratic liberty and justice will be betrayed.

Third, the religious liberty clauses lie close to the genius of the American experiment. Far more than a luxury, let alone a redundancy, the First Amendment is essential and indispensable to the character of the American republic. Not simply a guarantee of individual and communal liberty, the First Amendment's ordering of the relationship of religion and public life is the boldest and most successful part of the entire American experiment. Daring in its time, distinctive throughout the world both then and now, it has proved decisive in shaping key aspects of the American story. It is not too much even to say that as the religious liberty clauses go, so goes America.

Unless America's public philosophy respects and protects this remarkable American ordering, the civic vitality of the American republic will be sapped.

Fourth, the religious liberty clauses are the single, strongest nontheological reason why free speech and the free exercise of religion have been closely related and why religion in general has persisted more strongly in the United States than in any other comparable modern country. Social development in most modern countries seems to follow an almost ironclad equation: The more modernized the country, the more secularized the people. America, however, is a striking exception to the trend, being at once the most modernized country and having the most religious of modern peoples.

The reason lies in the effect of the American style of disestablishment. By separating church and state, but not religion and government or public life, disestablishment does two things. It undercuts the forces of cultural antipathy built up against religious communities by church-state establishments—historically speaking, established churches have contributed strongly to their own rejection and to secularization in general. At the same time, disestablishment throws each faith onto reliance on its own claimed resources. The overall effect is to release a free and unfettered competition of people and beliefs similar to the free-market competition of capitalism.

Unless America's public philosophy respects and protects this enterprising relationship, both American religious liberty and public discourse will be handicapped.

Fifth, the interpretation and application of the First Amendment today touches on some of the deepest and most revolutionary developments in contemporary thought. A generation ago it was common to draw a deep dichotomy between science and religion, reason and revelation, objectivity and commitment, and so on. Today such dichotomies are impossible. All thinking is acknowledged to be presuppositional. Value-neutrality in social affairs is impossible. To demand "neutral discourse" in public life, as some still do, should now be recognized as a way of coercing people to speak publicly in someone else's language and thus never to be true to their own.

Unless America's public philosophy respects and protects this new (or restored) understanding, the republican requirement of free democratic debate and responsible participation in democratic life will be thwarted.

One conclusion is inescapable: The place of religious liberty in American public life is not merely a religious issue, but a national issue. It is not only a private issue, but a public one. Far from being simply partisan or sectarian, religious liberty is in the interest of Americans of all faiths or none, and its reaffirmation should be a singular and treasured part of the American public philosophy.

Changes, Challenges, and Controversies

The second step in reforging the public philosophy is to analyze the factors behind the recurring conflicts over religion and public life and assess the challenge they pose for American religious liberty and the public philosophy today. The conflicts themselves need no elaboration, though it is helpful to draw a distinction between cases where religion itself is directly the issue and cases where its influence is indirect. Abortion is the principal example of the latter, and examples of the former are common—school prayer and New Age meditation, creation science, secular humanism, textbook tailoring, prayer before high school sporting events, Muslim prayer mats in government offices, Gideon's Bibles in hotel rooms, the Ten Commandments on school walls, blasphemy in films and novels, the Pledge of Allegiance, Mormon polygamy, "Christian Nation" resolutions, day care centers, and so on.

Some of these conflicts are critical, others less so. But they are all flashpoints along the contested boundaries between religion and public life. For a full generation now, this issue has been highly contentious, with an endless series of disputes and the whole subject surrounded by needless ignorance and fruitless controversy, including at the highest levels. Too often, debates have been sharply polarized, controversies dominated by extremes, resolutions sought automatically through litigation, either of the religious liberty clauses set against the other one, and any common view of a better way lost in the din of irreconcilable differences and insistent demands.

The temptation is to take a quick glance at the contestants, apportion the blame, enlist on one side or another, and treat the whole problem as largely political and capable of having a political solution. From that perspective, the problem is one that has been created by a series of overlapping conflicts:

an ideological clash (the fundamentalists versus the secularists) that over-laps with a constitutional clash (the accommodationist "low wallers" versus the strict separationist "high wallers") that overlaps with a historical clash (the biblical and republican tradition versus the Enlightenment and liberal tradition) that overlaps with a clash of social visions (the communitarian "rootsers" versus the libertarian "rightsers") that overlaps with opposing views of morality in public life (the maximalists versus the minimalists) that overlaps with a psychological clash (the "bitter-enders," who insist on com-mitment regardless of civility, versus the "betrayers," who insist on civility re-gardless of commitment). This has produced, in turn, two extremist tendencies (the "removers," who would like to eradicate all religion from public life, versus the "reimposers," who would like to impose their version of a past or future state of affairs on everyone else). All this, of course, is po-tently reinforced by technological factors, such as direct mail and its shame-less appeals to fear and anger.

Such analyses may be accurate as far as they go. But they stop before they take into account some of the deepest factors. All of the above con-flicts amount to a series of responses—which raises the question of what are the deeper forces to which they are responding. I would argue that be-hind the recent conflicts lie several developments that stem from the ex-plosive acceleration of modernization in the last generation. Two factors are especially important to this argument—the reversal of roles in the rela-tionship of church and state and the current expansion of pluralism.

"Church and state" has become a thought-numbing category that mis-leads as much as it illuminates. As Judge John Noonan has pointed out, the phrase is triply misleading because it suggests that in America there is a single church, a single state, and a simple, clear distinction between the two. But this confusion is only the beginning of the complexities. Harold J. Berman, the doyen of American scholars on law and religion, builds on that and shows that the framers' more common terms were religion and government, not church and state. But not only have religion and govern-ment each changed over the course of two hundred years under the im-pact of modernity, the relationship between them has also changed to the point of being a complete "exchange of roles."[4]

Berman analyzed the involvement of religion and government over two hundred years in three areas—family life, education, and welfare—and summarized the two main consequences of the role reversal:

> In the 1780s religion played a primary role in social life . . . and government played a relatively minor, though necessary, supportive role, whereas in the 1980s religion plays a relatively minor, though necessary, supportive role and government plays a primary role. On the other hand, the role played by government in the social life of America in the 1780s (and for almost a century and a half thereafter) was openly and strongly influenced and directed by religion, whereas in the 1980s that is much less true and in many respects not true at all, while the role played by religion in the social life of America in the 1980s is openly and strongly influenced and directed by government.[5]

Berman builds his case with care, but states his conclusion with force. "Whereas two centuries ago, in matters of social life which have a significant moral dimension, government was the handmaid of religion, today religion—in its social responsibilities, as contrasted with personal faith and collective worship—is the handmaid of government."[6] Not surprisingly, such a colossal reversal has sent out reverberations to every level of church-state relationships—constitutional interpretation, volunteerism in public life, and (supremely) religious liberty itself. The Williamsburg Charter states: "Less dramatic but also lethal to freedom and the chief menace to religious liberty today is the expanding power of government control over personal behavior and the institutions of society, when the government acts not so much in deliberate hostility to, but in reckless disregard of, communal belief and personal conscience."[7]

The second, and equally important, factor is the recent expansion of pluralism. This is a worldwide phenomenon that links current American tensions to similar trends around the globe. How do we live with each other's deepest differences? That simple question has been transformed by modernity into one of the world's most pressing dilemmas. On a small planet in a pluralistic age, the all-too-common response has been bigotry, fanaticism, terrorism, and state repression.

Multiculturalism and expanding pluralism are no strangers to the American experience. They have always been a major theme in the American story, with tolerance generally expanding behind pluralism. But in the last generation, religious pluralism has thrust forward in two significant ways. First, American pluralism now goes beyond the predominance of Protestant-Catholic-Jewish and includes sizable numbers of almost all the world's great religions—Buddhist and Muslim, in particular—though an astonishing 86.5 percent of Americans identify themselves as Christians. Second, it now goes beyond religion altogether to include a growing number of Americans with no religious preference. (In 1962, as in 1952, secularists—or the "religious nones"—were 2 percent of Americans. Today they are between 10 and 12 percent, and strikingly higher on the West Coast than anywhere else.)[8]

This latest expansion of pluralism is one of the social facts of our time, though consciousness of it has been reinforced and somewhat distorted through a combination of modern technologies and postmodern theories. The effect has been to complete the profound sea change initiated by the "new immigration" of the beginning of the century. The United States has shifted from a largely Protestant pluralism to a genuine multifaith pluralism that includes people of all faiths and those who claim no religious preference. The effect can be observed at two different levels in American society. In the first place, the effect of exploding diversity can be seen in the demographic makeup of contemporary American society. The state of California, for example, has America's most diverse as well as its largest population. It now accepts almost one-third of the world's immigration and represents at the close of the century what New York did at the start —the point of entry for millions of new Americans.[9]

California will undergo as challenging a project in culture-blending as New York experienced in nation-building nine decades ago, and as Boston experienced at the birth of the public school movement a century and a half ago. And, of course, this process affects the "natives" as well as the newcomers. Many Americans feel they are sharing the experience of new immigrants merely through staying at home. Growing up in one culture, they feel they are growing old in another.

The effect of the exploding diversity can also be seen in what is a form of cultural breakdown—collapse of the previously accepted understandings of the relationship of religion and public life and the triggering of the culture wars. As a result, a series of bitter, fruitless contentions over religion and politics has erupted, extremes have surfaced, the resort to the law court has become almost reflexive, many who decry the problems are equally opposed to solutions to them, and in the ensuing din of charge and countercharge any sense of common vision for the common good has been drowned.

As always with the trends of modernity, the consequences of increased pluralism are neither unique to America nor uniform throughout the world. The disruptive effects can be seen throughout the world, even in totalitarian societies and in democratic nations with long traditions of racial and linguistic homogeneity.

Nor are the consequences of pluralization simple. On the one hand, increased pluralism deepens old tensions. Under the challenge of "all those others," many are seemingly pressured to believe more weakly in their own faith, to the point of compromise—the more choice and change, the less commitment and continuity. In reaction, however, others tend to believe more strongly, to the point of contempt for the faith of others. On the other hand, increased pluralism helps develop new trends. Today's dominant tensions are not so much between distinct religions and denominations. As often as not, they are between the more orthodox and the more contemporary within the same denomination (for example, the recent divisions within the Southern Baptist Convention), or between an alliance of the more orthodox in several religions who oppose the more contemporary in those same groups (for example, the prolife coalition of conservative Protestants, Catholics, Mormons, and so on).

In sum, like it or not, modern pluralism stands squarely as both the child of, and the challenger to, religious liberty—whether because of its presence (given the democratic conditions arising out of the Reformation and the Wars of Religion), its permanence (given the likely continuation of these conditions in the foreseeable future), or its premise (that a single, uniform doctrine of belief can only achieve dominance in a pluralistic society by two means: through persuasion, which is currently unlikely because unfashionable, or through coercion by the oppressive use of state power, which at any time is unjust and unfree). If religious liberty makes pluralism more likely, pluralism makes religious liberty more necessary.

Not surprisingly, these developments and their logic have hit hard the trio of American institutions that have been so instrumental in tempering the forces of faction and self interest and helping transform American diversity into a source of richness and strength: the religious liberty clauses of the First Amendment, the public school movement, and the American public philosophy. The upshot is that the public schools have often become the storm center of the controversies, one or other of the twin clauses of the First Amendment has been looked to as the sole arbiter in the partisan conflicts, and the common vision for the common good becomes the loser. Only when the full extent of this damage and the full range of the causes have been taken into account can any prospective solutions be given realistic consideration.

Charter for the Third Century

The third step in reforging the public philosophy is to introduce the concept of covenantalism, or chartered pluralism, as the basis of the public philosophy. This means to examine its contribution to the civil society and to show its advantages over the two existing visions of religion and public life that are now deadlocked—namely, communitarianism, the social vision that degenerates into "tribalism," and libertarianism, the vision that degenerates into political "idiocy." Anyone who appreciates the factors behind the present conflicts is confronted with tough questions. Above all, can there be a healing of the schism of the spirit, a resolution to the culture wars, and an adjustment to the new pluralism without endangering the logic of religious liberty in public life? Can there be an agreed center of national unity that complements, rather than contradicts, American diversity? Is there a way in which diverse faiths can fulfill their respective responsibility to the requirements of order, freedom, and justice without favoring one of the three at the expense of the other two?

At first sight, the search for a just and commonly acceptable solution to these challenges seems as futile as squaring the circle or searching for esperanto. The question of the public role of religion in an increasingly pluralistic society appears to be a minefield of controversies, with the resulting ignorance, confusion, and reluctance an understandable outcome. Yet if it is correct to trace the problem to forces, such as pluralism, as much as to ideologies, individuals, and groups, then we have more victims than villains over this issue, and the wisest approach is to search together for a solution, not for a scapegoat.

In fact, the present stage of the conflict offers a strategic opportunity in the 1990s. Extreme positions and unwelcome consequences are readily identifiable on many sides, and a new desire for consensus is evident. But where and on what grounds could consensus emerge? As so often, the most constructive way forward is to go back—or, more accurately, to reforge the public philosophy through the renewal of a concept that is at the heart of American democracy and the American constitutional tradition—covenantalism.

The recovery of the idea of covenant as a key to American democracy and the American constitutional tradition is one of the freshest and most important findings of recent scholarship.[10] Far from being completely new and startlingly original, the Constitution of 1787 is now seen to be the climax of a long tradition of covenants, compacts, and charters that goes back to the earliest colonial experience. Far from being the legacy of John Locke in the seventeenth century or Whig and Enlightenment thinkers in the eighteenth century, the American constitutional tradition was in place and operating strongly by the 1640s, when John Locke was not yet a teenager and Charles-Louis Montesquieu, Jean-Jacques Rousseau, and William Blackstone had not been born.

Seen in this new light, the American Constitution and the constitutional tradition grew directly from the seedbed of Puritan ideals and institutions that were rooted in the notion of covenant. Dissenting English colonists relied on Swiss, Dutch, and German theologians who themselves relied on the biblical principles of a Jewish covenantal republic to create a distinctively American style of government. The term federalism did not come into use until later, but Puritan notions, such as "federal liberty," were the twin concepts to "federal theology" and all went back to the core of covenant. The foundational covenant was the one between God and human beings, but there were multiple extensions to different levels of community—the covenant of marriage, the local church, the town, the colony, and eventually the nation.

The Mayflower Compact on November 11, 1620, was the first explicitly political use of the religious covenant form and an historic milestone on the road to the more secular and national covenant of the "miracle in Philadelphia" in 1787. But in all the dozens of cases that made up the early American system of institutions and set of ideals, one feature was unmistakable: The covenant/compact/charter represents a distinctive combination of unity and diversity, commonality and independence, obligation and voluntary consent. Almost by itself, the principle of free consent carried all the promise and the perils of "federal liberty." For free consent, being as different as can be from a forced contract, is a matter of the spirit as well as the letter of the law. Therein lie the seeds of both the risk and the renewal of the unfinished American experiment. In the best traditions of covenantal agreement, the constitutional tradition would always have to remain the living faith of the dead rather than the dead faith of the living.

This idea of covenantal, or federal, liberty holds the promise of a resolution of our present problems through the concept of chartered pluralism. At the base of the notion is a defining feature of modern experience: The present state of intellectual divisions in modern pluralistic societies does not permit agreement at the level of the *origin* of beliefs (where justifications for behavior are theoretical, ultimate, and irreconcilable). But a significant, though limited, agreement is still possible at the level of the *outworking* of beliefs (where the expression of beliefs in behavior is more practical, less ultimate, and often overlapping with the practical beliefs and behavior of other people).

Covenantalism, or chartered pluralism, is therefore a vision of religious liberty in public life that, across the deep religious differences of a pluralistic society, guarantees and sustains religious liberty for all by forging a substantive agreement, or freely chosen compact, over three things that are the "Three Rs" of religious liberty: rights, responsibilities, and respect. The compact affirms: first, in terms of rights, that religious liberty, or freedom of conscience, is a fundamental and inalienable right for peoples of all faiths and none; second, in terms of responsibilities, that religious liberty is a universal right joined to a universal duty to respect that right for others; and third, in terms of respect, that the first principles of religious liberty, combined with the lessons of two hundred years of constitutional experience, require and shape certain practical guidelines by which a robust yet civil discourse may be sustained in a free society that would remain free.

The social vision of covenantalism is a modern form of "federal liberty" that combines the best, and avoids the worst, of the libertarian and communitarian visions. Put differently, the notion of chartered pluralism is an example of what John Rawls calls the "overlapping consensus" that is needed in a liberal democracy. The core of its principled pact over the Three Rs is a variation of what Jacques Maritain described as "a sort of unwritten common law, at the point of practical convergence of extremely different theoretical ideologies and spiritual traditions." Maritain used himself to provide the example of the difference between the theoretical and the practical levels:

> I am fully convinced that my way of justifying the belief in the rights of man and the ideal of liberty, equality, fraternity, is the only one which is solidly based on truth. That does not prevent me from agreeing on these practical tenets with those who are convinced that their way of justifying them, entirely different from mine, or even opposed to mine in its theoretical dynamism, is likewise the only one that is based on truth. Assuming they both believe in the democratic charter, a Christian and a rationalist will nevertheless give justifications that are incompatible with each other, to which their souls, their minds and their blood are committed, and about these justifications they will fight. And God keep me from saying that it is not important to know which of the two is right! That is essentially important. They remain, however, in agreement on the practical affirmation of that charter, and they can formulate common principles of action.[11]

The covenantal element in chartered pluralism is obvious. The social vision is solidly founded on such a principled pact that it can be seen to give due weight to the first of its two terms. It is therefore properly a form of *chartered* pluralism, or pluralism within the framework of a principled charter that spells out the rights, responsibilities, and respect required by religious liberty. So long as the pact over the Three Rs of religious liberty remains strong, the vision avoids the minimalist approaches to unity that rely solely on "process" and "proceduralism." (For example, claims that seek to go beyond proceduralism but only a little, such as "We are held together by the coherence of our moral disagreement and argument within an ongoing cultural conversation."[12]

But at the same time the area of public agreement is strictly limited in both substance and in scope. The pact does not pretend to include agreement over religious beliefs, political policies, constitutional interpretations, or even the philosophical justifications of the three parts of the compact. Chartered pluralism is an agreement within disagreements over deep differences that make a difference. It therefore gives due weight to the second of its two terms, and remains a form of chartered *pluralism*. By doing so, it avoids the equal but opposite maximalist approaches to unity, such as the dangers of majoritarianism, civil religion, or any form of overreaching consensus that is blind or insensitive to tiny minorities and unpopular communities. Thus social unity is maintained, but religious liberty and diversity are respected in that religious unity is either made dependent upon persuasion or deferred as a messianic hope to be fulfilled only at the end of time.

Several features of this compact at the heart of chartered pluralism need to be highlighted indelibly if the compact is to pass muster under the exacting challenges of the present situation. First, the character of the compact is not a form of civil religion or public theology. Its content does not grow from shared beliefs, religious or political, because the recent expansion of pluralism means that we are now beyond the point where that is possible. It grows instead from a common commitment to universal rights, rights that are shared by an overlapping consensus of commitment, although grounded and justified differently by the different faiths behind them.[13]

Second, the achievement of this compact does not come through the process of a general dilution of beliefs, as in the case of civil religion moving from Protestantism to "Judeo-Christian" theism. It comes through the process of a particular concentration of universal rights and mutual responsibilities, within which the deep differences of belief can be negotiated.

Third, the fact that religious consensus is now impossible does not mean that moral consensus (for example, "consensual" or "common core" values in public education) is either unimportant or unattainable. It means, however, that moral consensus must be viewed as a goal, not as a given; something to be achieved through persuasion and ongoing conversation rather than assumed on the basis of tradition. Thus chartered pluralism means that there is a way to give positive meaning to public life without coercive imposition, and at the same time to foster an emphasis on freedom and diversity that need not lead toward fragmentation.

Fourth, the fact that the different religious roots of the public philosophy are largely invisible in public does not mean that they are unimportant or that the public philosophy is secular in a secularist ideological sense. On the contrary, a cut-flower public philosophy will not work. So the health of the public philosophy depends not only on a public conversation of citizens across the division of creed and generation, but on the private cultivation of the first principles of the public philosophy within each home and faith community. Should the diverse roots of those first principles ever grow weak or be poisoned from some antidemocratic source, such a private crisis would have inevitable public consequences.

Fifth, chartered pluralism allows even "radically monotheist" religions, such as Judaism and the Christian faith, to balance the twin demands of theological integrity and civil unity. Such faiths can never be content with religious liberty as freedom *from;* to them it must always be freedom *for.* Chartered pluralism therefore allows them to exercise their responsibilities to their conceptions of order, freedom, and justice, yet without infringing on the rights of others or becoming socially disruptive. Whereas the "idiocy" bred by libertarianism can be notoriously casual about order, and the "tribalism" bred by communitarianism on the Right and the Left can grow blind to freedom and justice for others, the federal liberty of chartered pluralism makes room for the free exercise of transcendent faiths that can address all three concerns with their own integrity, yet without compromise to themselves or damage to civil unity. The only proviso is that such influence is generally best exercised spiritually rather than politically, indirectly rather than directly, and persuasively rather than coercively.

Doubtless, further questions are raised by these five points. Do all the different faiths mean the same thing when they affirm common rights? Do all have an adequate philosophical basis for their individual affirmations? Are all such divergences and inadequacies a matter of sheer indifference to the strength and endurance of the compact? Will such a principled pact always be enough in practice to keep self-interest from breaking out of the harness? The probable answer in each case is no, which is a reminder of both the fragility of the historical achievement of religious liberty for all and the sobering task Americans face if they are to sustain such freedom today. Indeed, the challenge might appear quixotic were it not for the alternatives.

Viewed in the light of the alternatives, chartered pluralism provides a way between communitarianism and libertarianism. Communitarianism, found on both the Left and the Right, virtually equates politics with morality. When transferred to the level of a public philosophy, it tends to see everything in terms of its ideology writ large all over public life. Whereas libertarianism, also found on both the Left and the Right, virtually excludes morality from politics. When transferred to the level of a public philosophy, it tends to see everything in terms of an individualism that sucks the commonness out of public life altogether.

Curiously, both social visions betray their inadequacies as candidates for the public philosophy, partly because of the ironies they exhibit and partly because they rule themselves out on the grounds of their own principles. In the politically unlikely event that communitarianism were to prevail as the public philosophy, it would become a form of majoritarianism. In seeking to impose a style of traditional solidarity on modern pluralism, it would end in denying pluralism (a smaller and milder recapitulation of the totalitarian error). On the other hand, if the communitarian vision does not seek to prevail as the public philosophy—which the majority of communitarians probably prefer anyway—the effect of communitarianism on public life would be to reinforce relativism, not community. For relativism in public life is less the planned offspring of a specific philosophical movement than an unwanted bastard born of general frustration with the apparently irreconcilable positions of different communities. Thus, ironically, if American public life is to retain and strengthen a sense of community, it cannot be on the basis of communitarianism as the public philosophy.

Libertarianism, in contrast, sets out to widen the sphere of public freedom by relativizing all faiths. Everyone will be more free if no one's position is "imposed" on anyone else because "everything depends on where you're coming from." But the effect is to relativize all positions except relativism and so to assert a new imposition in public life—that of a dogmatized relativism and a universalized libertarianism. Thus if communitarianism ends in denying the reality of pluralism, libertarianism ends in distorting it. For currently pluralism goes more closely with particularism than with relativism. Most believers who make up today's pluralistic society want to affirm their distinctiveness. They believe that the beliefs that make them different are finally right and important. They are committed to them in terms of absolutes—just as for many relativists relativism itself has become the last surviving absolute. Thus libertarianism rules itself out as a candidate for the public philosophy, too. Ironically again, if American public life is to retain and strengthen the sphere of liberty, it cannot be on the basis of libertarianism as the public philosophy.

Expressed differently, chartered pluralism owes much to John Courtney Murray's valuable insistence that the unity asserted in the American motto, *E pluribus unum,* is a unity with limits, and therefore that the religious liberty clauses are "articles of peace" rather than "articles of faith."[14] But Father Murray's distinction, which was borrowed from Samuel Johnson, must never be widened into a divorce. For one thing, the articles of peace are principled before they are procedural, and they need to stay principled if principled procedures are not to be sucked into the nihilism of empty proceduralism. The articles of peace are not sacred or ultimate themselves, but they derive from articles of faith and cannot be sustained long without them. For the same reason, genuine civility is substantive before it is formal. It is not a rhetoric of niceness, let alone a fear of nastiness. Nor is it a psychology of social adjustment. Civility is both an attitude and a discourse shaped by a principled respect for people, truth, the common good, and the American constitutional tradition.

For another thing, neither chartered pluralism nor the notion of articles of peace should be understood as leading to unanimity, but to that unity within which diversity can be transformed into richness and disagreement itself into an achievement that betokens strength. Again, the old term *federal liberty* carries rich meanings. As Murray wrote, "The one civil society contains within its new unity the communities that are divided among themselves; but it does not seek to reduce to its own unity the differences that divide them."[15] The introduction to the Williamsburg Charter includes a vivid current statement of this recognition:

> We readily acknowledge our continuing differences. Signing this Charter implies no pretense that we believe the same things or that our differences over policy proposals, legal interpretations and philosophical groundings do not ultimately matter. The truth is not even that what unites us is deeper than what divides us, for differences over belief are the deepest and least negotiated of all.
>
> The Charter sets forth a renewed national compact, in the sense of a solemn mutual agreement between parties, on how we view the place of religion in American life and how we should contend with each other's deepest differences in the public sphere. It is a call to a vision of public life that will allow conflict to lead to consensus, religious commitment to reinforce political civility. In this way, diversity is not a point of weakness but a source of strength.[16]

Understood properly, these three ideas—covenantalism, chartered pluralism, and federal liberty—are critical to reforging the aspect of the public philosophy that bears on questions of religion and American public life, especially in the light of the deficiencies of the alternatives. They therefore contribute vitally to keeping democracy safe for diversity. If this vision of a promise-keeping covenant gains acceptance in the three main arenas of conflict—public policy debates, the resort to law, and public education—and if it succeeds in addressing their problems constructively, chartered pluralism could serve as a public philosophy for the public square, truly a charter for religion and public life in America's third century of constitutional government.

Part V

NATURE AND GRACE

Transforming the Culture

GREGORY WOLFE

Gregory Wolfe is the founder and editor of *Image: A Journal of the Arts and Religion,* a quarterly featuring contemporary literature and art that grapple with religious themes. He is the author of *Malcolm Muggeridge: A Biography* and *Sacred Passion: The Art of William Schickel,* among other books. Wolfe is currently writing a book on the subject of religious humanism for the Free Press. This essay listed as one of the top 100 essays of the year in *The Best American Essays 1995,* was first published in *Image.*

The Christian Writer in a Fragmented Culture

Ours is the long day's journey of the Saturday. Between suffering,
aloneness, unutterable waste on the one hand and the dream of
liberation, of rebirth on the other. In the face of the torture of a child,
of the death of love which is [Good] Friday, even the greatest art and
poetry are almost helpless. In the Utopia of [Easter] Sunday, the
aesthetic will, presumably, no longer have logic or necessity. The
apprehensions and figurations in the play of metaphysical imagining, in
the poem and the music, which tell of pain and hope, of flesh which is
said to taste of ash and of the spirit which is said to have the savour of
fire, are always Sabbatarian. They have risen out of an immensity of
waiting which is that of man. Without them, how could we be patient?
—George Steiner, *Real Presences*

I T IS SAID that God alone can create *ex nihilo;* man creates only with the materials he is given. After spending many years laboring to launch

Image: A Journal of the Arts and Religion, I must admit that I've been close to heresy on this point. *Image* is, of course, the work of many hands, and expresses the hopes and passions of a large and diverse community. It is an exciting though daunting new venture, focusing on the best work in the Judeo-Christian tradition that writers and artists are producing today.

Ironically, it was just when *Image* appeared to be on the verge of succeeding that I was suddenly assailed by doubts about its mission.

This is how the voice in my mind phrases these doubts: "Focusing on the relationship between art and the perennial questions of man's origin and destiny is an occupation that any civilized person ought to relish. But should there be a journal devoted specifically to this relationship? After all, through most of Western history, the intersection between religion and art has been at the center of our culture. Founding a journal to highlight this intersection seems to relegate it to a specialty interest, like a hobby. Perhaps *Image* is really on a par with magazines like *Backpacker* or *Hot Rod*. Or worse, *Image* might be no better than one of those interminable scholarly journals, like *Sexual Semiotics Quarterly*. Publishing a journal where you can be guaranteed to find half a dozen poems about God in every issue seems artificial. Are you doing justice to this material, or just creating a petting zoo for religious artists? Maybe you better bow out gracefully and let this material appear where it should, in *The New Yorker* and the *Paris Review*."

I'm not ashamed of these doubts, because I think they come from a sound instinct. Art that bodies forth religious themes and experiences should not be relegated to the periphery of our culture. If *Image* is destined to become nothing but a quaint sideshow in American culture, it would be better to call the whole thing off.

But there is another inner voice reminding me that this process of marginalization has been going on for a century, as Western culture has become increasingly secularized and divided. We live in an age of fragmentation and discontinuity, and the response to that condition requires a certain amount of self-consciousness. In the preeminent poem about modernity, *The Waste Land,* T.S. Eliot sifts through the relics of an atomized culture. "I have shored these fragments against my ruin," he concludes. The danger of this approach is that this aesthetic hoarding of fragments yields only a jumbled assortment of "found objects," an imperfect synthesis, a failed fusion. In Eliot's case, however, it can be argued that his imagination was strong enough to absorb self-consciousness and eclecticism and forge a new and luminous whole.

There is an analogy here for a journal like *Image*—and for the Christian artist today. Looked at in one way, *Image* may appear to be nothing more than a "specialty" publication, appealing to people with certain "interests." But the journal's thrust is toward the center rather than the margin. After all, in the long perspective of Western history, art about God's ways with man *was* the center. In our fragmented culture, *Image* ought to function like a catalyst: not as an end product, but as an attempt to bring disparate elements into a creative and productive tension. *Image,* by demonstrating the vigor of art imbued with religious vision, can help to restore our awareness of where the true center of our culture lies.

That there is a cultural crisis in the West few would dispute. The banishment of religion from the public square has entailed a devastating loss of cultural cohesion and a corresponding crisis of authority. America's motto is *E pluribus unum*—out of many, one. But today the one is dominated by an aggressive and anarchic pack of the many.

There are individuals who have impeccable credentials in the area of civil liberties who now feel that the ideological assault on religion has gone too far. To take just one example, Stephen L. Carter, a liberal African-American, has written a book entitled *The Culture of Disbelief,* which argues that we have wrongly made the idea of separation between church and state absolute. This in turn leads to a loss of knowledge and memory. The banishment of religion from the classroom, and the decline of education in general, have led to a condition that E. D. Hirsch has called "cultural illiteracy." But the crisis of education, though acute, is not as threatening as the loss of cultural identity and institutional authority. American individualism, always a strong force in our history, used to be balanced by the communities created by church, neighborhood, and other mediating institutions. Battered by ideological attack and the exigencies of modern economics, the communities that once inculcated cultural traditions, socialized behavior, and provided identity, have been broken apart. Unfortunately, the breakup of the Judeo-Christian tradition has led people to find solidarity through more volatile means. Special interest groups pursue a new politics of righteousness, fueled by ideological abstractions about race and sex. The result is more and more frequently referred to as the "tribalization" of America.

One of the ironies of American history, however, is that many Christians have contributed to the divisions in our culture. From the earliest days of colonization, the tradition of religious separatism has induced believers to withdraw from the public realm, or at least certain sectors of it. More often than not, separatism has created tightly knit local communities, but has tended to weaken culture at broader levels. Both the Reformed denominations and the Roman Catholic Church have maintained ambiguous relationships with the public square. What these churches gained in terms of internal purity they tended to lose in their impact on the cultural mainstream. Lest it seem that I am straying too far into sociology, let me point out one highly relevant example of American religious separatism and its contemporary impact. It is widely known that in American publishing there are two vastly different markets, represented by the American Booksellers Association and the Christian Booksellers Association. In no other Western nation is there such a radical division in the republic of letters.

As the secularization of the modern era has progressed, Christians have adopted increasingly extreme positions. Fundamentalism and liberalism have come to dominate the fields of the Lord, and if you are not playing on one side, you will soon be recruited by the other. Hence the highly politicized atmosphere of Christian culture today. To adopt the terms used in H. Richard Niebuhr's seminal book, *Christ and Culture,* the two camps may be divided into those who see Christ standing *against* culture, and those who identify Christ *with* culture. You may recall that Niebuhr identifies three other positions between the extremes. The synthesist position, epitomized by Thomas Aquinas and medieval Christendom, represents a cultural balance that is no longer possible. The other two positions, including the tortured dualism of Luther and Kierkegaard and the conversionist philosophy of St. Augustine, are more complicated and require greater mental and emotional effort than many individuals today are willing to exert. That is why our public discussion of culture is dominated by fifteen-round slugfests between the likes of Jesse Helms and Andres Serrano, creator of the notorious "Piss Christ." Like any war, the "culture war" destroys what it promises to preserve.

It is not only our public culture that is divided. The Christian community itself suffers from massive fault lines that cause frequent quakes and aftershocks. Take, for example, the reactionary impulse. This impulse arises out of a legitimate fear of decadence and disorder, but it goes astray when it becomes too brittle. So many Christians have allowed their own anxiety about contemporary culture to give them an excuse to issue blanket condemnations of what they call "modern art." They are so busy fighting rear-guard actions against the wiles and seductions of the world that they dismiss any art that challenges their complacency, even if it comes from the pen or paintbrush of a devout believer. This is what separates a reactionary from a traditionalist: the reactionary believes that nothing valid has been produced since the demise of their favorite historical epoch, whereas the traditionalist believes that culture is a living thing, even in times of adversity. Since launching *Image* I have met quite a few intelligent and devout men and women who don't seem to care about the literature and art of their own time. They may appreciate the beauty and majesty of the classics, but they tend to forget how radical and innovative the classics were in their own day. Reactionaries pay homage to the classics, in part, because they see these works as if they were under glass, neatly labeled and pinned to the velvet. Reactionaries live in the past, precisely because the past does not live in them.

Liberals, on the other hand, have demonstrated their understanding of the importance of culture in recent decades. They have sought out the meanings and implications of modern art. Moreover, they evidence a deep-seated respect for the creative act. But liberals too have lost something vital. By being willing to identify Christ with culture, they have abandoned the critical perspective which religious faith demands. Forgetting that human beings are only sub-creators, under God, they have tended to idolize modern artists, finding spiritual significance in the most arrogant and absurd statements of those artists. Rarely do these artists show any real engagement with the religious concerns of their theological admirers. That is why liberal Christians at times look like cheerleaders swishing their pom-poms for a team that could care less about them. Having lost their confidence in the particularities of their faith, they embrace religious traditions indiscriminately, collapsing all distinctions and slowly melting into a New Age soup.

With all of this activity in the plate tectonics of American culture, can some of us be blamed if, like Californians sitting in their hillside homes, we wait apprehensively for The Big One?

There are hopeful signs, however. Despite the seriousness of our cultural crisis, the present moment offers significant opportunities for the Christian writer and artist. There are two signs to which I would like to call attention. First, there is a distinct advantage to living in a postmodern world, where the certainties of secular high modernism, such as Marxism and Freudianism, have been discredited. Each of these systems claimed that they possessed the ultimate form of reason, and in their failure to adequately explain the world, reason itself has been called into question. As Robert Royal has recently asserted: "Art has become more important in the postmodern world . . . because the truth claims of philosophy, theology, ethics, and even nature seem weak. The argument on many campuses over the canon has taken on added heat precisely because, where truth is assumed *a priori* not to exist, images and atmosphere will shape how most people think." Those of us who believe that Western civilization has long suffered from an overemphasis on reason at the expense of imagination will find this opportunity especially encouraging. Walker Percy reminded us that art, far from standing in opposition to reason, "is cognitive: it discovers and knows and tells, tells the reader how things are, how we are, in a way that the reader can confirm with as much certitude as a scientist taking a pointer-reading."

The other hopeful sign is that the grip secular modernism had on so many of our cultural institutions has now relaxed. In the decades after World War II, it was common to find critics dismissing literature or art with identifiably Christian themes. Under the influence of Freud, such critics argued that because religion was merely wish fulfillment it had no place in art, which ought to come to grips with the "real world." Dan Wakefield has written of the secular triumphalism of this period, when he and his generation echoed F. Scott Fitzgerald's claim: "All wars fought, all gods dead." In Wakefield's case, this arrogance took many years to crack.

In recent years, other cracks have become visible in the bulwarks of cultural power, including the pages of the *New York Times Book Review* and the *Washington Post Book World*. The critics in these publications are increasingly open to the idea that religious belief often calls for a fierce and anguished grappling with the realities of life. Jewish and Christian poets and novelists such as Chaim Potok, Shusaku Endo, Reynolds Price, Andre Dubus, Frederick Buechner, Annie Dillard, Louise Erdrich, Larry Woiwode, Mark Helprin, John Updike, Doris Betts, Paul Mariani, and Ron Hansen have received rave reviews for their books in these publications. Another important sign that the times are changing is the number of authors who are turning toward explicitly religious themes for the first time. Examples include the recent novels *Saint Maybe* by Anne Tyler and *A Prayer for Owen Meany* by John Irving.

Do these trends mean that we are about to undergo a new Great Awakening? Hardly. Much of the impetus behind these cultural changes has come from baby boomers who are now middle-aged and suddenly seeing their mortality in the bathroom mirror. Just as they are shelling out for hair replacements, they are looking for the transcendence they left behind in Sunday school. They tend to want their religion with large doses of nostalgia and sentimentality, and many are partial to New Age pantheism and/or the therapeutic methodologies of the self-help industry. Nonetheless, openness is better than closedness, and the Christian writer should be grateful that he or she is once more heard in the public square.

The Christian writer in America has always faced the same dilemma: how to find a way to heal the divisions running through the national psyche. Our first great Christian writer, Nathaniel Hawthorne, confronted the same divisions that assail us today. To his right were the descendants of his Puritan ancestors, whose lack of imagination pushed them in the direction of Philistinism and fundamentalism; to his left were Ralph Waldo Emerson and his followers, whose religious commitments had evaporated into a pantheistic liberalism. Hawthorne's answer was to evoke the power of evil and locate it in the human heart, in opposition to an age that wanted either to deny evil or locate it within human institutions. Instead of extolling Emerson's gnostic self-reliant man, Hawthorne held up for admiration Hester Prynne, a woman who is radically dependent on others. After she is scorned and abandoned by the conservative Christian community, she learns through suffering and sacrificial love to turn outward again. Hawthorne strove to articulate a theology of suffering and solidarity in *The Scarlet Letter.* Toward the end of his career, in *The Marble Faun,* he felt his way toward a more thoroughly sacramental vision.

The main line of descent from Hawthorne runs through T. S. Eliot to Flannery O'Connor and Walker Percy. All three of these twentieth-century writers attempted to address the same divisions that Hawthorne struggled to reconcile. Eliot spoke of the "dissociation of sensibility" which he believed took place in the seventeenth century, when faith and reason were separated by Descartes, and which gave rise to modern scientific rationalism. Eliot was all too aware of the fragmentation of Western culture. *The Waste Land* speaks of his desire to "shore these fragments against my ruin"—an apt description of the poem's form and method. Eliot's ambition was to create a body of poetry that would not only dramatize the major episodes in the decline of Christendom, but also discover how grace could be found in a decimated culture. At first he sought to oppose the romantic egotism of modern art by proclaiming his allegiance to classicism and the pursuit of objective knowledge. When he first began to speak of faith in his work, it was through indirection and allusion; the exhaustion of traditional religious language made him fear the deadening effect of cliché and the resistance of secular readers. In the end, however, Eliot found that only by reaching into his experience and speaking in a personal voice—in *Four Quartets*—could he discover the timeless moments of grace that touched the "still point of the turning world." For Eliot, the road to the objective could only be found through a process of probing the subjective. This process led to a redemption of the romantic impulse, correcting the pantheism of Wordsworth with the Christian intelligence of Coleridge.

Eliot's achievement, though small in quantity, was epic in scale, and has not been repeated in the fifty years since the publication of *Four Quartets.* So influential was Eliot on my own thinking that I used to think that the Christian writer in the modern era had to somehow match Eliot's achievement if he or she was to make an important contribution. But it has become clear to me that few artists can be expected to have the shoulders of Atlas, carrying the whole of Western civilization on their backs. Precisely because the fragmentation that Eliot observed has progressed, it is increasingly difficult to make such grand literary-philosophical gestures. Eliot's ambition was of a piece with the High Modernist aesthetic that gave us Joyce's *Ulysses* and Pound's *The Cantos,* but it is not a realistic ambition in the postmodern era.

O'Connor and Percy retained the philosophical depth of Eliot, but they chose smaller canvases for their art, in O'Connor's case the Georgia backwoods and in Percy's the country clubs and suburban subdivisions of the new South. O'Connor's parables took the modern Nietzschean "will to power" and incarnated it in the lives of wandering preachers, salesmen, and middle-aged society ladies. The secular pride of these folk has to be shattered by the violence of grace before they can be offered the chance to enter the kingdom. Percy's world is less violent and dramatic than that of O'Connor, for the good doctor from Covington was interested in the ways we have domesticated our despair. Drawing on European existentialists such as Kierkegaard, Marcel, and Camus, Percy gave us alienated seekers who tried to become anonymous, disappearing into the backwaters of a crassly materialistic culture. Because they were genuine seekers, they could run but not hide from the Big Questions.

What of our contemporary religious writers, those who have been publishing in the last twenty years? Like Percy and O'Connor, they have chosen to work on smaller canvases. Working from the concrete particulars of time and place, their imaginations reach out to universal truths. Significantly, they have not felt the need to employ indirection to the extent that Eliot, Percy, and O'Connor often did. Contemporary writers have felt more freedom to depict their characters' religious experiences and tensions. This is due in part to the cultural detente that has taken place in recent years. Ironically, it is also a factor of the marginalization of Christianity in mainstream culture. In a fragmented culture, Christianity seems to be just one more "lifestyle."

In the brief survey that follows, I will mention a few of the most distinguished writers in a number of somewhat arbitrary categories, focusing in on a younger, extremely promising writer in each area. The three categories

I would like to touch upon are historical fiction, regional fiction, and contemporary lyric poetry. What sets these writers apart is the way their vision helps to heal the divisions in our culture.

Perhaps because we have become so cut off from the past, Jewish and Christian writers are turning more and more to historical fiction. By placing the story in a historical period in which religion is woven into the fabric of life, and where it has not suffered from trivialization, these writers can explore the life of faith and examine the conflicts that lie in our past. Ron Hansen's *Mariette in Ecstasy,* set in a New York convent at the turn of the twentieth century, tells of a young postulant who receives the stigmata, the wounds of Christ, and of the tumultuous aftermath of this event. Mark Helprin's *A Soldier of the Great War* returns to World War I to examine a turning point in the modern world; it is suffused with many startling insights into the nature of love and art. In her novels *The Unquiet Earth* and *Storming Heaven* Denise Giardina has written of the West Virginia coal miners and their plight in the first half of this century. Frederick Buechner's novels about medieval saints, *Brendan* and *Godric,* at once debunk traditional hagiography and give us more moving portraits of sanctity than any saint's life could.

If I may be allowed to speak of a colleague's work, I would like to single out Harold Fickett's recent novel *First Light,* which is the first in a planned series of historical novels under the general title "Of Saints and Sinners." Fickett has set himself the goal of chronicling the generations of a prominent American evangelical family from the eighteenth century to the present. *First Light* introduces us to Abram White, who as a boy experiences grinding poverty in Ireland. Abram hears of the opportunities available to those who emigrate to the New World, and he decides to run off and do just that. His goal is to make his fortune and return to Ireland to rescue his family. In New York, after years at sea, he meets and marries a woman named Sarah. The choice of names is deliberate, of course: Fickett is structuring his multi-generational saga on the biblical narrative of Genesis. You can expect Hagar and Ishmael to turn up in future volumes. But historical figures, like Jonathan Edwards and George Whitefield, also make cameo appearances.

The historical and cultural territory Fickett has marked out is vast and uncharted. "Of Saints and Sinners" will recover one strand of American religion from obscurity and invest it with the dramatic weight and dignity that it deserves. Yet it does not sentimentalize its subject: unlike most of the historical novels that have been published by Christian houses, *First Light* is not populated by impossibly heroic and virtuous plaster saints. Abram and Sarah struggle with their faith. Abram's desire to rescue his family and establish a new life is balanced on a knife edge where pride and cruelty lie dangerously close to sacrifice and love. "Of Saints and Sinners" is a rescue operation in and of itself, a recovery of memory that pays tribute to a central religious tradition in America, while at the same time showing us its flaws. By telling us where we came from, Fickett helps us to struggle with our identity as a people. The restoration of memory helps heal the fragmentation that occurs when we are cut off from the past.

Another category where outstanding work is being done might be called the regional or local novel. This is a highly unsatisfactory label, because it covers a multitude of different narrative styles and subjects, but it will serve for the moment. What I mean by "regional" is that the author gives us a richly detailed picture of life in a specific place, either in the present moment, or reaching back into the recent past and moving toward the present. Religion is not necessarily the center of attention in these novels, but it is a part of the characters' lives, and plays an important role in the dramatic conflicts depicted in the story. Among the writers that might be placed in this category are Larry Woiwode, Louise Erdrich, Andre Dubus, Garrison Keillor, Kaye Gibbons, and Doris Betts. The South and the northern plains states (including the Dakotas and Minnesota) have been among the most fruitful regions.

One of the most exciting regional writers to emerge in recent years is Elizabeth Dewberry. Her first novel, *Many Things Have Happened Since He Died,* deserves to be more widely known. This first-person narrative is told by a twenty-year-old Alabama woman. She is pregnant, married to a loser, and alone in the world. Though she is almost unbelieveably naive, her passion for a better life is fierce. Though the resemblance may be faint, she is the descendent of Hester Prynne. Let down by Pharisaical fundamentalists, she must forge her own theology in the midst of suffering she barely understands. Late in the novel the narrator, heavily pregnant and thoroughly isolated, fears the ordeal that is soon to be upon her. She is worried about her unborn child, who she plans to put up for adoption, and about the pain of birth and death. She addresses God directly:

> Dear God maybe I am coming to You soon maybe when the baby is born. It wasn't suicide I just couldn't make myself go to the doctor I don't know why. Maybe because I know what is coming and I don't want the doctor to confirm it. Maybe because I am afraid the baby is a monster and he would tell me. I don't know. But now I feel that You are preparing me for death so I wanted to talk to You about that.
>
> Please save me. I don't necessarily mean don't make me die I just mean take me to Heaven. And please let Malone and Daddy be there when I get there. I haven't been real religious lately I haven't been to church in a while. But if I had more time I think I would have come to some sort of peace with You. I will do this I am not that scared of dying but would You please help me would You stay with me or send an angel or Malone or somebody to be with me. And would you please take care of the baby don't make the baby die please give it a nice home and parents and let it take piano lessons and be in the school band and grow up and go to college and be happy and get married to somebody nice and have good healthy children and when it dies please let it come to Heaven and be with us. I think she is a girl. I would name her Elizabeth. When you write her name in the Book of Life could you possibly put Elizabeth in parentheses beside it. If not that's okay.

Dewberry's novel has a breadth that can draw readers from all sectors of our fragmented culture. The novel's central concerns revolve around what might be called "women's issues," and yet the religious dimension cannot be downplayed. This woman does not wallow in self-pity or sublimate her anger in political activism. The narrator's fundamentalist upbringing may have let her down in many ways, but it does enable her to carry on a running debate with God that gives meaning to her suffering.

Among America's most distinguished poets are a number of Christians, including Richard Wilbur, Denise Levertov, Donald Hall, Dana Gioia, and Paul Mariani. Their mode is primarily the lyric, though a number of them have tried their hand at longer sequences.

I'd like to say a brief word about a Southern poet named Andrew

Hudgins. He has published several collections, including *Saints and Strangers* and *The Never-Ending*. His book-length narrative, *After the Lost War,* uses the voice and the life of the Southern poet Sidney Lanier to address such matters as Southern history, mortality, and the role of poetry. In his shorter poems, Hudgins often deals with Christian subjects without a trace of self-consciousness. One of his favorite approaches is to take a medieval or Renaissance painting of a New Testament subject, and interpret the painter's treatment of the story. But a number of his poems are themselves like these paintings: Christ and Mary and John and other biblical figures seem to be set against a background that is contemporary, just as Van Eyck put Flemish castles in the background of his paintings. The final poem from *The Never-Ending* is called "Psalm Against Psalms." It begins this way:

> God had Isaiah eat hot coals,
> Ezekiel eat shit, and they sang
> his praises. I've eaten neither, despite
> my childhood need to test most things
> inside my mouth. . . .
> Isaiah ate the blood-red ember.
> Ezekiel ate the dung. It went in fire
> and came out praise. It went in shit
> and came praise from his mouth. And this
> is where I stick. I pray: thank, ask,
> confess. But praise—dear God!—it clings
> like something dirty on my tongue,
> like shit. Or burns because it is a lie.
> And yet I try: I pray and ask
> for praise, then force the balking words
> out of my mouth as if the saying them
> could form the glowing coal—cool,
> smooth as a ruby—on my tongue.
> Or mold inside my mouth the shit
> that melts like caramel—and thereby,
> by magic, change my heart. Instead

I croak the harsh begrudging praise
of those who conjure grace, afraid
that it might come, afraid it won't.

The poet concludes that he is not capable of embodying the absolute
purity of either spirit (fire) or flesh (dung):

I'm smaller, human, in between,
a leavening of dirt with fire,
and I must be, with every passing day,
more careful of what goes into my mouth,
more reckless of what issues forth.

Hudgins does not conceal his doubts or the self-consciousness that is
so much a part of the modern era; they are incorporated into the piercingly
honest voice of the poem. Here is poetry that is truly confessional—not a
barbaric yawp of self-indulgence but an effort to measure the self against
the larger realities of the soul.

To return to the broad spectrum of American letters, there are two
modes of the imagination that do not have any American practitioners at
the moment. The first I would call the prophetic voice. Prophetic writers,
like Eliot, have moral intensity and a deep sense of history. They can be
scathing, full of Swiftian "savage indignation," but their attacks are
launched in the name of preserving moral and spiritual standards. Two of
the most compelling prophetic writers of our time are the British poet
Geoffrey Hill and the Russian novelist Aleksandr Solzhenitsyn.

The other type of writer that we are missing at the moment is the philosophical kind, such as O'Connor and Percy. This, I think, is our greatest
lack, because the philosophical artist, at his or her best, possesses the ability to link the foreground action of particular characters and settings to the
deep currents flowing beneath the surface of a culture. While we will have
to wait for authentically prophetic and philosophical writers, we can rejoice in what we have.

But what of the literary and religious communities into which these
works are launched? They too are divided, as I indicated earlier when
speaking of the split between the religious and trade markets in the book

industry. When it comes to their choice in books, Catholics and mainstream Protestants have been least affected by the phenomenon of cultural separatism. With a healthy instinct, they have not sought out specifically Christian novels or publishers. When they show an interest in serious literature at all, they tend to want to read the best writers, not merely the safe or acceptable ones. At the same time, many of them have accepted the dichotomy between art and faith that perpetuates cultural divisions. There is evidence that this dichotomy has begun to narrow, as the recent successes of Irving's *Owen Meany,* Tyler's *Saint Maybe,* and Hansen's *Mariette in Ecstasy* indicate.

The most interesting development in recent years has actually been occurring in the group broadly known as evangelical. A number of evangelicals have grown tired of the legacy of cultural separatism, of treating only some authors and publishers as officially approved and therefore safe. Though I cannot quantify this movement (some insist that it is very small), it is certainly having some impact. There are signs that many evangelicals are abandoning a brittle and triumphalistic stance, and searching for a vision that encompasses mystery, ambiguity, sacramentalism, and even tragedy. One practical manifestation of this is the development, within the evangelical world, of what are known as "crossover" publishers or imprints. These publishers are producing books with the intent of transcending the ABA/CBA distinction. Part of this is undoubtedly marketing strategy, but it also reflects a changing perspective. Whether the crossover publishers sell large quantities of books to a secular audience is almost irrelevant. By expecting their books to succeed on the merits of their narrative strength and humanity, rather than through cover quotes from the Bible or famous preachers, these publishers are, in essence, trying to say something to their own religious communities.

Our culture is undergoing a process of tribalization, a breakup into fierce armed camps inflamed by ideological abstractions. Of course, diversity has its virtues; I am not in favor of homogenization. But our mission now must be to dismantle the barriers. Christianity must once more be seen and heard in the public square. The faith must be made to speak, and not in the hectoring voice of the reactionary or in the attenuated and embarrassed tones the liberal. To return to Richard Niebuhr's terms, it is necessary to get away from the "Christ against culture" and "Christ in culture" perspectives, and to affirm a "transformationist" vision. Transformation is what faith and imagination have in common: they take the stuff of ordinary life and place it in the light of the ultimate questions of sin and redemption.

And this brings me back to where I began, to *Image* and my thoughts about its purpose.

Image is an ongoing effort to stake out the ground where faith and art can meet. We hope to bring together the most outstanding art and literature being produced in the Judeo-Christian tradition. We want to be a forum for the rich diversity of work that might not otherwise get the attention it deserves. We also want to build a community of readers bound by their interest in art that manifests a whole vision of the world. In other words, *Image* seeks to bring the healing power of art to a broken, fragmented culture. We want to move beyond the stale politicized debates between fundamentalists and relativists. We want to renew the tradition of Hawthorne, and Eliot, and O'Connor, and Percy. Of course, art in itself cannot save a single soul, much less a nation, but in this postmodern era, when reason has become suspect, the imagination helps us to see and speak the truth. It reminds us, in George Steiner's words, that we are on "the long day's journey of the Saturday," that Good Friday is behind us and Easter Sunday ahead.

JON D. LEVENSON

Jon D. Levenson is the Albert A. List Professor of Jewish Studies at Harvard Divinity School. He is the author of *Sinai and Zion: An Entry Into the Jewish Bible*, *Creation and the Persistence of Evil: The Jewish Drama of Divine Omnipotence*, and *The Hebrew Bible, the Old Testament, and Historical Criticism*. This essay was originally published in *First Things*.

The God of Abraham and the Enemies of "Eurocentrism"

HALF A CENTURY ago, on March 9, 1940, with the world collapsing into a war that was to exceed the worst nightmare, the great German novelist Thomas Mann delivered a brief radio address entitled "The Dangers Facing Democracy." "The streamlined, artificial anti-Semitism of our technical age," warned Mann, "is no end in itself; it is nothing but a wrench to unscrew bit by bit the whole machinery of our civilization."

> Anti-Semitism is like a hand grenade tossed over the wall to work havoc and confusion in the camp of democracy. This is its real end and main purpose.

Mann's goal was to shock out of their apathy those who were ashamed of racial hatred but leery of coming to the aid of the Jews. Broadcasting from New York, he warned that the peoples of Europe discovered too late that "the onslaught against the Jews was but the starting signal for a general drive against the foundations of Christianity."

That humanitarian creed for which we are forever indebted to the people of the Holy Writ originated in the old Mediterranean world. What we are witnessing today is nothing else than the ever-recurrent revolt of unconquered pagan instincts, protesting against the restrictions of the Ten Commandments. The Jews of Middle Europe had the misfortune, as living exponents of old Mediterranean culture, to earn the wrath of the younger Nordics first.

The Jews were thus only the first and most vulnerable target of the Nazis. The onslaught against them would inevitably become an attack on democracy, on Christianity, on the Mediterranean world in which the Western tradition was spawned, and ultimately on the moral life itself, the idea that instinct must yield to externally imposed restrictions. To Thomas Mann, Nazism signified the revolt of the pagan gods of northern Europe against the God of Israel, the Mediterranean Deity in Whose name a new moral order had been imposed upon the Nordics. That the revolt should have first targeted the people of Israel made perfect sense: this was the people whose very existence witnessed to that God and thus negated the deities of blood and soil with whom the Nazis struggled to replace Him. In the deepest sense, the war engulfing Europe even as Mann spoke was about more than politics: it was about theology. The conclusion of his radio address on that dark day expressed the hope that out of the suffering of the Jews might yet come something of universal value:

> Let us hope that this new Twilight will not bring about the pagan god's resurrection, but will be followed by Dawn. Let us pray that the martyrdom of the Savior's people may turn into salvation for a whole suffering world.

Eight years earlier, the Protestant theologian Paul Tillich had sounded the same note in an essay on "The Early Hegel and the Fate of Germany." Despite the focus on the youthful work of a philosopher dead for a century, the essay delivered an unmistakable message about Germany as it was about to sink into the degradation of the Third Reich: the Lord of time has vanquished the gods of space, the peoplehood of the modern Germans is inextricable from their Christianity, and their Christianity is necessarily and inevitably associated with Judaism.

Our history does not allow itself to be taken back, the polytheism of coexistence in space will not return. Through Judaism and Christianity, we have become a people bound up with time. The Jewish principle has become our peculiar destiny, and a *secessio judaica* would be a disconnection from our very selves.

The great contribution of Judaism, warned Tillich, was to break down the attachment to space, negating the polytheism of the nations through the principle that Hegel called "opposition": "bondedness to place, immediacy, and paganism are not the truth of human experience." For his own opposition to the neo-paganism of the Third Reich, Paul Tillich paid dearly. A year after "The Early Hegel and the Fate of Germany" was published, Tillich began his long exile in the United States.

Were the Nazi position so clearly paganistic as Mann and Tillich represented it, the question of why so many churchmen went along with the movement—some even hailing and lionizing it—would be an enduring conundrum. Surely, the church had a stake in the preservation of the legacy of the Mediterranean culture that gave it birth and would have resisted an effort to replace Jesus with Wodan or Thor. The truth is that even apart from the theology of the *Deutsche Christen* (Christians of Nazi persuasion), the claim that the Nazis sought to replace the Christian deity with the Nordic deities falls short of doing justice to the movement. It would be more accurate to say that they sought to *reconstruct* Christianity so as to make it appropriate for Nordic peoples (as they conceived them, that is) to reformulate Christianity so that it would no longer be biased toward the Jews and other Mediterraneans. The Nordic reformulation of Christianity is not only more subtle than the rank paganism of blood and soil that Mann and Tillich described, but also more insidious, and—I maintain—a more durable challenge to Western monotheism than has generally been recognized.

In the cultural program of Alfred Rosenberg, the chief theorist of the National Socialist Movement, for example, a prime objective was to recover Jesus from the Jewish falsification of him to which the church had early on capitulated. "There is no proof," wrote Rosenberg, "for the often-made claim that Jesus was a Jew. Indeed, there is much to show the contrary. Jesus possibly was an Aryan, or partially so, showing the Nordic type strongly." For Rosenberg and other Nazis, the "Nordic type" was not only a physical characteristic but a matter of fundamental spiritual posture. According to them, the true Nordic practices an ethic that is the polar opposite of the ideal of humility, subservience, and nonviolence that has so long been enforced by reference to the authority of Jesus. That this was indeed an imposition upon the historical Jesus Rosenberg sought to establish by citing the earliest gospel, Mark:

> But to resist evil and to turn the left cheek when the right one is struck are womanish exaggerations which are not to be found in Mark. These are falsified additions by other persons. Jesus' entire existence was a fiery rebellion. Only inwardly bastardized men have laid value on a doctrine of cowardice. . . .

Engineering this imposition was the Roman Church, acting from an ambition to dominate.

> It was in the interest of the Roman Church, with its lust for power, to represent subservient humility as the essence of Christ in order to create as many servants as possible for this motivated ideal. To correct this representation is a further ineradicable requirement of the German movement for renewal.

Behind the self-interested distortion of Christianity imposed by Rome lay, in turn, a non-Aryan religion that could never succeed in its goal of vanquishing the Nordic spirit: "This Syrian-African superstition, despite fire and sword, could never be forced upon Europeans." Indeed, the pagan deities reappeared in Europe precisely in the guise of saints of the Church Militant: "These [Nordic] gods lived and breathed as St. Oswald, St. George, St. Martin and as armed horsemen." In his own time, Rosenberg believed, the Aryan peoples had it at long last within their power to liberate themselves from the Jewish God and the ethic of cowardice imposed in His name: "Finally, today, there is occurring a fundamental awakening from this power hypothesis: we are not confronting life from the point of an enforced principle that is still of Jewish-Roman-African ancestry." The liberation of the oppressed Aryans from the spiritual oppression that they had internalized required the de-Judaization of Christianity, and this, as always in the history of the Church, entailed the expunction of the Old Testament.

> Accordingly, the so-called Old Testament must be abolished once and for all as a book of religion. By this, the unsuccessful attempt of the last one-and-a-half thousand years to make us spiritually into Jews will be eliminated. This is an attempt for which we, among other things, had to thank our terrible materialistic Jewish rulers.

Alone, however, this would not suffice, for the Jewishness that had ruined Christianity and, through it, the entire Western world was not confined to the first of the two testaments of the Church's scripture. It also infected the second:

> Thus, Matthew and Paul have provided us with the misfortune of the entire Western cultural world. . . . Our Pauline churches are therefore, in essentials, not Christian. They are the product of the Jewish-Syrian leanings of the apostles.

Rosenberg preferred the fourth gospel because of what he perceived as John's "anti-Jewish spirit hostile to the Old Testament." But beside the expunction of most of the Bible, he also saw an urgent need for new scripture. This was to be composed by someone who understood the spiritual imperatives of the time, as most of the established church did not.

> The necessary fifth Gospel cannot naturally be added by a synod. It will be the creation of a man who experiences the longing for purification very deeply. He probably will have studied the theology of the New Testament.

The tentativeness of the last sentence captures nicely Alfred Rosenberg's ambivalence about Christianity. On the one hand, he recognized that too much of German culture was invested in the church to allow for a simple revival of the Norse religion as he imagined it. "Beyond question," he wrote, "an epoch of German History—the age of myths—would have come to an end even without the attack of armed Roman-Syrian Christianity," and "no matter how the [Etruscan-Jewish-Roman] system had spread, *it has become ennobled through the devotion of millions of Germans.*" To renounce that heritage would be to repudiate the major symbols of the last millennium and more of German culture.

On the other hand, at the basis of the same heritage lies a book still revered and obeyed by Jews and another book influenced by the Jewish spirit and ethic in ways that are hardly incidental. For Rosenberg, then, a reversion to paganism could never work. Instead, he called for a reformulation of Christianity that would liberate the Nordics from Mediterranean domination and enable them once more to exercise their innate and yet unvanquished capacity for martial heroism. This would be a kind of second Protestant Reformation—with one ominous difference, however: what would be recovered from centuries of Roman hegemony would not be the gospel of all the apostles, but the original Nordic spirit of Jesus, long suppressed by force, but never uprooted from the peoples of the north. This new Reformation was to be the spiritual wing of the German awakening that later plunged the world into war and worse.

Viewed from a certain angle, these theories of Alfred Rosenberg and other Nazis may seem as antiquated as they are repugnant. Nearly half a century since the Third Reich collapsed, Germany is a stable Western democracy, and those who admire Hitler and the positions he espoused have been relegated to the status of a fringe group without access to the democratic processes they despise. Moreover, right-wing racist philosophies of history stand in no higher repute anywhere else, and the few intellectuals willing to express anything even faintly reminiscent of them immediately find themselves the target of broad-based opposition.

As for Rosenberg's view of the Old and New Testaments, here the situation is only slightly more complex. It does seem to be the case that the continuity of Jesus with the Judaism of his time and after are still not so well recognized as they ought to be, with many Christians, simple or learned, much preferring to identify Judaism with the Old Testament and to see it as the problem ("the law," "the God of wrath") for which Jesus and the New Testament conveniently provide the answer ("grace," "the

God of love"). Most New Testament scholars are still more at home in the Greek literature of the first two Christian centuries than in the Hebrew, and this does, on occasion, produce a dubious picture of the earliest period of Christianity as more Hellenic than Hebraic. Seldom the result of explicit prejudice, however, this is usually owing to the character of education in the West, in which the Greek and Roman classics are more central than the Dead Sea Scrolls and the Talmud, and Hebrew and Aramaic are thought exotic even among humanistic scholars. But while not without some analogues in the biblical scholarship of his time, Rosenberg's reconstruction of the historical Jesus today commands the allegiance of no credible New Testament scholar. In this case as elsewhere, right-wing racialist historiography is seen not only as amateurish and tendentious, but also as pernicious. Perhaps having been belatedly heeded, the warnings of Thomas Mann and Paul Tillich can be dispensed with in our time.

If one approaches the neo-paganism of the Nazis with an eye to its fundamental assumptions and inner logic, however, the picture is one with a vast and troubling resonance in contemporary American culture. The assumption at the foundation of Rosenberg's edifice of Aryan supremacy was that culture is determined mostly by biology, so that one ethnic group's acceptance of another's cultural legacy is unnatural and takes place only because of violence—"the fire and sword," for example, through which the "Syrian-African superstition" that is Christianity was "forced upon Europeans." If the cultural system is already implicit in the biological self (i.e., the body), then any large-scale cultural shift, such as the Christianization of northern Europe, must be altogether owing to domination and in no sense the result of the greater persuasiveness of the new order, in this case the putatively greater persuasiveness of the Christian than the Nordic view of life.

Still less, needless to say, could the change be owing to the gracious providence of God. This being the case, Rosenberg's idealization of martial heroism rests on more than just the romanticization of the Nordic past. It rests also on a thoroughgoing skepticism about even the possibility of reasoned discourse across cultural boundaries. The ostensibly reasonable positions argued in the discourse are only a cover for self-interest, and the self that advances its interest is defined by its biology; it reduces to its body. With reason thus exposed for what it is, coercion is the weapon of choice in the encounter of cultures.

II

Detached from their particular Nazi applications, these assumptions will be immediately familiar to anyone who labors in the intellectual vineyards today. They are most frequently heard in the challenges flung at the "canon" of the classical liberal arts curriculum. Here I am not speaking of those who argue that the great works of blacks, women, and others have been unjustly denied the attention they deserve because of prejudicial attitudes to these groups still dominant within traditional American social structures. For their argument still presupposes standards by which to judge whether a work is great, and its exponents merely seek admission into the larger discourse for works they believe meet these standards—a petition that rests on a view of culture that is eminently traditional in American liberal arts education. Indeed, exceedingly few are the professors who would deny that the "canon" of the humanities has traditionally lacked the fixity and authority that this rather inappropriate theological term implies. I am speaking, instead, of those who regard race, gender, and sexual instinct as the *principal criteria* for determining the worth of authors or artists to be studied, so that opposition to any given candidate is immediately ascribed to the race, gender, or sexual instinct of the opponent himself. Here again the possibility of reasoning across the boundaries is implicitly—and often explicitly—denied and intellectual discourse rapidly degenerates into politics, as the various groups are redefined as factions and the campus comes to resemble the national convention of a political party more than the groves of academe.

There are a number of ways in which equilibrium can be restored when this happens. One of them is to allocate slots in the curriculum and appointment structure according to the proportions of the duly accredited victimized minority groups in American society. (As we know, many minorities, even some with histories of extraordinary victimization, are denied consideration in the allocation process—e.g., evangelicals, Catholics, Jews, Southerners, Mormons.) Beneath this solution for restoring quiet lies the assumption that the university (or the seminary) is a community primarily political in character and that its proper form of politics is a kind of vulgar democratism. Acceptance of this assumption places the affirmation of any given cultural tradition at a disadvantage, since no culture has historically subscribed to an interpretation of itself and its artifacts as political through and through. The subversion and deconstruction of tradition are thus features of the current politicizing of scholarship that are more than adventitious.

And in the last analysis, the restoration of equilibrium through proportional representation still implies the reduction of culture to biology, for any ethnic group will then command only as much attention as the fertility rate of its recent generations allows: higher numbers, more representation; lower numbers, less representation. The irony is that this solution to the academic problem posed by cultural diversity is often advocated by people for whom child-bearing and rearing are not objects of elevated esteem. In the event, vulgar democratism is usually advocated alongside a moral argument with which it cannot be easily harmonized—that is, the experience of the accredited group has something of *value* to which all communities should pay heed. The tensions in this mixed argument are rarely exposed and almost never faced.

On occasion one hears a solution to the problem of cultural diversity that is more directly and crudely biological. There is, for example, the theory of the chairman of a black studies department in New York who has been reported to hold that the Ice Age deformed the genes of white people, whereas those of blacks were enriched by exposure to the warming rays of the sun. This is, it must be noted, an extreme case, which is why it has received considerable attention in the news media. The implications of this black professor's linkage of culture to genetics are as anti-democratic as those of Rosenberg's Aryan supremacy; couched in terms of multiculturalism, however, such anti-democratic thinking can find a sympathetic hearing in academic life today. One reason for this is that *biological essentialism* does seem to play a large role in the thinking of many advocates of multiculturalism. Given the way that race, class, and sexual instinct have come to dominate the discussion, it is hard to see how matters could be otherwise. The addition of social class to the mix should, at least in theory, dampen the biological essentialism a bit. But most discussions in which race, gender, class, and sexual instinct are high on the agenda suffer from an amalgam of biological *and* social determinism that makes an affirmation of transcendence well-nigh impossible. Indeed, transcendence has become a prime target of the two great guns of academic nihilism in our time, deconstruction and the hermeneutics of suspicion. Thus fades the "opposition" to "bondedness to place, immediacy, and paganism" that Hegel and Tillich associated with the faith of Abraham and the opportunity for transcendence. More ominously, as we shall soon see, "the co-existence of polytheism in space" that Tillich said "will not return" in fact threatens to return.

Advocacy of multiculturalism is inevitably associated with opposition to "Eurocentrism"—that is, a concentration on the European heritage to the disadvantage of other cultures, especially those with roots in Africa and the pre-Columbian Americas. As a critique of provincialism, an argument against Eurocentrism could be built on themes that are themselves prominent in both the Hebraic and the Hellenic roots of European civilization and thus part and parcel of that heritage. Usually, however, the attack on Eurocentrism takes a very different form, one of opposition to the traditional curriculum and the culture to which it gives expression on the grounds that this curriculum is irrelevant or inapplicable to some particular community. Thus the oft-heard rejection of DEWM—"dead European white males," whose work and ideas are assumed to be of no benefit to the non-European, the non-white, the female, and (logic dictates) the living as well. Now national origin joins race and gender as *predetermining* the cultural identity of an individual or group (and not simply *influencing* it, as almost everyone would concede). In this way, the "bondedness to place" that Hegel and Tillich thought the faith of Abraham had dislodged reestablishes itself with a vengeance. That a person without European ancestors might become culturally European is either denied altogether or lamented as an election of inauthenticity. This being the case, it is unclear why persons of European descent ought, in turn, to occupy themselves with something as distant as the cultures of Africa or the

Andes. The critique of provincialism thus yields to the powerful forces of the new determinisms, and narrowness acquires a theoretical foundation of high prestige.

One of the oddities of the critique of Eurocentrism is the ubiquitous assumption that Europe somehow constitutes a cultural unit, an assumption to which not a few conservative champions of the older curriculum have been known to subscribe as well. The less-sophisticated opponents of Eurocentrism often equate Europe and even the Caucasian race with imperialism, as if Africa had been carved up in the nineteenth century among the Lithuanians, the Jews, the Basques, and the Irish. When race, a biological category, overtakes culture, a historical category, it is again hard to see how the matter could be otherwise. The irony here is that in the very name of multiculturalism, the cultural heritage of numerous students is once more neglected. A telling instance of this is those schools in which the study of Jewish civilization does not count for the ethnic studies program or the "diversity" requirement. You would think that whites have generally been preoccupied with Talmudic Law, medieval Torah commentaries, and the Yiddish short story.

That Europe is a cultural unity is one illusion from which Alfred Rosenberg did not suffer. For him, as we have seen, the great divide lay between people of Nordic extraction and those of "Jewish-Roman-African ancestry," with the former representing purity, honor, and heroism, and the latter incarnating the corresponding negatives. In our present cultural situation, a reexamination of Rosenberg's theories drives home a keen awareness of how particular and localized is the origin of what often is glibly called "European culture" by both defenders and despisers. The foundation of that culture does not lie in the Germanic north or the Slavic east of Europe. Instead, it lies in what Thomas Mann in that radio address of 1940 termed the "old Mediterranean world," of which the "Jews of Middle Europe had the misfortune [of being] living exponents." It is from their Mediterranean homelands that the modes of thought and practice of Jerusalem and Athens have spread in every direction, and it is this diffusion that, for all their differences, the Nazis and the opponents of Eurocentrism both attack. To describe the offending culture as European or white is thus to neglect key features of the very diffusion that is now so regretted. From Jerusalem, it is roughly the same distance to London as to Nairobi: the God of Abraham is no more native to the Angles and the Saxons than to the Kikkuyu and the Kamba. Whether any of these groups ought to have put away their traditional gods to accept Him is a matter of legitimate debate, as is the perennial question of whether either Jerusalem or Athens ought to have attained cultural hegemony over the other. Without resort, however, to a biological essentialism reminiscent of Nazism and, to put it mildly, of very dubious worth, appeal to ethnicity alone cannot resolve these knotty issues.

Thus, for all the differences between humanism and Hebraism, on this point defenders of traditional liberal education and believers in the God of Abraham can come to agreement: culture, whether personal or communal, is not reducible to genetics or ethnicity because man is always capable of transcending his origins, that is, of ending his journey in a different and better place than he began it. Indeed, to end our journey in a better place than that of our origin is, in different ways, the objective of both Abrahamic religious life and traditional liberal arts education. In the religious framework, Abraham's experience is paradigmatic; even if they were begun amidst the pollution of Ur, our lives can end in the purity of Hebron.

The Abrahamic paradigm presents a formidable obstacle to those Christians eager to align the church with Third World liberation movements. For, to the extent that such movements seek to undo the legacy of European imperialism, they must also, if they are to be consistent, seek their own de-Christianization and the restoration of the indigenous religions that the church eradicated, suppressed, or diluted through syncretism. That Christianity can be enlisted in the movement to rectify social, economic, and political injustice in and against the Third World is beyond dispute, for this is still to appeal to norms esteemed in the "old Mediterranean culture" that Jesus of Nazareth exemplified. Things become more complicated, however, when that culture and its European successors are defined, even at their best, as inevitably part of the problem. This places in danger the essential Pauline principle that through faith in the Christ a Gentile is grafted onto the tree of Israel and attains the status of a descendant of Abraham (Romans 4 and 11). It implies that what Paul called the "native wild olive" has no need of the "cultivated olive" onto which it has been grafted graciously, mysteriously, and conditionally (Romans 11:19–24). And this un-Christian implication is one that Alfred Rosenberg—who, it will be recalled, hated Paul for his Jewish leanings—would have seconded with enthusiasm. Rejection of the God of Abraham makes strange bedfellows.

III

Anyone under the impression that the hyper-romantic program of recovering the gods of soil and nature died with the Third Reich has not spent much time in liberal religion departments and divinity schools lately. In many of these, radical feminists of a particular kind have mounted an extraordinarily successful assault on traditional Christianity and Judaism in the name of the goddesses these traditions have suppressed or eradicated. Sometimes the agenda involves reclaiming the pagan deity whom, it is argued, the normative traditions have masked.

In *Changing of the Gods: Feminism and the End of Traditional Religion,* Naomi R. Goldenberg writes that "behind [the Virgin Mary's] sanitized figure lurk all the great pagan goddesses of the ancient world. . . . Mary has become castrated by popes, cardinals, priests, and theologians, by all who fear the sexual and emotional power of natural womanhood." Goldenberg's Mary is analogous to Rosenberg's St. Oswald, St. George, and St. Martin, the putative Christian masks of the Nordic gods, except that for Goldenberg the original Mary "of natural womanhood" did not survive her Christianization. Instead of a renewed Christianity or Judaism, Goldenberg thus turns to such phenomena as witchcraft where, she tells us, "a woman's will is sacred," and "Once she has learned to visualize her wishes, a witch uses her will to bring them to reality." The Nietzschean implications suggested here are immediately disavowed: "The only rule that restricts the play of the will is an injunction not to use it for destructive purposes."

But this qualification is in tension with an element in witchcraft that Goldenberg tells us conventional minds find repellent. Witchcraft provides:

> No *rigid law of discipline*. The absence of a need to keep base human instincts in control is unthinkable to most Jews and Christians. . . . Both conscious and unconscious elements of the person are considered self-regulating and self-governing. . . . No higher moral law is called upon to keep any lower nature in check.

One wonders why the rule that prevents the witch's will from being used "for destructive purposes" is not a "higher moral law" necessary to keep our "lower nature in check." One can go further: why are those "destructive purposes" wrong in an ethic that celebrates naturalness and instinct? Surely, natural history presents abundant evidence for destruction, including the destruction of whole species, and the instinct to kill is hardly unique to males or even human beings. The lower nature, liberated from higher moral law that keeps it in check, is at least as likely to give us Rosenberg's Nazis and the Holocaust as it is to produce Goldenberg's benign witches and female empowerment.

In *Laughter of Aphrodite: Reflections on a Journey to the Goddess,* Carol P. Christ speaks of two intuitions that nourish what she calls her the*a*logy (from the Greek *thea,* "goddess"):

> The first is that the earth is holy and our true home. The second is that women's experience, like all human experience, is a source of insight about the divine.

The second intuition is hardly new or repugnant to Jewish and Christian traditionalists. It underlies the prophet Hosea's understanding of Israel's relationship to God as a marriage, for example, and the traditional Jewish and Christian interpretations of the Song of Songs as an allegory of God's love for Israel and Christ's for his Church, respectively. But these images drawn from traditional notions of courtship and marriage are not what Carol Christ has in mind when she speaks of "women's experience." Indeed, in words reminiscent of the theology that Hosea lambasted, she speaks warmly of her liberation from "male Gods who are defined in opposition to the powers of earth, nature, myself" and reports that "I began to feel that my loyalties were with those castigated by my tradition as idolators."

The substantive values of writers like Goldenberg and Christ are obviously very different from those of the Nazi theorist Alfred Rosenberg—indeed, often diametrically opposed to them. Whereas he saw the Christian ethic as one of nonviolence and self-giving love and therefore Jewish and effeminate, Carol Christ identifies the biblical God as a "God of War [who] stands for too much that I stand against." It must also be noted that whereas Rosenberg was a vehement anti-Semite, Christ rejects the Western theological traditions in part because of the Holocaust and contributes a chapter "On Not Blaming Jews for the Death of the Goddess." But in her case, as in Goldenberg's, it must still be asked whether all who liberate themselves from the God "defined in opposition to the power of earth, nature, and myself" will feel drawn to her ethic and her the*a*logy. Will not some be reasonably drawn to the blood and soil mysticism of Alfred Rosenberg and correctly recognize in the Jews the living exponents of the order they reject? And will not some replace the God of Abraham with goddesses inimical to Carol Christ's the*a*logy—with Athena, the Greek goddess of war, for example, or with her Canaanite counterpart, the bloodthirsty Anat?

If goddess worship of the sort presented in Goldenberg's and Christ's books seems exotic, consider this: according to a reliable press report, the "goddess movement" is being advanced in part by a course entitled "Cakes for the Queen of Heaven" (see Jeremiah 44). Produced under Unitarian auspices, the course has now been used not only by at least 800 of the 1,000 congregations of the Unitarian Universalist Association, but also by Congregationalist, Methodist, and Episcopal groups and even by an order of nuns. The inclusion by mainline ecclesiastical bodies of forms of religion that their own scriptures and traditions have pronounced abominable and idolatrous is one of the most remarkable transformations of our times. It is not altogether without precedent.

IV

The midrash relates that a philosopher once posed a question about circumcision to Rabbi Hoshayah, one of the great authorities in the Land of

Israel early in the third century. "If circumcision is precious," asked the philosopher, "why was it not given to Adam?" Rabbi Hoshayah answered:

> Everything created during the six days of creation requires that something be done to it. Mustard, for example, requires sweetening, lupin requires sweetening, wheat requires grinding—even man requires perfecting.

The assumption underlying the rabbi's response is that Abraham, to whom the commandment of circumcision is first given (Genesis 17), is to be a perfecting of Adam, and life in covenant with God, therefore, an improvement upon life in the state of nature. The philosopher's implicit critique of Abraham is formidable. For the commandment of circumcision comes bound up with the promise of progeny and the Land, two of the most natural of things, and yet circumcision is an invasion of nature and not, as one might expect in this context, an affirmation of it.

The point of Rabbi Hoshayah's reply is that the covenantal life of the Jewish people is neither a denial of nature, on the one hand, nor an unqualified expression of it, on the other. Neither "opposition" (to use Paul Tillich's term) nor "the powers of earth, nature, myself" (to use Carol Christ's) captures the spirituality of covenant in the Abrahamic mode. Rather, to borrow a phrase from the late Arthur A. Cohen, each member of the people Israel is called to be both a natural and a supernatural Jew. The natural and supernatural Jew seeks neither to love nature nor to conquer it, but only to bring nature—including the natural vitalities of nationalism and sexuality—to the service of its Creator and thus to elevate, ennoble, and sanctify it. To keep nature and that which is beyond nature in their proper relationship is not a task for Jews alone, but for all who call Abraham their father. As in the dark days when Thomas Mann and Paul Tillich issued their warnings, so now, this is a task of mounting urgency.

WILFRED M. McCLAY

Wilfred M. McClay is associate professor of history at Tulane University and is currently a Guest Scholar at the Woodrow Wilson International Center for Scholars. His book *The Masterless: Self and Society in Modern America* won the 1995 Merle Curti Award from the Organization of American Historians. McClay is a frequent contributor to such publications as *Commentary, First Things,* and *Books and Culture.* He is currently writing the authorized biography of the sociologist David Riesman. This is an original, previously unpublished essay.

Filling the Hollow Core: Religious Faith and the Postmodern University

WHAT IS MEANT by the term *Christian scholarship*? There is no simple answer. Does the term designate work done by a scholar who happens to be Christian? Or by a Christian who happens to be a scholar? Of course, it does both, in varying degrees. But which of the two words should take priority in shaping the term's practical meaning, and in defining the aims of those identified with it? How powerful is that modifier *Christian* to be?

This is (or ought to be) a central issue for Christians in every occupation, simply because they are called to see all aspects of their lives, including their work, in the light of God's will. But it is never easy to know how to conform to that will, no matter what work one does—even pastoring a church. The problem seems especially compelling, and often baffling, for those involved in the business of academic scholarship. This may be partly because writers

231

and intellectuals are prone to imagine, narcissistically, that their lives are somehow more complicated than everyone else's. Still, there is something to their perception—at least, so far as their professional life is concerned.

Consider, by way of contrast, the work of plumbers or dentists. A Christian plumber will pay the most painstaking attention to his craft, show the most scrupulous regard for his customers, and thereby stand as a powerful witness to his faith. But his faith will not dictate the methods he uses to unclog your drain. Nor will the skilled Christian dentist argue that the ministry of the Holy Spirit ought to supersede the knowledge and techniques learned in dental school. There are those who would approach the problem of Christian scholarship in just the same way. In this view, one should strive to be a professional's professional, excelling at one's work on the world's terms, standing above reproach in one's conduct—letting the light of one's achievements so shine before colleagues and students that they will, perhaps, be led to wonder about the faith behind such exemplary deeds.

This is good advice, with a fitting intellectual modesty and accountability attached to it. Yet the rightful claims of Christian scholarship would seem to be more extensive than that. All scholarly writing relies upon, and in turn reinforces, certain suppositions about the nature and meaning of the phenomena being studied. It should make a very big difference in one's view of the world whether one believes that there exists a God Who created the world, fashioned human beings in His own image, revealed Himself through the Holy Scriptures, became incarnate in the person of Jesus Christ, and so on. And that difference would seem to entail more than just being a responsible and humane teacher. "Do not conform any longer to the pattern of this world," urged Paul, in what is perhaps the definitive scriptural statement on the matter, "but be transformed by the renewing of your mind" (Romans 12:2). And how could it be otherwise? Is it not self-evident that Christian beliefs about the nature of ultimate reality should so dramatically transform the act of scholarship that the work of Christian scholars, even those employed in secular institutions, should be propelled by a distinctive energy and purposefulness?

Self-evident, perhaps. But as the historian George Marsden has recently pointed out in a provocative and engaging book, ironically entitled *The Outrageous Idea of Christian Scholarship,* it is generally not the case. On the contrary, Marsden asserts what we all know to be the sad truth of the matter: Most Christian scholars learn early on to "keep quiet about their faith as the price of full acceptance" in the scholarly community. The unstated commitment to self-censorship extends to every facet of academic life, from graduate training to hiring, tenuring, promotion, and access to the most prestigious and influential venues. So deeply internalized is this commitment that Christian scholars are themselves often among the most vigilant in promulgating it.

Of course, if one takes the longer historical view, there were good reasons for this turn of events. American higher education originated in a climate of established Protestantism, an atmosphere of pervasive cultural Christianity in which free intellectual inquiry nearly always took a back seat to the imperatives of character formation, and in which a faculty member's range of permissible opinions—and acceptable personal characteristics—was severely circumscribed. The fundamental outlook of many of today's American academics, particularly (though not exclusively) Jews and other non-Christians who would formerly have been excluded from full participation in the life of the academy, has been heavily conditioned by the knowledge or memory of those earlier days. The movement to disestablish Protestant Christianity in American higher education was, in many respects, a good thing, addressing genuine inadequacies and injustices, and resulting in genuine benefits.

But that was then, and this is now. Today it increasingly appears that we have merely exchanged one religious establishment for another, having moved from established Protestantism to what Marsden calls "established unbelief." As in so much of contemporary American public discourse, such as our construal of the First Amendment, we seem unable to distinguish between the cultivation of genuine intellectual pluralism that encourages religious expression and the imposition of a secularist orthodoxy that proscribes all such expression. The near-complete banishment of Christian perspectives from the discourse of today's American academy—a proscription of religious expression that seems to be peculiarly directed at Christianity—represents the latter rather than the former, and as such is a profound overreaction to a long-vanished Protestant hegemony.

In short, the tables have been turned completely, so that what began as liberation from orthodoxy now itself resembles a new orthodoxy, and a constraint upon free inquiry. But given the fact that an ideal of "diversity" is uniformly embraced by all of the most prominent and influential academics of our day, it is reasonable to ask: Why are the perspectives of believing Christians not accounted a legitimate part of that diversity? Or is the otherwise commendable ideal of "diversity" being used as a cover word, designed to veil the imposition of a new uniformity—namely, a dogmatic naturalism that regards religion in general, and Christianity in particular, with unveiled hostility?

No one has explored these matters with greater sensitivity and depth than Marsden; as he has pointed out, one can even deploy the vocabularies of multiculturalism and postmodernism in support of the Christian perspective, and against the very anti-religious position their proponents generally embrace. If we are all agreed that scholarship is unavoidably "situated" in various ways (according to such desiderata as race, gender, class, and sexual orientation), and if we are all agreed that every scholar operates on the basis of certain nondemonstrable beliefs, then what grounds can there be for discriminating against the expression of Christian or other religious perspectives, so long as the scholars that do so play by the pragmatic rules, wait their turn, and do not hog the stage? Even the ritualistic invocation of "the separation of church and state" now seems, even aside from its slogan-like crudeness and inaccuracy, wildly inappropriate to the situation in which we find ourselves in the centerless, drifting, dissension-ridden fin-de-siécle academy. Perhaps there is no longer any good reason, in a post-Enlightenment era, to privilege the "nonsectarianism" of secularism—or, indeed, to regard it as especially nonsectarian.

Yet the problem of Christian scholarship may not be only, or even primarily, the result of mainstream hostility. Christian scholars who might be expected to be broadly sympathetic to such arguments often react to it with surprising discomfort and nervousness. Have they gotten too fearful, or comfortable, in their confinement? Are they too eager to court the approval of those who disdain them? Or perhaps they do not want to be seen as trading on their religious commitments, like businessmen who put fish symbols on their business cards as a way of attracting clients and disarming criticism. Or, perhaps most likely, they may simply find it hard to imagine what difference the Christian perspective could, and should, make in their own professional work, aside from questions of personal demeanor. It is easy to see that Christians should distinguish themselves by their scholarly civility, and the fairness and charity with which they engage in debate. But it is less apparent how their perspective can also influence the questions they pose, and the conclusions they reach. Nothing in their professional training and socialization has prepared them to consider such matters.

Such a Christian perspective will not necessarily generate a specific or uniform agenda. Christianity is not an ideology, and it almost never leads its adherents to identical positions on questions of policy or politics. But it will profoundly shape the way questions are posed, for it brings a characteristic disposition and moral urgency to bear on the subject at hand. Christian faith serves to "sacralize" (in Robert Wuthnow's term) and ennoble the intellectual life, restoring to it a high seriousness and consequentiality that it has slowly but surely lost in strictly secularist hands. A Christian perspective is intrinsically holistic, for it supposes that all truth is one—because the Author of all truth is One. Because its holism affirms the comprehensive order of the world, it becomes a powerful critique of, and reproach to, all our tendencies toward reductionism and fragmentation, a persistent reminder of their inadequacy.

George Marsden has pointed to three other distinctive features that Christian scholarship ought to possess, features that (not coincidentally) correlate with the three persons of the Trinity. The Christian understanding of creation affirms that there is a moral law grounded in God's unchanging nature, a fact that thereby restores a plausible basis for just the kind of moral judgments (about distributive justice, human rights, business ethics, and so on) that many secular academics would like to be able to make, but find themselves unable to justify within the epistemological constraints they have embraced. The doctrine of Incarnation confers honor and potentiality upon the body of the natural world by conjoining it to the spiritual realm, neither exploiting nature nor deifying it, but revealing the deeper meanings that course through its veins. And its acknowledgement of the spiritual dimension of reality, in tandem with the sense of human limitation expressed in the doctrine of original sin, makes it a powerful counterforce to an arrogant humanity's tendency to exalt itself.

Given the nature of these potential contributions, then, it would seem to be a mistake for Christians to lean too heavily upon the language of postmodernism and multiculturalism to secure a place at the academic table. In the first place, it would be dangerous to assume that postmodern assertions about the Enlightenment's bankruptcy command general assent among academics. Indeed, there is an intense and growing reaction against postmodernism taking place in many quarters of the academy. The near-universal *Schadenfreude* with which academics greeted the Alan Sokal hoax of last year, in which an intrepid professor of physics at New York University managed to palm off a bogus science-debunking parody as a genuine work of postmodernist scholarship, thereby fooling the editors of the ultra-fashionable pomo journal *Social Text,* is a clear indication of this contempt. Christians should resist the temptation to make common cause with those who believe there is no truth; otherwise, their ships will sink together.

They should also resist the temptation (which surfaces in Marsden's book) to claim that Christian scholars, like African Americans, Hispanics, women, gays, lesbians, and other marginalized groups before them, deserve to be permitted a distinct "voice," based upon their distinctive "background beliefs," as part of the pluralism of a decentered academy. One can well understand why it might be tempting to adopt the language of identity politics, at a time when such language commands almost automatic respect in the academy; there can be little doubt that Christian scholars are discriminated against in that environment. But such arguments are unlikely to carry the day in this instance, if only because most advocates of diversity are committed secularists with little desire to promote intellectual diversity.

Even if such arguments succeeded, the success would come at too great a price. For in advancing such an argument, one gives one's blessing to a vision of the academy as hopelessly, permanently, and systematically fragmented, incapable of anything like a common discourse. In addition, and perhaps more importantly, such an argument runs the risk of minimizing the profound truth-claims Christianity makes, and downplaying the profound hope it offers a fragmented world. In adopting this argument, Christian scholars would win their place at the table by classifying themselves as just another identity group, just another particularism in a vast, noisy dining hall of particularists. In this day and age, what could be less outrageous—and less challenging to the status quo?

Such a fate would be especially ironic in light of the bracing sentence with which George Marsden begins *Outrageous Idea:* "Contemporary university culture is hollow at its core." Surely this emptiness at the core is the condition we most urgently need to address; and it is a condition about which Christianity has much to say, beginning as it does with the premise that all truth is one. Far from supporting a "diversity" argument, however, such a premise suggests a diametrically opposite argument, of the sort advanced most memorably in John Henry Newman's *Idea of a University*—a theologically grounded conception of higher education. That conception is well summarized by two sentences drawn from Newman's distinguished work: "In a word, Religious Truth is not only a portion, but a condition of general knowledge. To blot it out is nothing short, if I may so speak, of unraveling the web of University Teaching."

For Newman, the firm possession of a theological center was the precondition of there being any coherent organization of knowledge at all. Such a view hearkens back, in some respects, to the older, Protestant-focused American ideal of higher education. The modern university has decisively abandoned this ideal, and despite the academy's growing resemblance to Babel, no one is advocating a Protestant restoration. But if there is to be no religious center to higher education, and no recourse to what Robert Nisbet called "the academic dogma" of rational, objective, and universal discourse, then where are we to turn in addressing the problem of the hollow core? Even if the re-establishment of "religious truth" at the core of the university is an unfeasible proposition, except in a handful of special situations, there remains an immense burden on those who would offer a compelling vision of the university that does not invoke equally "commanding" truths.

There are, then, two very different and seemingly antithetical reasons for bringing Christian scholarship up out of the catacombs and into the public square. On the one hand, there is the desire to stake a claim of legitimate minority status for Christians in a pluralistic academy that no longer has any reason to fear Christian coercion—indeed, may have far more to fear from the coercive dogma of "established unbelief." On the other hand, there is the irrepressible hope that Christian scholarship can lead the way in the reintegration of knowledge and reunification of a decaying, dispirited, and disintegrating modern university. That there is a tension between these two reasons would seem obvious. If today's stubbornly fragmented academy has nothing to fear from Christians, can it really have anything to hope for from them either? In the pluralist dispensation, won't the institutional presence of Christianity always be conditional upon the acceptance of a prior restraint? Or, to put it a little differently, can one separate the Christian worldview's claim to "model" the integration of human knowledge with the fullness of life from that worldview's claim to be the truth?

Be that as it may, Christians will want to affirm both of these reasons. Taken together, they mirror the "betweenness" of the Christian life itself, which must be lived suspended between fall and redemption, between the reality of brokenness and the promise of wholeness, between Good Friday and Easter Sunday—between being fully engaged in a suffering world and yet deriving one's ultimate citizenship, and one's ultimate identity, from another source. In this connection, it is illuminating to consider Stanley Fish's odd contention that religious people "should not want to enter the marketplace of ideas, but to shut it down," since they are (presumably) already in possession of the truth. This represents a common enough belief, even among some Christians—but it is dead wrong, at least insofar as it refers to a genuine and deeply meditated Christianity. For the freedom to make choices is at the heart of what it means to be made in the image of God. The Christian faith teaches that God desires not only that we know the truth, but that we choose to embrace it; and it is His will that we be provided the opportunity to make that choice, and perhaps to make it wrongly. In the same way, He desires to receive our uncoerced, heartfelt love and our voluntary obedience, rather than programming us to live in robotic holiness and fealty.

In short, the Christian God tolerates error and untruth for the sake of moral and spiritual freedom. This fact may, curiously enough, be a powerful reason why Christian scholars ought to defend the modern university, despite all its hollowness, chaos, and waste, as a place where Christians can choose to be salt—though, as always, they must count the cost in doing so. Yet there are great benefits to be derived thereby. One of the great drawbacks to the "established" Protestantism that dominated earlier universities was the same drawback presented by "Christendom" itself: its tendency to substitute the seductive comforts of a "cultural Christianity" for the opportunity to make that costly choice—freely, courageously, counterculturally—and, in so doing, be forced to forge a more vigorous and distinctive brand of Christian scholarship. Today we face a very different set of problems, and a very different set of opportunities.

Of course, schools are not merely marketplaces of ideas. We used to call them *seminaries,* a word that suggests garden plots, places of cultivation and formative discipline—places of "culture," in the fullest sense of that word. And so there is an inescapable tension in the expectations we have for all schools, and for the university in particular—a tension between its formative role, as a place in which cultural legacies are transmitted and young souls are shaped, and its liberatory role, as a place where, in C. vann Woodward's memorable words, "the unthinkable can be thought, the unmentionable can be discussed, and the unchallengeable can be challenged." The debates over religious establishment and academic freedom in the past, and over the various forms of "political correctness" in the present, have much to do with this tension, and we should not expect to see it resolved with any finality.

It is important to remember, however, that no marketplace can exist in a cultural vacuum. To be successful, free institutions must be able to draw upon habits and attitudes ingrained by constraints. Liberal institutions must be able to rely upon the discipline imparted by certain illiberal institutions—notably the family—to form the citizens and workers that make a liberal society work. Markets require a solid foundation of non-market-derived values—notably the legal and moral codes that underwrite the reliability of contracts and fairness of competition—to function properly. There is always, in short, an optimal balance to be sought between the formative and the libertarian. Christians, who believe the only true freedom comes through obedience to God, should grasp this fact instinctively.

That balance, however, cannot be found in the modern secular universities, and it is probably illusory to hope for it there, although we can certainly expect that their deans and presidents will continue prattling on about "values" for the foreseeable future. Such talk is either empty posturing or protective cover, designed to conceal the hollowness at the core of the modern research university. But such a balance cannot be found in the overwhelming majority of religious colleges and universities, either because (as in the case of most Catholic institutions) they have become overwhelmingly secular in their ethos, or (as in the case of most evangelical Protestant colleges) the formative function predominates over all others, including the spirit of free inquiry. All the more reason, then, to emphasize diversity—institutional diversity—as a way of compensating for the inevitable incompleteness of any one kind of school. The two kinds of educational institutions (marketplace and seminary, open libertarian forum and enclosed formative institution) may have trouble existing at the same time in the same place; they may even seem antagonistic. But the fact is, they need one another.

In this view, then, there is an enormously important place for the Christian colleges, Protestant and Catholic alike, not only as protective undergraduate environments but as distinctive and relatively homogeneous intellectual microcultures where the integration of faith and knowledge can be pursued with the highest degree of energy and confidence. Just as there need to be churches—enclosed and consecrated places into which Christians have been "called out," places that form Christian disciples around sound doctrine, moral instruction, and corporate worship—so, too, there need to be church-like schools, which also proceed from a formative blueprint based upon Christian convictions. Flawed though they be there is no substitute for them.

At the same time, however, it is high time to acknowledge the need for a space (though a very different kind of space) for the mainstream academic activity that scholars like George Marsden are advocating. In part, this is a simple question of equity, and of the universities' living up to the standards of openness, diversity, and inclusivity they profess. But the possibility of such activity is also important for the health and tempering of the Christian mind. Again, the church comparison is revealing. Just as Christians neither grow in their faith nor obey its imperatives if they do nothing more than snuggle in the safety of their churches, so Christian intellectuals need to venture out of their safe venues and take their insights and questions to the Mars Hills of today. Considered apart, these two very different environments for Christian scholarship would seem to be at war. But taken together, they can correct and complement one another, modeling in their very being how it is that Christianity sustains the promise of wholeness while accepting the reality of brokenness.

Part VI

FLESH AND SPIRIT

A Sacramental Vision

WENDELL BERRY

Wendell Berry is a poet, novelist, essayist, and cultural critic. A native of Kentucky, he has lived with his family on a 125-acre farm in Henry County for the past three decades. He has received fellowships from the Guggenheim and Rockefeller Foundations and won the Lannan Foundation Award for Nonfiction in 1989. Among his many books are *What Are People For?*, *Collected Poems: 1957–1982,* and *Remembering,* a novel. This essay is reprinted from Berry's collection *Sex, Economy, Freedom and Community.*

Christianity and the Survival of Creation

I

ICONFESS THAT I have not invariably been comfortable in front of a pulpit; I have never been comfortable behind one. To be behind a pulpit is always a forcible reminder to me that I am an essayist and, in many ways, a dissenter. An essayist is, literally, a writer who attempts to tell the truth. Preachers must resign themselves to being either right or wrong; an essayist, when proved wrong, may claim to have been "just practicing." An essayist is privileged to speak without institutional authorization. A dissenter, of course, must speak without privilege.

I want to begin with a problem: namely, that the culpability of Christianity in the destruction of the natural world and the uselessness of Christianity in any effort to correct that destruction are now established clichés of the conservation movement. This is a problem for two reasons.

First, the indictment of Christianity by the anti-Christian conservationists is, in many respects, just. For instance, the complicity of Christian priests, preachers, and missionaries in the cultural destruction and the economic exploitation of the primary peoples of the Western Hemisphere, as of traditional cultures around the world, is notorious. Throughout the five hundred years since Columbus's first landfall in the Bahamas, the evangelist has walked beside the conqueror and the merchant, too often blandly assuming that their causes were the same. Christian organizations, to this day, remain largely indifferent to the rape and plunder of the world and of its traditional cultures. It is hardly too much to say that most Christian organizations are as happily indifferent to the ecological, cultural, and religious implications of industrial economics as are most industrial organizations. The certified Christian seems just as likely as anyone else to join the military-industrial conspiracy to murder Creation.

The conservationist indictment of Christianity is a problem, second, because, however just it may be, it does not come from an adequate understanding of the Bible and the cultural traditions that descend from the Bible. The anti-Christian conservationists characteristically deal with the Bible by waving it off. And this dismissal conceals, as such dismissals are apt to do, an ignorance that invalidates it. The Bible is an inspired book written by human hands; as such, it is certainly subject to criticism. But the anti-Christian environmentalists have not mastered the first rule of the criticism of books: you have to read them before you criticize them. Our predicament now, I believe, requires us to learn to read and understand the Bible in the light of the present fact of Creation. This would seem to be a requirement both for Christians and for everyone concerned, but it entails a long work of true criticism—that is, of careful and judicious study, not dismissal. It entails, furthermore, the making of very precise distinctions between biblical instruction and the behavior of those peoples supposed to have been biblically instructed.

I cannot pretend, obviously, to have made so meticulous a study; even if I were capable of it, I would not live long enough to do it. But I have attempted to read the Bible with these issues in mind, and I see some, virtually catastrophic discrepancies between biblical instruction and Christian behavior. I don't mean disreputable Christian behavior, either. The discrepancies I see are between biblical instruction and allegedly respectable Christian behavior.

If because of these discrepancies Christianity were dismissible, there would, of course, be no problem. We could simply dismiss it, along with the twenty centuries of unsatisfactory history attached to it, and start setting things to rights. The problem emerges only when we ask, "Where, then, would we turn for instruction?" We might, let us suppose, turn to another religion—a recourse that is sometimes suggested by the anti-Christian conservationists. Buddhism, for example, is certainly a religion that could guide us toward a right respect for the natural world, our fellow humans, and our fellow creatures. I owe a considerable debt myself to Buddhism and Buddhists. But there are an enormous number of people—and I am one of them—whose native religion, for better or worse, is Christianity. We were born to it; we began to learn about it before we became conscious; it is, whatever we think of it, an intimate belonging of our being; it informs our consciousness, our language, and our dreams. We can turn away from it or against it, but that will only bind us tightly to a reduced version of it. A better possibility is that this, our native religion, should survive and renew itself so that it may become as largely and truly instructive as we need it to be. On such a survival and renewal of the Christian religion may depend the survival of the Creation that is its subject.

II

If we read the Bible, keeping in mind the desirability of those two survivals—of Christianity and the Creation—we are apt to discover several things about which modern Christian organizations have kept remarkably quiet or to which they have paid little attention.

We will discover that we humans do not own the world or any part of it: "The earth is the Lord's, and the fullness thereof: the world and they that dwell therein."[1] There is in our human law, undeniably, the concept and right of "land ownership." But this, I think, is merely an expedient to safeguard the mutual belonging of people and places without which there can be no lasting and conserving human communities. This right of human ownership is limited by mortality and by natural constraints on human attention and responsibility; it quickly becomes abusive when used to justify large accumulations of "real estate," and perhaps for that reason such large accumulations are forbidden in the twenty-fifth chapter of Leviticus. In biblical terms, the "landowner" is the guest and steward of God: "The land is mine; for ye are strangers and sojourners with me."[2]

We will discover that God made not only the parts of Creation that we humans understand and approve but all of it: "All things were made by him; and without him was not anything made that was made."[3] And so we must credit God with the making of biting and stinging insects, poisonous serpents, weeds, poisonous weeds, dangerous beasts, and disease-causing microorganisms. That we may disapprove of these things does not mean that God is in error or that He ceded some of the work of Creation to Satan; it means that we are deficient in wholeness, harmony, and understanding—that is, we are "fallen."

We will discover that God found the world, as He made it, to be good, that He made it for His pleasure, and that He continues to love it and to find it worthy, despite its reduction and corruption by us. People who quote John 3:16 as an easy formula for getting to Heaven neglect to see the great difficulty implied in the statement that the advent of Christ was made possible by God's love for the world—not God's love for Heaven or for the world as it might be, but for the world as it was and is. Belief in Christ is thus dependent on prior belief in the inherent goodness—the lovability—of the world.

We will discover that the Creation is not in any sense independent of the Creator, the result of a primal creative act long over and done with, but is the continuous, constant participation of all creatures in the being of God. Elihu said to Job that if God "gather unto himself his spirit and his breath; all flesh shall perish together."[4] And Psalm 104 says, "Thou sendest forth thy spirit, they are created." Creation is thus God's presence in creatures. The Greek Orthodox theologian Philip Sherrard has written that "Creation is nothing less than the manifestation of God's hidden Being."[5] This means that we and all other creatures live by a sanctity that is inexpressibly intimate, for to every creature, the gift of life is a portion of the breath and spirit of God. As the poet George Herbert put it:

> Thou art in small things great, not small in any . . .
> For thou art infinite in one and all.[6]

We will discover that for these reasons our destruction of nature is not just bad stewardship, or stupid economics, or a betrayal of family responsibility; it is the most horrid blasphemy. It is flinging God's gifts into His face, as if they were of no worth beyond that assigned to them by our destruction of them. To Dante, "despising Nature and her goodness" was a violence against God.[7] We have no entitlement from the Bible to exterminate or permanently destroy or hold in contempt anything on the earth or in the heavens above it or in the waters beneath it. We have the right to use the gifts of nature but not to ruin or waste them. We have the right to use what we need but no more, which is why the Bible forbids usury and great accumulations of property. The usurer, Dante said, "condemns Nature . . . for he puts his hope elsewhere."[8]

William Blake was biblically correct, then, when he said that "everything that lives is holy."[9] And Blake's great commentator Kathleen Raine was correct both biblically and historically when she said that "the sense of the holiness of life is the human norm."[10]

The Bible leaves no doubt at all about the sanctity of the act of world-making, or of the world that was made, or of creaturely or bodily life in this world. We are holy creatures living among other holy creatures in a world that is holy. Some people know this, and some do not. Nobody, of course, knows it all the time. But what keeps it from being far better known than it is? Why is it apparently unknown to millions of professed students of the Bible? How can modern Christianity have so solemnly folded its hands while so much of the work of God was and is being destroyed?

III

Obviously, "the sense of the holiness of life" is not compatible with an exploitive economy. You cannot know that life is holy if you are content to live from economic practices that daily destroy life and diminish its possibility. And many if not most Christian organizations now appear to be perfectly at peace with the military-industrial economy and its "scientific" destruction of life. Surely, if we are to remain free and if we are to remain true to our religious inheritance, we must maintain a separation between church and state. But if we are to maintain any sense or coherence or meaning in our lives, we cannot tolerate the present utter disconnection between religion and economy. By "economy" I do not mean "economics," which is the study of money-making, but rather the ways of human housekeeping, the ways by which the human household is situated and maintained within the household of nature. To be uninterested in economy is to be uninterested in the practice of religion; it is to be uninterested in culture and in character.

Probably the most urgent question now faced by people who would adhere to the Bible is this: What sort of economy would be responsible to the holiness of life? What, for Christians, would be the economy, the practices and the restraints, of "right livelihood"? I do not believe that organized Christianity now has any idea. I think its idea of a Christian economy is no more or less than the industrial economy—which is an economy firmly founded on the seven deadly sins and the breaking of all ten of the Ten Commandments. Obviously, if Christianity is going to survive as more than a respecter and comforter of profitable iniquities, then Christians, regardless of their organizations, are going to have to interest themselves in economy—which is to say, in nature and in work. They are going to have to give workable answers to those who say we cannot live without this economy that is destroying us and our world, who see the murder of Creation as the only way of life.

The holiness of life is obscured to modern Christians also by the idea that the only holy place is the built church. This idea may be more taken for granted than taught; nevertheless, Christians are encouraged from childhood to think of the church building as "God's house," and most of them could think of their houses or farms or shops or factories as holy places only with great effort and embarrassment. It is understandably difficult for modern Americans to think of their dwellings and workplaces as holy, because most of these are, in fact, places of desecration, deeply involved in the ruin of Creation.

The idea of the exclusive holiness of church buildings is, of course, wildly incompatible with the idea, which the churches also teach, that God is present in all places to hear prayers. It is incompatible with Scripture. The idea that a human artifact could contain or confine God was explicitly repudiated by Solomon in his prayer at the dedication of the Temple: "Behold, the heaven and the heaven of heavens cannot contain thee: how much less this house that I have builded?"[11] And these words of Solomon were remembered a thousand years later by Saint Paul, preaching at Athens:

> God that made the world and all things therein, seeing that he is lord of heaven and earth, dwelleth not in temples made with hands . . .
>
> For in him we live, and move, and have our being; as certain also of your own poets have said.[12]

Idolatry always reduces to the worship of something "made with hands," something confined within the terms of human work and human comprehension. Thus, Solomon and Saint Paul both insisted on the largeness and the at-largeness of God, setting Him free, so to speak, from *ideas* about Him. He is not to be fenced in, under human control, like some domestic creature; He is the wildest being in existence. The presence of His spirit in us is our wildness, our oneness with the wilderness of Creation. That is why subduing the things of nature to human purposes is so dangerous and why it so often results in evil, in separation and desecration. It is why the poets of our tradition so often have given nature the role not only of mother or grandmother but of the highest earthly teacher and judge, a figure of mystery and great power. Jesus' own specifications for his church have nothing at all to do with masonry and carpentry but only with people; his church is "where two or three are gathered together in my name."[13]

The Bible gives exhaustive (and sometimes exhausting) attention to the organization of religion: the building and rebuilding of the Temple; its furnishings; the orders, duties, and paraphernalia of the priesthood; the orders of rituals and ceremonies. But that does not disguise the fact that the most significant religious events recounted in the Bible do not occur in "temples made with hands." The most important religion in that book is unorganized and is sometimes profoundly disruptive of organization. From Abraham to Jesus, the most important people are not priests but shepherds, soldiers, property owners, workers, housewives, queens and kings, manservants and maidservants, fishermen, prisoners, whores, even bureaucrats. The great visionary encounters did not take place in temples but in sheep pastures, in the desert, in the wilderness, on mountains, on the shores of rivers and the sea, in the middle of the sea, and in prisons. And however strenuously the divine voice prescribed rites and observances, it just as strenuously repudiated them when they were taken to *be* religion:

> Your new moons and your appointed feasts my soul hateth: they are a
>   trouble unto me; I am weary to bear them.
> And when you spread forth your hands, I will hide mine eyes from you:
>   yea, when you make many prayers, I will not hear; your hands are full
>   of blood.
> Wash you, make you clean; put away the evil of your doings from before
>   mine eyes; cease to do evil;
> Learn to do well; seek judgment, relieve the oppressed, judge the
>   fatherless, plead for the widow.[14]

Religion, according to this view, is less to be celebrated in rituals than practiced in the world.

I don't think it is enough appreciated how much an outdoor book the Bible is. It is a "hypaethral book," such as Thoreau talked about—a book open to the sky. It is best read and understood outdoors, and the farther outdoors the better. Or that has been my experience of it. Passages that within walls seem improbable or incredible, outdoors seem merely natural. This is because outdoors we are confronted everywhere with wonders; we see that the miraculous is not extraordinary but the common mode of existence. It is our daily bread. Whoever really has considered the lilies of the field or the birds of the air and pondered the improbability of their existence in this warm world within the cold and empty stellar distances will hardly balk at the turning of water into wine—which was, after all, a very small miracle. We forget the greater and still continuing miracle by which water (with soil and sunlight) is turned into grapes.

It is clearly impossible to assign holiness exclusively to the built church without denying holiness to the rest of Creation, which is then said to be "secular." The world, which God looked at and found entirely good, we find none too good to pollute entirely and destroy piecemeal. The church, then, becomes a kind of preserve of "holiness," from which certified lovers of God assault and plunder the "secular" earth.

Not only does this repudiate God's approval of His work; it refuses also to honor the Bible's explicit instruction to regard the works of the Creation as God's revelation of Himself. The assignation of holiness exclusively to the built church is therefore logically accompanied by the assignation of revelation exclusively to the Bible. But Psalm 19 begins, "The heavens declare the glory of God; and the firmament sheweth his handiwork." The word of God has been revealed in facts from the moment of the third verse of the first chapter of Genesis: "Let there be light: and there was light." And Saint Paul states the rule: "The invisible things of him from the creation of the world are clearly seen, being understood by the things that are made."[15] Yet from this free, generous, and sensible view of things, we come to the idolatry of the book: the idea that nothing is true that cannot be (and has not been already) written. The misuse of the Bible thus logically accompanies the abuse of nature: if you are going to destroy creatures without respect, you will want to reduce them to "materiality"; you will want to deny that there is spirit or truth in them, just as you will want to believe that the only holy creatures, the only creatures with souls, are humans—or even only Christian humans.

By denying spirit and truth to the nonhuman Creation, modern proponents of religion have legitimized a form of blasphemy without which the nature- and culture-destroying machinery of the industrial economy could not have been built—that is, they have legitimized bad work. Good human work honors God's work. Good work uses no thing without respect, both for what it is in itself and for its origin. It uses neither tool nor material that it does not respect and that it does not love. It honors nature as a great mystery and power, as an indispensable teacher, and as the inescapable judge of all work of human hands. It does not dissociate life and work, or pleasure and work, or love and work, or usefulness and beauty. To work without pleasure or affection, to make a product that is not both useful and beautiful, is to dishonor God, nature, the thing that is made, and whomever it is made for. This is blasphemy: to make shoddy work of the work of God. But such blasphemy is not possible when the entire Creation is understood as holy and when the works of God are understood as embodying and thus revealing His spirit.

In the Bible we find none of the industrialist's contempt or hatred for nature. We find, instead, a poetry of awe and reverence and profound cherishing, as in these verses from Moses' valedictory blessing of the twelve tribes:

> And of Joseph he said, Blessed of the Lord be his land, for the precious things of heaven, for the dew, and for the deep that croucheth beneath,
> And for the precious fruits brought forth by the sun, and for the precious things put forth by the moon,
> And for the chief things of the ancient mountains, and for the precious things of the lasting hills,
> And for the precious things of the earth and fullness thereof, and for the good will of him that dwelt in the bush.[16]

IV

I have been talking, of course, about a dualism that manifests itself in several ways: as a cleavage, a radical discontinuity, between Creator and creature, spirit and matter, religion and nature, religion and economy, worship and work, and so on. This dualism, I think, is the most destructive disease that afflicts us. In its best-known, its most dangerous, and perhaps its fundamental version, it is the dualism of body and soul. This is an issue as difficult as it is important, and so to deal with it we should start at the beginning.

The crucial test is probably Genesis 2:7, which gives the process by which Adam was created: "The Lord God formed man of the dust of the ground, and breathed into his nostrils the breath of life: and man became a living soul." My mind, like most people's, has been deeply influenced by dualism, and I can see how dualistic minds deal with this verse. They conclude that the formula for man-making is man equals body plus soul. But that conclusion cannot be derived, except by violence, from Genesis 2:7, which is not dualistic. The formula given in Genesis 2:7 is not man equals body plus soul; the formula there is soul equals dust plus breath. According to this verse, God did not make a body and put a soul into it, like a letter into an envelope. He formed man of dust; then, by breathing His breath into it, He made the dust live. The dust, formed as man and made to live, did not *embody* a soul; it *became* a soul—that is, a whole creature. Humanity is thus presented to us, in Adam, not as a creature of two discrete parts temporarily glued together but as a single mystery.

We can see how easy it is to fall into the dualism of body and soul when talking about the inescapable worldly dualities of good and evil or time and eternity. And we can see how easy it is, when Jesus asks, "For what is a man profited, if he shall gain the whole world, and lose his own soul?"[17] to assume that he is condemning the world and appreciating the disembodied soul. But if we give to "soul" here the sense that it has in Genesis 2:7, we see that he is doing no such thing. He is warning that in pursuit of so-called material possessions, we can lose our understanding of ourselves as "living souls"—that is, as creatures of God, members of the holy community of Creation. We can lose the possibility of the atonement of that membership. For we are free, if we choose, to make a duality of our one living soul by disowning the breath of God that is our fundamental bond with one another and with other creatures.

But we can make the same duality by disowning the dust. The breath of God is only one of the divine gifts that make us living souls; the other is the dust. Most of our modern troubles come from our misunderstanding and misvaluation of this dust. Forgetting that the dust, too, is a creature of the Creator, made by the sending forth of His spirit, we have presumed to decide that the dust is "low." We have presumed to say that we are made of two parts: a body and a soul, the body being "low" because made of dust, and the soul "high." By thus valuing these two supposed-to-be parts, we inevitably throw them into competition with each other, like two corporations. The "spiritual" view, of course, has been that the body, in Yeats' phrase, must be "bruised to pleasure soul." And the "secular" version of the same dualism has been that the body, along with the rest of the "material" world, must give way before the advance of the human mind. The dominant religious view, for a long time, has been that the body is a kind of scrip issued by the Great Company Store in the Sky, which can be cashed in to redeem the soul but is otherwise worthless. And the predictable result has been a human creature able to appreciate or tolerate only the "spiritual" (or mental) part of Creation and full of semiconscious hatred of the "physical" or "natural" part, which it is ready and willing to destroy for "salvation," for profit, for "victory," or for fun. This madness constitutes the norm of modern humanity and of modern Christianity.

But to despise the body or mistreat it for the sake of the "soul" is not just to burn one's house for the insurance, nor is it just self-hatred of the most deep and dangerous sort. It is yet another blasphemy. It is to make nothing—and worse than nothing—of the great Something in which we live and move and have our being.

When we hate and abuse the body and its earthly life and joy for Heaven's sake, what do we expect? That out of this life that we have presumed to despise and this world that we have presumed to destroy, we would somehow salvage a soul capable of eternal bliss? And what do we expect when with equal and opposite ingratitude, we try to make of the finite body an infinite reservoir of dispirited and meaningless pleasures?

Times may come, of course, when the life of the body must be denied or sacrificed, times when the whole world must literally be lost for the sake of one's life as a "living soul." But such sacrifice, by people who truly respect and revere the life of the earth and its Creator, does not denounce or degrade the body but rather exalts it and acknowledges its holiness. Such sacrifice is a refusal to allow the body to serve what is unworthy of it.

V

If we credit the Bible's description of the relationship between Creator and Creation, then we cannot deny the spiritual importance of our economic life. Then we must see how religious issues lead to issues of economy and how issues of economy lead to issues of art. By "art," I mean all the ways by which humans make the things they need. If we understand that no artist—no maker—can work except by reworking the works of Creation, then we see that by our work we reveal what we think of the works of God. How we take our lives from this world, how we work, what work we do, how well we use the materials we use, and what we do with them after we have used them—all these are questions of the highest and gravest religious significance. In answering them, we practice, or do not practice, our religion.

The significance (and ultimately the quality) of the work we do is determined by our understanding of the story in which we are taking part.

If we think of ourselves as merely biological creatures, whose story is determined by genetics or environment or history or economics or technology, then, however pleasant or painful the part we play, it cannot matter much. Its significance is that of mere self-concern. "It is a tale / Told by an idiot, full of sound and fury, / Signifying nothing," as Macbeth says when he has "supp'd full with horrors" and is "aweary of the sun."[18]

If we think of ourselves as lofty souls trapped temporarily in lowly bodies in a dispirited, desperate, unlovable world that we must despise for heaven's sake, then what have we done for this question of significance? If we divide reality into two parts, spiritual and material, and hold (as the Bible does *not* hold) that only the spiritual is good or desirable, then our relation to the material Creation becomes arbitrary, having only the quantitative or mercenary value that we have, in fact and for this reason, assigned to it. Thus, we become the judges and inevitably the destroyers of a world we did not make and that we are bidden to understand as a divine gift. It is impossible to see how good work might be accomplished by people who think that our life in this world either signifies nothing or has only a negative significance.

If, on the other hand, we believe that we are living souls, God's dust and God's breath, acting our parts among other creatures all made of the same dust and breath as ourselves; and if we understand that we are free, within the obvious limits of mortal human life, to do evil or good to ourselves and to the other creatures—then all our acts have a supreme significance. If it is true that we are living souls and morally free, then all of us are artists. All of us are makers, within mortal terms and limits, of our lives, of one another's lives, of things we need and use.

This, Ananda Coomaraswamy wrote, is "the normal view," which "assumes . . . not that the artist is a special kind of man, but that every man who is not a mere idler or parasite is necessarily some special kind of artist."[19] But since even mere idlers and parasites may be said to work inescapably, by proxy or influence, it might be better to say that everybody is an artist—either good or bad, responsible or irresponsible. Any life, by working or not working, by working well or poorly, inescapably changes other lives and so changes the world. This is why our division of the "fine arts" from "craftsmanship," and "craftsmanship" from "labor," is so arbitrary, meaningless, and destructive. As Walter Shewring rightly said, both "the plowman and the potter have a cosmic function."[20] And bad art in any trade dishonors and damages Creation.

If we think of ourselves as living souls, immortal creatures, living in the midst of a Creation that is mostly mysterious, and if we see that everything we make or do cannot help but have an everlasting significance for ourselves, for others, and for the world, then we see why some religious teachers have understood work as a form of prayer. We see why the old poets invoked the muse. And we know why George Herbert prayed, in his poem "Mattens":

> Teach me thy love to know;
> That this new light, which now I see,
> May both the work and workman show.[21]

Work connects us both to Creation and to eternity. This is the reason also for Mother Ann Lee's famous instruction: "Do all your work as though you had a thousand years to live on earth, and as you would if you knew you must die tomorrow."[22]

Explaining "the perfection, order, and illumination" of the artistry of Shaker furniture makers, Coomaraswamy wrote, "All tradition has seen in the Master Craftsman of the Universe the exemplar of the human artist or 'maker by art,' and we are told to be 'perfect, *even as* your Father in heaven is perfect.'" Searching out the lesson, for us, of the Shakers' humble, impersonal, perfect artistry, which refused the modern divorce of utility and beauty, he wrote, "Unfortunately, we do not desire to be such as the Shaker was; we do not propose to 'work as though we had a thousand years to live, and as though we were to die tomorrow.' Just as we desire peace but not the things that make for peace, so we desire art but not the things that make for art. . . . we have the art that we deserve. If the sight of it puts us to shame, it is with ourselves that the reformation must begin."[23]

Any genuine effort to "re-form" our arts, our ways of making, must take thought of "the things that make for art." We must see that no art begins in itself; it begins in other arts, in attitudes and ideas antecedent to any art, in nature, and in inspiration. If we look at the great artistic traditions, as it is necessary to do, we will see that they have never been divorced either from religion or from economy. The possibility of an entirely secular art and of works of art that are spiritless or ugly or useless is not a possibility that has been among us for very long. Traditionally, the arts have been ways of making that have placed a just value on their materials or subjects, on the uses and the users of the things made by art, and on the artists themselves. They have, that is, been ways of giving honor to the works of God. The great artistic traditions have had nothing to do with what we call "self-expression." They have not been destructive of privacy or exploitive of private life. Though they have certainly originated things and employed genius, they have no affinity with the modern cults of originality and genius. Coomaraswamy, a good guide as always, makes an indispensable distinction between genius in the modern sense and craftsmanship: "Genius inhabits a world of its own. The master craftsman lives in a world inhabited by other men; he has neighbors."[24] The arts, traditionally, belong to the neighborhood. They are the means by which the neighborhood lives, works, remembers, worships, and enjoys itself.

But most important of all, now, is to see that the artistic traditions understood every art primarily as a skill or craft and ultimately as a service to fellow creatures and to God. An artist's first duty, according to this view, is technical. It is assumed that one will have talents, materials, subjects— perhaps even genius or inspiration or vision. But these are traditionally understood not as personal properties with which one may do as one chooses but as gifts of God or nature that must be honored in use. One does not dare to use these things without the skill to use them well. As Dante said of his own art, "far worse than in vain does he leave the shore . . . who fishes for the truth and has not the art."[25] To use gifts less than well is to dishonor them and their Giver. There is no material or subject in Creation that in using, we are excused from using well; there is no work in which we are excused from being able and responsible artists.

VI

In denying the holiness of the body and of the so-called physical reality of the world—and in denying support to the good economy, the good work, by which alone the Creation can receive due honor—modern Christianity generally has cut itself off from both nature and culture. It has no serious or competent interest in biology or ecology. And it is equally uninterested in the arts by which humankind connects itself to nature. It manifests no awareness of the specifically Christian cultural lineages that connect us to our past. There is, for example, a splendid heritage of Christian poetry in English that most church members live and die without reading or hearing or hearing about. Most sermons are preached without any awareness at all that the making of sermons is an art that has at times been magnificent. Most modern churches look like they were built by robots without reference to the heritage of church architecture or respect for the place; they embody no awareness that work can be worship. Most religious music now attests to the general assumption that religion is no more than a vaguely pious (and vaguely romantic) emotion.

Modern Christianity, then, has become as specialized in its organizations as other modern organizations, wholly concentrated on the industrial shibboleths of "growth," counting its success in numbers, and on the very strange enterprise of "saving" the individual, isolated, and disembodied soul. Having witnessed and abetted the dismemberment of the households, both human and natural, by which we have our being as creatures of God, as living souls, and having made light of the great feast and festival of Creation to which we were bidden as living souls, the modern church presumes to be able to save the soul as an eternal piece of private property. It presumes moreover to save the souls of people in other countries and religious traditions, who are often saner and more religious than we are. And always the emphasis is on the individual soul. Some Christian spokespeople give the impression that the highest Christian bliss would be to get to heaven and find that you are the only one there—that you were right and all the others wrong. Whatever its twentieth-century dress, modern Christianity as I know it is still at bottom the religion of Miss Watson, intent on a dull and superstitious rigmarole by which supposedly we can avoid going to "the bad place" and instead go to "the good place." One can hardly help sympathizing with Huck Finn when he says, "I made up my mind I wouldn't try for it."[26]

Despite its protests to the contrary, modern Christianity has become willy-nilly the religion of the state and the economic status quo. Because it has been so exclusively dedicated to incanting anemic souls into heaven, it has been made the tool of much earthly villainy. It has, for the most part, stood silently by while a predatory economy has ravaged the world, destroyed its natural beauty and health, divided and plundered its human communities and households. It has flown the flag and chanted the slogans of empire. It has assumed with the economists that "economic forces" automatically work for good and has assumed with the industrialists and militarists that technology determines history. It has assumed with almost everybody that "progress" is good, that it is good to be modern and up with the times. It has admired Caesar and comforted him in his depredations and defaults. But in its de facto alliance with Caesar, Christianity connives directly in the murder of Creation. For in these days, Caesar is no longer a mere destroyer of armies, cities, and nations. He is a contradicter of the fundamental miracle of life. A part of the normal practice of his power is his willingness to destroy the world. He prays, he says, and churches everywhere compliantly pray with him. But he is praying to a God whose works he is prepared at any moment to destroy. What could be more wicked than that, or more mad?

The religion of the Bible, on the contrary, is a religion of the state and the status quo only in brief moments. In practice, it is a religion for the correction equally of people and of kings. And Christ's life, from the manger to the cross, was an affront to the established powers of his time, just as it is to the established powers of our time. Much is made in churches of the "good news" of the Gospels. Less is said of the Gospel's bad news, which is that Jesus would have been horrified by just about every "Christian" government the world has ever seen. He would be horrified by our government and its works, and it would be horrified by him. Surely no sane and thoughtful person can imagine any government of our time sitting comfortably at the feet of Jesus while he is saying, "Love your enemies, bless them that curse you, do good to them that hate you, and pray for them that despitefully use you and persecute you."[27]

In fact, we know that one of the businesses of governments, "Christian" or not, has been to reenact the crucifixion. It has happened again and again and again. In *A Time for Trumpets,* his history of the Battle of the Bulge, Charles B. MacDonald tells how SS Colonel Joachim Peiper was forced to withdraw from a bombarded château near the town of La Gleize, leaving behind a number of severely wounded soldiers of both armies. "Also left behind," MacDonald wrote, "on a whitewashed wall of one of the rooms in the basement was a charcoal drawing of Christ, thorns on his head, tears on his checks—whether drawn by a German or an American nobody would ever know."[28] This is not an image that belongs to history but rather one that judges it.

ANDREW KIMBRELL

Andrew Kimbrell is an attorney, activist, and author. In 1994 he established the International Center for Technology Assessment, based in Washington, D.C. The center examines the economic, ethical, social, environmental, and political impacts that result from the applications of technology. He has appeared frequently on radio and television, including interviews on such programs as "Today," "Crossfire," and "Good Morning America." In 1994 the *Utne Reader* named Kimbrell as one of the 100 most innovative thinkers in America. His books include *The Human Body Shop: The Engineering and Marketing of Life* and *The Masculine Mystique.* This essay is a revised and adapted version of an essay first published in *The Intercollegiate Review.*

Second Genesis: The Biotechnology Revolution

"We can hold in our minds the enormous benefits of technological society, but we cannot so easily hold the ways it may have deprived us, because technique is ourselves. All descriptions or definitions of technique which place it outside ourselves hide from us what it is."
—George Parkin Grant in *Technology and Empire*

A TECHNOLOGICAL revolution has begun. This revolution could affect each of us in the most intimate, yet permanent fashion. It could indelibly change the destiny of mankind and the other members of the living kingdom. The growing technology revolution is being made a reality by dizzying advances in the biological sciences and the application of that knowledge to a variety of techniques, most importantly recombinant DNA technology. It is now becoming possible to insert, recombine, re-arrange, edit, program, and produce human and other biological materials just as our ancestors were able to heat, burn, melt, and solder together various inert materials. A growing group of engineers are in the process of manipulating, and creating, new combinations of living matter just as the machine makers of the past centuries created new shapes, combinations, and forms of inanimate matter. We are in a historical transition from the Age of Pyrotechnology to the Age of Biotechnology.

Over the last decade, the achievements of biotechnology seem more like science fiction than science fact. The accomplishments of the engineers of life have triggered visions of a utopia on earth, and concerns over the creation of a "brave new world." Consider just a few recent successes:

- Researchers in Scotland announce that they have produced genetically duplicate sheep from the biological information contained in a single adult body cell. This "cloning" of larger mammals is a significant step towards large-scale cloning of human beings.
- Two scientists at George Washington University in Washington, D.C, publish their research involving basic techniques of cloning human embryos. The scientists are able to produce 42 identical embryos.
- Scientists at the National Institutes of Health (NIH) gain approval for first experiments in gene engineering of somatic human cells. Many call for approval of germline genetic "surgery" that is aimed at altering the genetic makeup of future generations.
- Surgeons in Denver, Colorado, perform the first U.S. transplant of fetal organ parts into the brain of a victim of Alzheimer's disease. Meanwhile, researchers in California report successful transplants of fetal organs into laboratory mice. Fetal organs and tissues suddenly become valuable commodities.
- Congress approves a massive $3 billion scientific effort to map the entire human genetic structure. Researchers claim that in the next few years, diagnostic tests will be able to determine an individual's genetic traits and predispositions to physical and emotional disorders. Critics raise the

specter of a new form of social discrimination based on genetic makeup. Corporate employers and insurance companies express an interest in mandatory genetic screening of workers and insurance applicants. Prenatal screening increases sex-selection and other "eugenic" abortions.

- Researchers successfully place human growth genes into the permanent genetic code of mice and pigs. Other scientists create hundreds of transgenic animals, including cows and fish containing human genes. In one bizarre experiment, researchers insert the gene that emits light in a firefly into the genetic code of a tobacco plant. The leaves of the plant glow 24 hours a day.

- U.S. Patent officials announce that all genetically engineered animals, including those with human genes inserted into their permanent genetic code, are patentable. The Patent Office also allows the patenting of human genes, cells, and embryos. Under this new interpretation of the Patent Act, life forms including human embryos have the legal status of "manufactures" and are indistinguishable from nonliving commodities. More than 40 animals have been patented, with over 500 patents pending. Hundreds of human genes, cells, and cell lines have been patented.

- Corporations and universities are releasing genetically engineered viruses and bacteria, as well as genetically engineered plants and animals, into the open environment. If one of these new genetically engineered organisms becomes dangerous, the results could be catastrophic, since these living organisms mutate, reproduce, and have extraordinary mobility, they cannot be recalled.

- As part of its biological warfare research program, the Department of Defense is using new genetic technology in experimenting with virtually every known dangerous microorganism in 129 university, corporate, and military laboratories across the country. Scores of these experiments involve controversial gene-splicing technology.

- Dozens of "baby brokers" have set up shop in the U.S., contracting with women to become surrogate mothers. Amniocentesis and other prenatal genetic tests are used to ensure that the child contracted for is "fit." Under the contract, "abnormal" children are aborted upon request of the paying client. Since the famous Baby M case, over two dozen lawsuits have been filed challenging the controversial business. More than 10,000 babies have been born to surrogate mothers and then surrendered to paying clients.

As societies scramble to cope with each new techno-dilemma, the new cadre of biological technicians and decision-makers are slowly beginning to assume a novel, though controversial, role in the natural scheme. Scientists and engineers, often with the best of intentions, are assuming the roles of creator and designer of the living kingdom, from microbe to man. They are using their newfound abilities to alter the very blueprint of life—to apply traditional engineering values such as efficiency, utility, quantifiablity, and predictability to the manipulation of life forms. Driven by billions of research dollars and massive profit possibilities, these techniques, whether in the areas of human health and childbearing or in the manipulation of animals, plants, and microbes, are invading the most intimate aspects of human life, and the most hidden areas of the natural world.

There can be little question that extension of the techniques and ideology of the industrial age to the living kingdom, including the human body, is among the most significant technological and philosophical transitions in recorded history. The question of whether we should embark on a long journey in which we become the architects of life is among the most important technological issues ever to face humanity.

Those overseeing and promoting biotechnology assure us that the consequences of the technological revolution can be managed. *The New York Times* in a recent editorial noted that "life is special, and humans even more so, but biological machines are still machines that now can be altered, cloned, and patented. The consequences will be profound but, taken a step at a time, they can be managed."[1] Biotech's supporters also point out that, whatever the short-term dislocations, these novel techniques and practices will bring dazzling social benefits. The engineers and salesmen of biotechnology confidently predict cures for cancer and AIDS; they hail the coming abolition of man's most pernicious hereditary diseases; they pronounce an end to human infertility; they herald a new biotech "green" revolution that will help end world starvation.

Those questioning the new technology are skeptical of these claims. As part of the generation brought up with a plethora of techno-booster bro-mides ("Progress Is Our Middle Name," "Better Living Through Chem-istry," "Cheap and Clean Nuclear Power," and even "DDT Is Good for Me"), they find the promises of utopian technologists hollow, even tragi-comic. Certainly, for a society viewing a new genre of social threats (in-cluding the destruction of the family, disintegration of communities, urban blight, and growing crime) and a new genre of global environmental threats (including ozone depletion, deforestation, species extinction, and global warming), it is now painfully evident that every new technological revolution has both benefits and costs. Society's experience with industrial technology demonstrates that the more powerful a technology is at expro-priating and controlling the forces of nature, the greater the disruption of our society and destruction of the ecosystems that sustain life.

The biological revolution is no exception to the technological rule. Though less than two decades old, it has spawned unprecedented envi-ronmental, economic, and ethical concerns. Environmentalists have raised alarms about biological pollution as the prospect of the release of thou-sands of genetically engineered microbes, plants, and animals comes closer to reality. Farmers, researchers, and workers around the world anx-iously await the economic consequences of corporate controlled genetic engineering techniques and novel life forms replacing more traditional production methods and native plant and animal species.

Perhaps most compelling, the biorevolution is creating an upheaval in the way in which we define, understand, and use life. As we transplant and engineer human organs, tissue, and genes into other animals, we blur the line between human and nonhuman. As we engineer, patent, and clone life forms as if they were "biological machines," we obscure the line be-tween life and nonlife. In our haste to better harvest human materials, in-cluding the newly defined "brain dead" and fetuses, we throw into confusion traditional concepts of life and death. As we seek to cure infer-tility with in vitro fertilization, egg and sperm donors, and surrogate mother contracts, we no longer have clear lines on what constitutes moth-erhood or fatherhood. As we screen our unborn for abnormalities, we force eugenic decisions on what constitutes a life worth living. As we patent life forms, we turn the entire life community into corporately owned commodities. As we open up a market for "contract" children and human body parts, we initiate bio-slavery for the economically disenfranchised who are lured into selling the irreplaceable.

Virtually all past civilizations believed that the human form was sacred. In the Judeo-Christian tradition, it is understood that human kind was made in the "image" of God. For millennia this concept of humanity and the human body, taken directly from Genesis, formed the basis of Western ethics. The biblical understanding affirmed that all life was divinely authored and was by definition, "good." The Christian tradition gave the body added significance through the belief that God became incarnate and suffered the joys and pains of being human. Subsequently, the body was given the ultimate sacramental value as the early church taught that the union of human beings and God was to be obtained through ingesting the "body and blood" of Christ. And the body was to be exalted. The church promised those worthy that their bodies, albeit now "glorified," would be resurrected with them in heaven.

The traditional understanding of the human body has been shattered. Increasingly in recent years, advances in science and technology have confused and obscured any fixed definition of human life. The body is no longer seen as analogous to the divine, but rather simply as the new raw material for the bio-industrial age. The body has become a commodity.

We are, today, unprepared to cope with the myriad theological, ethical, economic, and political consequences of the biotechnology revolution. Clearly, the questions raised by the manipulation and marketing of life are among the most important ever to face the human family, yet we have done little to establish adequate bio-policies to guide us through the moral morass. Furthermore, despite its epochal impact, biotechnology's chief decision-makers are not world leaders or elected officials. The issues surrounding the technology are not decided by democratic decision-making or popular opinion. Rather, the managers of biotechnology are a haphazard group of researchers, bureaucrats, doctors, businessmen, scientists, and judges. Their choices are, more often than not, made through corporate board decisions, arcane bureaucratic regulations, and local and federal court opinions. They do not constitute a conspiracy, nor do they all share the same political ideology. In fact, they are generally guided in their decision-making by the narrowest of notions concerning efficiency and marketability.

Unfortunately, then, those now authorized to make decisions on regulating or limiting genetic engineering are not inclined, or able, to guide society in addressing the policy challenges of biotechnology. Often goaded by scientific curiosity, the drive to cure disease, or raw personal profit, current actors in the forefront of the biorevolution do not seem to have the breadth of vision to confront the implications of what they are bringing to society. Perhaps it should not surprise us that those who spend their lives looking through microscopes tend to develop microscopic vision.

Even those employed as so-called bioethicists seem to be incapable of saying no to any new advance in the marketing of life, no matter how questionable. As the ethicists line up in favor of the continuing extension of biotechnology into the body's organs, cells, genes—even offspring— they seem intent on guiding the unthinkable on its passage to becoming debatable, and then toward being justifiable, and on to finally becoming routine. We are in an ethical free fall.

How will society limit biotechnology in order to reduce its risks and still reap its benefits? The prospect is far from reassuring. After all, we have never limited a technology to its beneficial uses. And, so far, there are no new answers. The biotechnology revolution is being managed and regulated in the same manner as have the other major technological breakthroughs of the last several decades. Author Langdon Winner has termed this mode of dealing with technology the "utilitarian-pluralistic" approach. The problem of technology is primarily seen as a question of benefits and costs. The utilitarian-pluralistic approach attempts to assess the possible risks of a technology as against the benefits it provides. Questions arising from this approach are routine public policy fare: "What are the trade-offs between eliminating various sources of air pollution and possible productivity costs for industries affected by the restrictions? What are the trade-offs between preserving wilderness areas and the loss of jobs to the lumber industry? What are the trade-offs between the environmental threat of nuclear power as against the need for more energy?"

Biotechnology is following the pattern. Regulating biotechnology now involves various federal agencies in the United States, and similar international bodies, preparing a variety of risk assessments on sundry actions involving the use of genetic engineering techniques. Environmental agencies assess the risks of releasing genetically engineered organisms into the environment. Other regulators gauge potential health risks of genetically engineered foods (some of these foods border on the bizarre—tomatoes with flounder genes to enhance resiliency, pork produced by engineering human genes into pigs to create "leaner" meat). Advisory panels look into the risks posed by engineering the human germline. The Department of Defense evaluates the dangers of using biotechnology to create new biological-warfare weapons as measured against possible advantages for national security.

Once risks and benefits of a technology are assessed, the next major regulatory issue required by the utilitarian-pluralistic approach becomes distribution. The pluralistic approach to technological regulation attempts to ensure that the benefits of a technology are distributed equally and that the costs are allocated so that no sector of the population is overly burdened.

The utilitarian-pluralistic approach has been the dominant approach to technology by government and social activists alike. The environmental, consumer, and social justice movements have all taken this route. Social and environmental legislation is based on this approach to technology. Congress, scientists, and regulatory decision-makers use this approach almost exclusively. Even Marxism is primarily based in the pluralistic mode of viewing technology. The central social question as presented by Marxism becomes the relationship of various classes to the ownership of the means of production.

The utilitarian-pluralistic model of technology controls is woefully inadequate to the task. The major difficulties about technology are not its side effects, or projected "trade-offs" necessitated by its introduction, but rather the fact that technologies ultimately become controlling influences on the very fabric of human thought and activity.

Man does not only reshape nature through technology; technology shapes man and his thinking. The discovery of the clock gave us the "clockwork universe" of the early Enlightenment thinkers, and it also gave us the idea that living organisms (including our own bodies) are machines. "Living bodies, are even in the smallest of their parts, machines *ad infinitum,*" noted Gottfried Wilhelm von Leibniz. As technology developed into the great motors of the industrial age, experts in thermodynamics such as Helmholz assured us that "the animal body does not differ from the steam engine." In more recent times, we see ourselves as computers. Computer mavin Marvin Minsky has compared the brain to a "meat-machine." Scientists see genes as information chips that can be manipulated as if they were parts of a computer. The utilitarian-pluralistic approach to technological thinking cannot deal with the tendency of technology to embody, and even create, social and political beliefs. Indeed, the utilitarian approach is merely another technological solution to the problems of technology. As noted by Langdon Winner:

> The utilitarian-pluralistic approach sees that technology is problematic in the sense that it now *requires legislation.* An ever-increasing array of rules, regulations, and administrative personnel is needed to maximize the benefits of technological practice while limiting its unwanted maladies. Politics is seen as the process in representative government and interest group interplay whereby such legislation takes place.[2]

The alternative approach to understanding technology, an approach necessary if we are to control the biotechnology revolution, begins with the crucial awareness that technology *is* legislation, that technology and its bureaucratized forms of human regulation and control determine a large majority of what we are and what we believe. Technology is itself a political, social, and theological phenomenon.

As such, technology is not in any sense neutral. A nuclear power plant, for example, regardless of how efficiently its risks are dealt with or how democratically it is owned or operated, contains certain political suppositions in the technology itself. For the technology to be used, a society must be capable of amassing large capital expenditures in the building of the facilities; a society must have centralized control of energy production and dissemination, either state-controlled or utility-controlled or both (no individual or smaller community could or would use such a large and potentially hazardous power source). There must be a massive bureaucracy to ensure safety of facility operations and disposal of nuclear waste. A scientific elite is required to build and supervise the plant. A military elite is necessary to guard against sabotage and use of the nuclear by-products. The social vision inherent in nuclear power involves a society that is capital-intensive, committed to centralized control of resources, extensive bureaucracy, and scientific and military elites. Compare this with the politics of solar power; this technology involves low capital accumulation, individual or community control of energy, no bureaucracy of risk assessment, and no need for a scientific or military elite. Clearly, every technology encodes a vision of the individual and of society. Different technologies realize different concepts of social and political life.

But that is not all. The biotechnology revolution demonstrates that technologies can also have a metaphysical content. A pig genetically engineered to contain the human growth hormone gene in order to make it a leaner, larger pig for the production of pork (a pig then patented as a "manufacture") reflects a view of life as machine and genes as information chips that can be inserted in the same manner as changing the program of a computer. Genetic screening of the newborn to find and abort those with abnormalities encodes the belief that the value of life is in "quality" of life, not in the eternal life of the soul. The engineering, sale, and patenting of human fetal tissue from induced abortions represents an historic and morally grotesque reductionism of the very concept of human life.

But the biotechnology prospect is even broader. The biotechnologists are attempting to recreate nature in the image of efficiency. In fact, the genetic engineers envision little less than a second genesis—a genetic mixing and matching of the living kingdom to create more useful and efficient life forms. This time, the genesis is not of sacred origin but rather a secular creation based on the technological imperative. The view that life can be remade through biotechnology is the most breathtaking example of the tendency of the technological ethos itself to challenge traditional religious and cultural understandings of life—and life as a given good. As Gregory S. Butler argues:

The unlimited application of science and technology . . . involve[s] the intelligent control and manipulation of both human and non-human nature so that the material ends of the collective are better served and the deficiencies of nature finally overcome. A necessary part of the unbridled technological ethos, furthermore, is a conscious act of rebellion against the traditional moral authority given in classical and Christian metaphysics, especially insofar as the authority posits limitations on the creative powers of man by a claim to a knowledge of the nature of things. If a deficient creation is to be overcome or recreated, one must break free from those who persist in talking about eternal justice of a benevolent creator-God, or about the inherent worth and dignity of the individual before that God. The will to re-create is strong; it tends to eschew any understanding of man or God which might limit the progressive building of the future.[3]

The biotechnology revolution tends strongly in the direction of an anti-sacred, mechanistic view of life and the human. The Biblical understanding that we are created in the image of God falls by the wayside. Scientists see the new technology as reifying the mechanistic worldview set out centuries ago by René Descartes and his critic/follower Julien Offray de La Mettrie. Dr. Robert Haynes, a keynote speaker at (and president of) the 16th Congress of Genetics, firmly reminded his audience that the doctrine of mechanism is a key organizing principle for the age of biotechnology. "For 3,000 years at least, a majority of people have considered that human beings were special, were magic. It's the Judeo-Christian view of man," said Haynes. "What the ability to manipulate genes should indicate to people is the very deep extent to which we are biological machines. The traditional view is built on the foundation that life is sacred . . . . Well, not anymore. It's no longer possible to live by the idea that there is something special, unique, even sacred, about living organisms."[4]

Advances in biotechnology will further embody this mechanistic view of life. The new medical and genetic engineering technologies of the last few decades have and will save lives and perhaps will provide new cures for humanity, but, without resistance, these technologies and the ideology behind them will also lead to the devaluation and commercial exploitation of the human body, and the living kingdom of which it is part. Biotechnologies are becoming ever more sophisticated. Additionally, extraordinary profits on body elements and processes are awaiting the scientists and biotechnologists who are pushing the new technologies.

Unless checked, these advances in biotechnologies will significantly accelerate current trends. Advances in utilization of fetal parts for curing disease or for enhancement therapy will make the unborn ever more valuable commodities for the medical marketplace. As reproductive technologies become refined and increase the percentage of successful births via artificial insemination, egg donation, and embryo transfer, sperm, eggs, embryos, and children will be subject to increased marketing and will soon be legally defined as property by the courts and legislatures. As genetic screening of the unborn allows prospective parents to know a wide range of genetic traits of their offspring, eugenic abortions based on sex and other nondisease characteristics will expand.

Greater understanding of the location and functions of genes will accelerate the marketing and patenting of valuable genes. Discoveries in genetic links to undesirable physical or social traits will also continue to lead to increased genetic manipulation of humans, including proposals to permanently change the genetic code of certain individuals through germline genetic surgery. Genetic engineering will also allow for even more transfer of human genes into animals, animal genes into plants, and plant genes into foreign species. Finally, breakthroughs in cloning could change the modes of reproduction for all members of the living kingdom, including the reproduction of humans. The warning is clear. Unless human choices control biotechnology, biotechnology will control human choices.

As biotechnology begins to change our traditional views of central aspects of our being—life, death, birth, our bodies, motherhood, nature—we are shocked into a revelation about the history of our politics over the last century. During that time, the near cataclysmal struggle was between the market system and the communist economic vision. The great cold war was essentially fought over different views about the ownership of the means of production. Because the market system triumphed, some view the end of that struggle as the "end of history" itself.[5] However, the extraordinary issues surrounding biotechnology and our other modern technologies now demonstrate, to paraphrase Burke, that Marxism was not a revolution made or failed, but rather one avoided. By fighting over the ownership of the means of production, society neglected the real political duty of our time—namely, the stuggle over the means of production themselves.

Each technology encodes an ideology. The technology becomes the embodiment of the ideology. As that technology becomes part of the means of production, it brings with it the full plethora of theological and social suppositions contained within it. Those suppositions then become an inherent and inextricable part of the social structure. Different ideas of God, what man is or is not, what a community is, or what is sacred require different technologies for their realization. The politics of technology is therefore the real politics of the next century.

Technological politics cannot be fought in the utilitarian-pluralistic framework—inside the regulatory forum. There is little reason to hope that current government agencies, themselves the product of a spiritually impoverished Enlightenment liberal culture, will recant from the development and use of technologies that encode their basic beliefs and begin constructing technologies consonant with a sacred view of life.

Clearly, the major constituency capable of reshaping our technological future and limiting the biotechnology revolution is the religious community. In particular it is the religious humanist tradition that can best "re-sacralize" creation by fighting for the ethic of love over that of efficiency, by seeing life not as a commodity but as a divine gift, and by experiencing the earth's life forms not as a collection of exploitable objects but as a community of subjects—ends in themselves worthy of respect. This humanist religious tradition has in the past and must continue to profess this sacramental vision though art (novels, movies, music, paintings, poetry and sculpture). It must also reinhabit the "naked public square" by fighting in the courts and legislatures to halt desacralizing technology and support technologies that reify their beliefs.

G. K. Chesterton noted that every revolution is a revival. We now need such a revival if we are to remake the technology of the next millennium in the image of the sacred. The revival will be artistic and political, joyous and combative. However, the continuing advances in technology make the task for Christian humanists ever more daunting and urgent.

FREDERICA MATHEWES-GREEN

Frederica Mathewes-Green is a regular commentator for National
Public Radio's "All Things Considered" and *Odyssey News,* a cable
television newsmagazine. She is a founder of Common Ground,
an organization devoted to bringing forces on different sides of
the abortion issue together. Her books include *Facing East: A Pilgrim's Journey into the Mysteries of Orthodoxy* and *Real Choices: Listening to Women Looking for Alternatives to Abortion.* This essay is
adapted from a lecture given at the first national conference of the
Common Ground Network for Life and Choice.

Abortion and the Search for Common Ground

AN ANTHROPOLOGIST curious to see the widest public display of
Scripture verses, rosaries, and Christian artifacts would be well ad-
vised to head for the nearest pro-life protest. In any number of cultural
battles the attributes of faith may be exhibited, but nowhere as vehe-
mently or comprehensively as here. A pro-life demonstration looks like
God's Country.

As someone who's been involved in the pro-life cause for a number of
years now, I'm not sure this is good. The sad fact is that no one is surprised
to hear that God is opposed to abortion. No one reads a pro-life placard,
smacks his forehead, and says, "Whoa, who knew? I never thought of
that!" Instead, they think, "Oh, you're one of *those.* You belong in this familiar little box over here. What a relief; now I don't have to listen to you
anymore."

But pro-lifers feel understandably conflicted over this. To conceal the influence of our faith in this debate—well, wouldn't that amount to being "ashamed of the Gospel"? Isn't the most heinous aspect of this issue the violence against children created in God's image? Isn't this as outrageous as the slaughter of the innocents in Bethlehem? It's difficult for Christians to imagine unborn children being torn apart by abortion, four thousand times a day, without being stirred at a level deeper than mere political opinion. Something that moves one to beseeching prayer is likely to come into the daylight with the attributes of prayer still attached.

The problem is that alluding to God's will in this issue does the opposite of what the Christian pro-lifer thinks it will. Citing God's position is meant to universalize the appeal to conscience, meant to appeal to the grandest of all final authorities. Instead, it shrinks the moral position to the dimensions of a stereotyped and stigmatized group, people who are presumed to be narrow-minded, mean-spirited, and woman-hating. It's an infernal rhetorical sleight of hand: name God and, to your secular opponent, He immediately disappears. All that's left is your obnoxious self, now quite easy to dismiss.

I am not pro-life because I am a Christian. I could be a Godless-secular-humanist-atheist-pinko and be pro-life. My opposition to abortion is built on a simple frame—that it is wrong to kill children. This is something everyone knows; it's built into human nature to be revolted at the idea of killing children. People can only favor abortion by convincing themselves that the life in the womb somehow doesn't qualify as "one of us," but all those arguments have a desperate and self-serving flavor. None convince. Opposing abortion is the path of obvious reason, consistent and clear; it rings true. It doesn't take religious faith, it just takes common sense (and an open mind, which may not be as common).

But I am a pro-life activist because I am a Christian. This fight is an ugly one. People who speak in favor of the unborn get tarred and feathered and dragged over the hedge. It would be much easier to sit this one out, to choose a more fashionable cause or just to watch the world go by from the comfort of sofa and TV. But I am not free to do that. I am not my own; I was bought with a price. I must speak out on abortion.

This is a vital distinction. Yes, it is religious feeling that, in most cases, compels pro-lifers to get involved in the cause. But church precepts aren't what form the conviction in the first place. We know abortion is wrong because our very hearts tell us so; everyone knows it's wrong to kill children.

Over the last several years I have been meeting in dialogue with pro-life and pro-choice activists, discovering ways that we can get over high walls of misunderstanding and communicate with each other. I have found that one of the first steps is to put aside religious language; it is usually as incomprehensible as Urdu. Whatever we find we have in common will be rooted elsewhere.

In June 1996 I was able to attend the first national conference sponsored by the Common Ground Network for Life and Choice, and I gave a presentation titled "Critiquing Your Own Side." I shared this workshop with feminist strategist and author Naomi Wolf, whose groundbreaking article in the *New Republic,* "Our Bodies, Our Souls," aroused much controversy. In that article, Wolf granted that pro-choicers have failed to adequately understand the value of the fetus; she said that abortion must be viewed as a "moral iniquity." I wrote a letter in response remarking that, though serious disagreements remained and we weren't yet close enough to meet in the middle, we were close enough to "wave at each other and holler." Sharing this event with Wolf brought us a good bit closer, and we continue to meet and talk.

An unusual aspect of this workshop was that I was free not to dwell on the negative aspects of abortion and the value of unborn life; ironically, I could rely on Wolf to do that (within the parameters of her convictions, of course). Instead, I focused on the elements of pro-life rhetoric that were counterproductive, with an eye to improving communication and breaking through the present deadlock. My remarks to the group attending that day could apply just as well to anyone interested in presenting the case for life effectively—persuading, not just proclaiming. Some of the more vehement things pro-lifers do and say may feel pleasantly cathartic, but they don't work. The abortion debate has been at gridlock for more than twenty years; when we put away the placards, we may just be able to get somewhere.

I've been involved with the Common Ground movement for several years now, both nationally and in the local group in Washington, D.C. Common

Ground matters to me because I was pro-choice at one point, and then came over to a pro-life position; because of that I think there's a logic to the pro-choice position that deserves respect, even as we engage it critically. It is possible to disagree with opponents without calling them baby-killers, without believing that they are monsters or fiends. It is possible to disagree in an agreeable way.

But there's another reason I'm drawn to Common Ground. I was a feminist back in the early 1970s, back even before people called it feminism. I was a "women's libber"—not the most fluid of terms—in the time when it was just a Bob Hope joke about bra-burners. Back then there wasn't the proliferation of feminisms that there is now, and I remember sitting on the floor in the dormitory with the other women, talking dreamily about how different it would be if women ruled the world: "We're peace-loving, we're peacemakers, we're listeners, we're compassionate," we said. "If only women ruled the world, there'd be no more war."

I believe the abortion conflict is the first chance we've had to prove that, and we have failed miserably. The abortion argument is essentially an argument among women, and it doesn't show much evidence of peacemakers. It's been a bitter and ugly debate, and I find that embarrassing. For me, that gives a special urgency to my involvement in Common Ground.

Conflicts are by definition difficult, and this is a particularly difficult one. In any kind of conflict, though, as you come to peace, there's a common pattern. In trying to reach agreement you must back up until you can see far enough into the horizon to locate a point upon which you actually agree. As people on each side come to Common Ground, they typically believe they know what that point of agreement will be, and then are disappointed to find out that it's not. Many pro-choice people come to Common Ground, for example, thinking that we'll agree to prevent abortion through promoting contraception and sex education. They're surprised when pro-lifers decline the invitation, saying, "I don't think so. That's doesn't fit my values." On the other side, pro-lifers think that pro-choicers will be glad to pitch in with pregnancy support services, maternity homes, and post-birth care. But pro-choicers say, "That really isn't where my interest is."

We fall short on agreement because we have not looked far enough into the horizon. What the sides have in common is this: We'd like to see a world where women no longer want to have abortions. We'd like to see the demand for the procedure reduced, by resolving women's problems and alleviating the pressure for abortion. We can go along this road together as far as we can—and there will come a time when pro-choicers are satisfied, and pro-lifers want to keep going, but that doesn't mean we can't go together for now. I don't believe that even among the most fervent pro-choice people there is anyone who rejoices over abortion. I think we all wish that there were better solutions that could make it unnecessary, or prevent the situation in the first place.

I discovered an important piece of common ground when something I wrote kept coming back to me. A couple of years ago I wrote in a magazine article, "There is a tremendous sadness and loneliness in the cry, 'A woman's right to choose.' No one wants an abortion as she wants an ice cream cone or a Porsche. She wants an abortion as an animal, caught in a trap, wants to gnaw off its own leg."

What surprised me was where that quote appeared. Friends started mailing me clips: the quote in Ellen Goodman's column, as "Quote of the Month" in the Pro-Choice Network Newsletter, and as "Quote of the Week" in the Planned Parenthood Public Affairs Action Letter. I realized that I'd stumbled across a scrap of common ground—we all know that nobody leaves the abortion clinic skipping. Instead of marching against each other, maybe we could envision a world without abortion that we could be marching for together.

The problem —and I believe the pro-life movement has been especially complicit in this—is that we have focused only on abortion, and not on women's needs. That is where I think we've made our big mistake. We have perpetuated a dichotomy wherein it's the baby against the woman, and we're on the baby's side. You can look over twenty-five years of pro-life rhetoric and basically boil it down to three words: "It's a baby." We have our "Little Feet" lapel pins, our "Abortion Stops a Beating Heart" bumper stickers, and we've pounded on that message.

In the process we have contributed to what I think is a false concept, an unnatural and even bizarre concept: that women and their unborn children are mortal enemies. We have contributed to the idea that they've got to duke it out, it's going to be a fight to the finish, and one of these combatants must lose its life. Either the woman is going to lose control of her life, or the child is going to literally lose its life.

It occurred to me eventually that there's something wrong with this picture. When we presume this degree of conflict between women and their own children, we're locating the conflict in the wrong place. Women and their own children are not naturally mortal enemies, and the problem is not located inside women's bodies, but within society. Social expectations make unwanted pregnancy more likely to occur and harder for women to bear. Unwed mothers are supposed to have abortions to save the rest of us from all the costs of bringing an "unwanted" child into the world.

How can we continue to call for the sort of workplace options that allow women to care for their own children—flextime, part-time, and home-commute jobs—if the socially expected solution is that she'll have an abortion instead? When we say, "It's her against the baby," society thinks, "So let them fight it out." It looks like, thanks to abortion, there's really no problem there; it's not broke, so why fix it? It's a capitulation instead of social change, and it's not moving us toward an abortion-free society.

So I believe that the big flaw in pro-life rhetoric was emphasizing the baby's rights, rather than keeping the mother and child together to solve their problems in a positive way. I'm talking now about the rhetoric, the things we in the movement tend to say—not necessarily what we do, because there has been a strong crisis pregnancy movement giving individual women hands-on help for almost thirty years. But when we came up to the podium, it was all baby versus mom.

There was a sort of naive belief that if we can only make abortion illegal, that would solve all the problems. The abortion rate in this country is about a million and a half a year, and although there's been a little dip the rate's held fairly stable for about fifteen years. If you divide that figure by 365, you end up with about 4,100 abortions every day.

So this morning in America, 4,100 women woke up and thought, "Today is the day of my abortion." Imagine for a moment that in the middle of the country there is a big, central abortion store, and outside it 4,100 women got in a long line, one behind the other—and that's just today. It's a sobering image. And I think the shortsighted pro-life response has been, "Put a padlock on the abortion store." But that's not going to solve the problem. You cannot reduce the demand by shutting off the supply. It doesn't work that way. If 4,100 women were lining up every day to get breast implants, we'd be saying, "What's causing this demand? What's going on here?" We'd be looking for sources of pressure, trying to figure out why women felt so bound to alter their bodies to comply with unnatural ideas of beauty. Likewise, we've got to look at why women are undergoing surgery to accommodate pressures that punish them for being pregnant. You can't fix that by merely shutting off the supply. So I think we need some larger thinking here.

I can understand why my allies put the emphasis on "It's a baby." It's a powerful message, and it tends to be the conversion point for people who come over from being pro-choice. However, polls on American attitudes toward abortion show that between 70 and 80 percent already agree that it's a baby—especially since the advent of sonograms. So when we say, "It's a baby," we're answering a question nobody's asking anymore. I believe there is a question they are asking, though: "How could we live without it?" Abortion has become a part of our social machinery; it undergirds the sexual and workplace expectations laid on women. How *could* we live without it?

There are three drawbacks to emphasizing "It's a baby" as the sole message. One is that it contributes to the present deadlock in this debate, and I hate the deadlock as much as you do. I think that's why we're here; we hate the thought that the argument is running endlessly like trains on parallel tracks. We say "It's a baby," and our friends on the pro-choice side say, "No, it's her right," and the arguments don't even engage each other. It's an interminable argument that can go on for another twenty-five years if we don't find a way to break through. It perpetuates the idea that the woman and her own baby are enemies, which I think is a sign of a sick culture.

Second, the "It's a baby" message alienates the woman distressed by a difficult pregnancy. There's a pro-life message I sometimes hear that makes me cringe: "Women only want abortions for convenience. They do this for frivolous reasons. She wants to fit into her prom dress. She wants to go on a cruise." My side takes the role of defending that baby against her, and we treat her motives as suspect. But this alienates the very person to whom we need to show compassion. If we're going to begin finding ways to live without abortion, we need to understand her problems better.

I want to repeat that, of course, there has been a wing of the pro-life movement that has been addressing itself to pregnant women's needs for a long time, and that is the crisis pregnancy center movement. Centers like these have been giving women maternity clothes, shelter, medical care, job training, whatever they have for thirty years. But you wouldn't know that from the things the movement says. It's been a curious case of walking and talking different things. I once saw a breakdown of the various sorts of pro-life activities, and more than half of the movement's energy was going into direct aid to pregnant women. Yet you don't hear this at the podium, you don't hear it in the rhetoric, and you don't hear it in the debate. What you hear it is, "Those terrible baby-killers." You don't see the softer side that's actually trying to help women.

The third problem with this rhetoric is that it enables the great mushy middle to go on shrugging off the problem. While both sides know that women don't actually want abortions in any positive sense, the middle is convinced they do. And that's because both sides are telling it they do. Pro-lifers say, "She wants an abortion because she's selfish"; pro-choicers say, "She wants an abortion because it will set her free." No wonder the middle believes us—it's one of the few things we appear to agree on. But, as I found out by the widespread currency of my steel-trap metaphor, both sides actually know that abortion is usually a very unhappy choice. If 4,100 women are choosing something they don't really want, every single day, it's not a situation anyone should be happy with. It's not liberation that we've won. But our "It's a baby, and she's just selfish" rhetoric keeps the middle thinking that abortion really is what women want, so there's no need for change and nothing to fix. I want to recognize my side's complicity in contributing to this deadlock and confusion.

How can we solve the problems that contribute to the demand for abortion? If this were easy, I guess we would have done that by now. It's not easy. But when you consider the question, "How can we can live without it?" there are two obvious components: preventing the unwanted pregnancy in the first place, and assisting women who slip through the cracks and become pregnant anyway.

The obvious tool for pregnancy prevention is contraception, but the pro-life movement has been very reluctant to support the contraceptive option. I come from a religious tradition that accepts non-abortifacient contraception, so it's not been a theological problem for me. So when I started considering this, I thought, "This is great! I'll get a helicopter, fill it with condoms, get a snow shovel, and just fly over the country tossing 'em out. We'll close all of the abortion clincs tomorrow!"

Then I began to analyze it a little deeper. There's a line by Adrienne Rich that really opened my eyes. She said, "The so-called sexual revolution of the 60s was briefly believed to be congruent with the liberation of women. . . . [But] it did not mean that we were free to discover our own sexuality, but rather that we were expected to behave according to male notions of female sexuality." This struck me deeply, because I was in college in the early days of the sexual revolution. There was one great shining moment when it seemed like a pretty carefree enterprise; there wasn't the explosion of sexually transmitted diseases we're seeing now, or AIDS. Condoms, pills, and diaphragms were all available, and abortion had just been legalized. Recreational sex looked like harmless fun. But I gradually began to think that maybe a con game was being played on women. We were "expected to behave according to male notions of sexuality," as Rich says; we were expected to accommodate a *Playboy* ethic of sex without consequences. Instead of gaining respect and security in our bodies, we were expected to be physically more available, more vulnerable than ever before, and with very little offered in return.

I believe that the pro-life movement needs to make a strong stand in favor of preventing these unintended pregancies. But I've become skeptical about the contraceptive solution, when—for example—about two-thirds of births to teenage moms in California involved a dad who was an adult, and other studies have found teen mothers had been forced into sex at the average age of eleven, that the men who molested them had an average age of twenty-seven. Well, you're not going to solve that problem by tossing a handful of condoms at it. A friend of mine was brought to an abortion clinic by her molesting older brother when she was twelve; they gave her a bag of condoms and told her to be more careful. This just doesn't solve the problem.

Even leaving out the question of abuse, I think the sexual revolution overlooked the basic emotion-based nature of women's sexuality. What women found out is that we have hearts in here along with all our other physical equipment, and you can't put a condom on your heart. So in answering the question, "How do we live without it?" I'd say we need to look at restoring respect and righting the balance of power in male-female sexual relationships.

Second, what can we do to help women who get pregnant and would rather not be? That was a question I sought to answer in my book *Real Choices*. I didn't consider politics or any means of restricting abortion; instead, I wanted to find out why women have abortions, and what we can do to solve their problems today. I presumed that I'd find most abortions are prompted by problems that are financial or practical in nature, and that some could be solved with outside help, and some could not.

But as I went around the country talking to women who'd had abortions, and the pregnancy center volunteers who provide care for pregnant women, I found something very different. To my surprise, what I heard most frequently was that the reason for the abortion was not financial or practical; it had to do with a relationship. It was either the father of the child, or else her own mother, who was pressuring her to have the abortion. The core reason I heard was, "I had the abortion because someone I love told me to."

When I asked, "Is there anything anyone could have done? What would you have needed in order to have had that child?" I heard the same answer over and over: "I needed a friend. I felt so alone. I felt like I didn't have a choice. If only one person had stood by me, even a stranger, I would have had that baby." Over and over I learned that women had abortions because they felt abandoned, they felt isolated and afraid. As one woman said, "I felt like everyone would support me if I had the abortion, but if I had the baby I'd be alone." In order to support women who have unwanted pregnancies, we have to offer them whatever financial and practical resources we can, but we also must offer simple friendship and support. Women told me over and over that this would have made the difference for them.

Another aspect of resolving the problems of unwanted pregnancy have to do with the situation after the birth. You know, we keep analyzing this situation as if it were a problem of pregnancy. It's not; the problem has to do with child rearing. Getting through the pregnancy isn't nearly the dilemma that raising a child for eighteen years is. In most families, marriage lightens the load, but sometimes that isn't the best solution. A neglected option is adoption, which can free the woman to resume her life while giving the child a loving home.

The numbers on this, however, are shocking. The national adoption rate is about 2 percent. Among clients at pregnancy care centers, it's not any better. Adoption is a difficult sell to make for a number of complex reasons, but the bottom line is that 80 to 90 percent of the clients who go through pregnancy care centers and have their babies end by setting up single-parent homes. This is very serious. Pregnancy care centers know this, but aren't sure what to do about it. I've been strongly encouraging that there be more emphasis on presenting adoption to clients, and equipping center volunteers so they feel comfortable with the topic and enabled to discuss it. Adoption is not a one-size-fits-all solution, but it's got to fit more than 2 percent. More women should try it on for size.

In summary, my critique of the pro-life movement centers around our narrow emphasis on "It's a baby." Rather, I want to encourage viewing the pregnant woman and child as a naturally linked pair that we strive to keep together and support. I'm enough of an old ex-hippie, granola-based life form that I tend to automatically look for guidance to what appears in nature. What I see in this case is that nature puts the mother and the child together; it doesn't make them enemies, doesn't set one against the other in a battle to the death. If our rhetoric is tearing them apart, we're the ones who are out of step. We need to try to follow the path of non-resistance, coming in line with what is healthful and natural as much as we can. I believe that the pro-life movement should be answering the question, "How can we live without abortion?" by keeping mother and child together, looking into pregnant women's needs and examining how to meet them, and encouraging responsible sexual behavior that will prevent those pregnancies in the first place.

VIGEN GUROIAN

Vigen Guroian is professor of theology and ethics at Loyola College in Baltimore, Maryland. He has also served on the faculty of the Ecumenical Institute of Theology at St. Mary's Roman Catholic Seminary in Baltimore. He is the author of *Ethics After Christendom: Toward an Ecclesial Christian Ethic* and *Incarnate Love: Essays in Orthodox Ethics,* and he is currently writing a book about children's literature and the moral imagination. This excerpt is taken from his book *Life's Living Toward Dying: A Theological and Medical-Ethical Study* (1996).

The Culture of Death

MOST AMERICANS are familiar with Walt Disney's animated feature *Bambi.* Far fewer are familiar with the classic children's book upon which it is based, Felix Salten's *Bambi: A Life in the Woods.* The Disney version of the story is an archetypal American tale of romantic love, oozing with sentimentality. Salten's original, on the other hand, is a profound fable about living in the face of death without allowing it to rob life of hope or meaning. It speaks to the ways in which we in this culture hide death from view and refuse to deal seriously with it as a moral or metaphysical problem.

Salten tells the story of a young buck named Bambi who comes under the tutelage of a mysterious, solitary old stag. The stag shows Bambi how to live independently and always be alert to the dangers of the forest. "We must learn to live and be cautious," says the stag.[1] Man, the hunter with his gun, is the greatest threat to the woodland animals. For all of the other creatures, including Bambi's mother, he symbolizes death and inspires

285

awe and dread so deep that the animals rarely mention those who have perished by his hand.

The stag, however, is not crippled by this fear. He has taken careful measure of human beings, and while he is fully acquainted with their capacity to unleash lethal force, he knows that man is neither omnipotent nor immortal. As Bambi grows to become a buck, the stag instructs him and passes along his wisdom, including the sure knowledge that there is a transcendent and providential Being who is greater even than man. One day the old stag leads Bambi to the still and bloodied body of a dead poacher.

> "Do you see, Bambi," the stag went on, "Do you see how He's lying there dead, like one of us? Listen, Bambi. He isn't all-powerful as they say. Everything that lives and grows doesn't come from Him. . . . Do you understand me Bambi?" asked the old stag.
>
> "I think so," Bambi said in a whisper.
>
> "Then speak," the old stag commanded.
>
> Bambi was inspired, and said trembling, "There is Another who is over us all, over us and over Him."
>
> "Now I can go," said the old stag.[2]

Death and the Loss of the Transcendent

The woods in which we live are likewise filled with demons of violence and death that terrify and stultify the lives of many people. Twenty-five years ago, Arthur McGill judged that our society was moving rapidly toward a post-Christian era, that people were abandoning their belief in a creative, nurturing, and redemptive reality that overarches their lives and beginning to "see the world as filled with shapeless ferocities that come and go."[3] Indeed, death has increasingly come to overshadow all of life in our culture; we are gripped by anxiety in the face of the untreatable diseases and random violence that threaten to snatch away our health and our lives.

Many people in our society have cut their ties to the sort of larger sacral context that has traditionally assigned meaning to the experiences associated with illness and dying. Apart from these sacral structures, many have difficulty dealing with such painful experiences. Every day they are exposed to reports of divorce, spousal battery, and the physical and sexual abuse of children. Every day they encounter stories of the violence occurring all around them—burglaries, holdups, muggings, rapes, murders, riots, genocidal wars. They hear incessant warnings about the depletion of the ozone layer, pesticides in their food, radon in their basements, asbestos in their schools, secondhand cigarette smoke in their workplace, and countless other noxious and invisible threats surrounding them. And every week a new batch of experts crowds the talk-show circuit to describe the latest physical and psychological maladies. After long exposure to this barrage of bad news, many are gripped with a fear that they are poised precariously on the edge of an abyss, completely surrounded by destructive and lethal powers. They have become convinced that ultimately life itself is arbitrary and absurd. The best that many can hope for in the face of this constant threat of suffering and death is the protection offered by advanced medical technology—but that has turned out to be a mixed blessing. Increasingly people are as reluctant to surrender themselves entirely to the physicians and the dehumanizing machinery of medicine as they are to surrender themselves to disease. And even if medical treatment is effective in restoring them to health, many people come away from the treatment feeling defeated on some level, newly convinced that they remain at the mercy of both the microbes and the medical technicians.

In his novel *The Poorhouse Fair,* John Updike presents his readers with Connor, an administrator of a home for the elderly who believes that it is his special calling to protect people from the surrounding destructive powers. He ridicules traditional religious faith and its claim that suffering and death have meaning. Hook, one of the old people under his care, a Southerner and Christian believer, argues against Connor's atheistic humanitarianism. He defends biblical theism and the belief that creation issues from the hands of a benevolent God and that life is good. Connor is unswayed: "People speak of loving life. Life is a maniac in a closed room."[4] He is Updike's version of Dostoevsky's Grand Inquisitor. The setting, however, is not the church of a sacral age but a total health care institution in a secular society. Connor believes that "pain is evil" and that the home he runs is the only "heavenly" reward its wards will ever receive. Hook disagrees. "It is an error to believe that the absence of evil will follow from the elimination of pain," he says.[5] "There is no goodness, without belief. Only busyness. And if you have not believed, at the end of your life you shall know you have buried your talent in the ground of this world and have nothing saved to take into the next."[6] But in this post-Christian, postbiblical culture, Hook's convictions seem as timeworn and anachronistic as the old Southerner himself.

Aversion and Obsession

William F. May argues that death is the last sacral power in a post-Christian culture. Modern people avoid death "because they recognize in the event an immensity that towers above their resources for handling it. In effect, death (or the reality that brings it) is recognized as some sort of sacred power that confounds the efforts of man to master it."[7] In the modern American funeral home, the parlor in which the body rests is furnished as if it were a living room in anyone's home. The dead body is beautified; the face is made hardly recognizable with cosmetics that cover up death's pallor in order to leave the impression of life.

The effects of this denial and expulsion of death on our perceptions and expectations are sometimes quite bizarre. During a trip I made to Russia in the fall of 1991, the group I was with visited the parish church of Fr. Alexander Men, a charismatic Orthodox priest who, only a year before, had been brutally axed to death—many believed by agents of the KGB. The small wooden church was crowded with Sunday worshipers and pilgrims who had come to pay homage at this holy site of a modern-day martyr. Like many Orthodox churches, this one had no pews. Everyone stood, and in the middle of this crush of people lay an open casket that displayed the body of an old babushka. People occasionally made their way up to the casket, touching and kissing the wrinkled and shrunken old woman. After a time, an Episcopal priest who was standing next to me whispered: "Is it a common practice to place such mannequins in Orthodox churches?" This clergyman in his sixties, who had buried many people during his lifetime, simply could not see death in front of him when it had not been disguised, sanitized, and set apart from real life.

We needn't look very far to observe sillier but no less telling examples of denial and aversion in the face of death. In the winter of 1994, the *Baltimore*

Sun ran a wire story entitled " 'Dead End' Dead in Sensitive Colorado City" that underscores our uneasiness with anything that even reminds us of death. "Signs warning of dead-end streets apparently are too macabre for some people," the article explained, "so the City Council [of Longmont, Colorado] voted to replace them with less sensitive panels reading 'no out-let.'" One resident who favored the change was quoted as saying, "We just moved into a condo, right outside there's a dead-end sign. . . . Every time you come, you have to go by this sign, and it just isn't very pleasant."

When I read this story I couldn't help recalling John Cheever's hilarious and sardonic tale "The Death of Justina." The protagonist, who has the suspiciously symbolic name of Moses, discovers his wife's old cousin Justina "sitting on the living-room sofa [in his home] with a glass of good brandy, [having] breathed her last."[8] Moses meets one obstacle after an-other as he tries to arrange for the removal of Justina's body from the house for a proper burial. He learns that several years earlier, in order to stop a funeral home from being built in the neighborhood, the town passed a zoning regulation making it illegal either to die or to be buried in Proxmire Manor. Thus, Moses is unable to obtain the death certificate for Justina that the undertaker requires in order to transport the dead body. The mayor tells Moses that he cannot make an exception to the rule be-cause that would set a bad precedent. "People don't like to live in a neigh-borhood where this sort of thing goes on all the time," he explains.[9] Moses does eventually manage to get Justina's body taken to a funeral home, however, and Cheever grants him the honor of having the last word:

> The dead are not, God knows, a minority, but in Proxmire Manor their un-exalted kingdom is on the outskirts, rather like a dump, where they are transported furtively as knaves and scoundrels and where they lie in an at-mosphere of perfect neglect. Justina's life had been exemplary, but by end-ing it she seemed to have disgraced us all. *How can people who do not understand death hope to understand love, and who will sound the alarm?*[10]

Pornography and the Obsession with Death

While people in our culture have demonstrated a clear aversion to thoughts of death, they have also demonstrated an almost compulsive fascination with it. Who that saw them can forget the pictures of Rock Hudson taken in 1985 as he was being transferred on a stretcher from a privately chartered Boeing 747 to an awaiting ambulance—his face, a once-vital icon of masculine good looks, reduced by AIDS to a cadaverous death mask? English sociologist Geoffrey Gorer has shown how both our aversion to and obsession with death are manifested in a new kind of pornography. Gorer contends that that pornography is a "concomitant of prudery. . . . In contrast to obscenity, which is chiefly defined by situation, prudery is defined by subject; some aspect of human experience is treated as inherently shameful or abhorrent."[11] The Victorians dealt with sex this way, and despite our culture's presumptions about sexual liberation, sex remains a potent taboo for us as well. But death has edged out sex to become our preeminent taboo, says Gorer. "The natural processes of corruption and decay have become disgusting, as disgusting as the natural processes of birth and copulation were a century ago."[12] In recent years, so-called sex thrillers like *Fatal Attraction* and *Basic Instinct* and erotic horror movies like *Interview with the Vampire* have exploited this. These movies combine death with sex, pandering to the subterranean desire of audiences to flirt with these two great modern taboos without risking guilt, grief, or embarrassment. In *Basic Instinct* (the prototype of many such films), orgasm and murder occur in the same bed, as the woman, like the female praying mantis, kills and consumes the male lover.

The earmark of pornography, Gorer continues, is its hallucinatory and delusory character. Private fantasies extrude into public expression intended for popular consumption. The 1990s have reaped a harvest of art that fits this description. In reporting on a major European art exhibit held in 1993, Paul Griffiths, an art critic for *The New Yorker,* noted that "if there is a single stylistic tic that fills both the pavilions and the work of the younger artists . . . it is the display of death, decay, and violence." Griffiths describes the work of several artists, including Jean-Pierre Reynaud's floor tiles of "thousands of unvarying images of skulls" and American artist Andres Serrano's exhibit "The Morgue," which displays "huge photographs of corpses." "Other than death," writes Griffiths, "the set subject is sex . . . with lots of genital imagery."[13]

As Freud understood, death and sex are deeply intertwined in the human psyche, perhaps pathologically among modern people. Our fascination with sex is a form of our fascination with death. So we can explain in Freudian terms why modern moviemakers have turned to the sex thriller and contemporary artists choose sex and death for their subjects. Sex and erotic love point to a union and communion often frustrated by egoism, pride, lust, and a proclivity for violence. But sexual orgasm and its aftermath of exhaustion and impotence are also reminders of death. Ruth, the down-and-out prostitute with whom Harry Angstrom adulterously cohabits in John Updike's early novel *Rabbit, Run,* tells Harry after their lovemaking that orgasm "is like falling through." Harry asks Ruth, "Where do you fall to?" She answers, "Nowhere." Later in the novel Ruth says to Harry, "You're Mr. Death himself."[14]

Denial of Death, Denial of Life

Fear and anxiety about death should not be confused with aversion to death. In his seminal study *Western Attitudes Toward Death,* Philippe Ariès explains the difference. In earlier Western societies where Christianity dominated, death was very much a part of life, Ariès observes. For a variety of reasons involving social organization and the primitive state of medicine, death was a near and familiar occurrence. People died at home in the company of family and friends. Then as now, death could be ugly, messy, and tragic, and it was certainly feared and respected, but on the whole people were neither as repulsed nor as terrified by death as are modern folk. In part, the frequency and immediacy of death rendered it less alien and hence less threatening, but it was also the case that religion and belief in an afterlife, supported by familiar rituals of dying and mourning, enabled people to cope with death better as a part of living. According to Ariès, earlier Western culture did not make as strong a distinction as contemporary culture does "between the time before and the time after, this life and the afterlife. . . . On both sides of death, one is still very near the deep wellspring of sentiment."[15]

At the close of the movie *Forrest Gump,* Forrest stands by the grave of his deceased wife and says, "Momma always said that dyin' was a part of life. I sure wish it wasn't." Throughout the film, Forrest demonstrates a fundamental wisdom in response to the events in his life despite his IQ of 75. He experiences truth deeply and suffers from it when it is hard. Perhaps it is because he's "not a smart man" that Forrest can't dodge the truth the way the rest of us can. He wishes it wasn't so that death is a part of life, but he knows his Momma is right—death and dying are in the very midst of life and living. Forrest's religious beliefs are never defined in the film, but he does seem to express an implicit belief in life after death when he talks to his wife at her grave and delivers a note from their son to her. There is no reason to think that Forrest doesn't believe that his Jenny can hear him when he talks to her, since he means pretty much everything else he says in the film literally. In talking about his grief to his wife, he uses the same tone as he did in conversations with her when she was alive. But this last communication amounts to a religious act in that it hints of a real communion that transcends death. Forrest clearly remains near the wellspring of sentiment on both sides of death. It is less clear whether he has received any of the comforts that traditional Christian belief offers in these circumstances. While it is inarguably the case that death is a part of life insofar as it takes place in the midst of the living, it is also the case that death has been transformed into a passage toward a transcendent destiny that replaces the sting of separation with the joy of presence.

I would not uncritically lament the loss of the religious manner in which our ancestors tamed or domesticated death. There are both good and bad things that might be said about that. Nonetheless, two points that Ariès makes about the history of death in Western culture are especially helpful in thinking about a contemporary theological ethic of death and dying. First, in the modern era, "despite the apparent continuity of themes and ritual," death is "furtively pushed out of the world of familiar things."[16] Even self-consciously religious people tend to respond to death with an otherworldliness that suggests a weakened belief in Providence and no real sense of grace. Second, vast numbers of contemporary people have difficulty making anything good out of the process of dying and death itself. And all that remains for many mourners today is a vague hope that they are sending the deceased to some "far off" better place. By the nineteenth century, argues Ariès, even within the family that "believed in the afterlife . . . death became the unaccepted separation, the death of the other, 'thy death,' the death of the loved one."[17]

Ariès argues that more and more modern people react against this sort of otherworldly piety by embracing a one-dimensional this-worldly secularism. In the end, however, this makes little difference: like its weak religious counterpart, the secular outlook is typically characterized by dread of death and propensity to expel it from the world of the living. "Thus death gradually assume[s] another form, both more distant and more dramatic, more full of tension."[18] Death becomes unnamable. "Everything henceforth goes on as if neither I nor those who are dear to me are any longer mortal," says Ariès. "Technically, we admit that we might die; we take out insurance . . . to protect our families from poverty. But really, at heart we feel we are non-mortals. And surprise! Our life is not as a result gladdened!"[19]

The Rise of the New Therapeutic Naturalism

Today new answers are being proposed for the old problem of death. The modern therapists of death and dying are trying hard to transmute the secular view of death left in the wake of the decline of traditional religion into an acceptance of death as something quite natural. Sherwin B. Nuland's recent best-seller *How We Die* is an exceptionally sensitive and compelling expression of this project. Nuland relates stories from his life as a physician to show the reader how the banishment of death—real death, not the Hollywood variety—demeans and devalues life, and he sharply criticizes the medical profession for having become an accomplice in this denial of death. In 1950, Nuland notes, 50 percent of American deaths happened in hospitals; today that figure has reached 80 percent. Death is thus moving out of the field of vision of most Americans, moving behind the curtains and the banks of medical equipment. "The cultural symbolism of sequestering the dying," says Nuland, "is here as meaningful as the strictly clinical perspective of improved access to specialized facilities, and for most patients even more so. The solitary death is now . . . well recognized."[20] Nuland contends that people who die in this way, isolated from most aspects of their life prior to illness and hospitalization and adrift in the unfamiliar environment of modern medical treatment, will have a more difficult time finding meaning in the experience of dying.

To his credit, Nuland recognizes that much of what goes on in medicine today demonstrates how much we have been stripped of traditional religious and moral resources for facing death without loss of hope or meaning. In many cases, the art of caring for the dying has given way to an art of saving life at all cost. He adds that this new science of saving life is mostly concerned with the physician's need to be in control and the patient's need to feel that someone is in control. For the doctor who internalizes or flaunts the image of the physician as shaman or soldier, "even a temporary victory justifies the laying waste of the fields in which a dying man has cultivated his life."[21]

This is good stuff. But in the end I disagree with Nuland's naturalism. He sums up his ethic near the end of *How We Die:*

> A realistic expectation also demands our acceptance that one's allotted time on earth must be limited to an allowance consistent with the continuity of the existence of our species. Mankind, for all its unique gifts, is just as much a part of the ecosystem as any other zoolic or botanical form, and nature does not distinguish. We die so that the world may continue. We have been given the miracle of life because trillions upon trillions of living things have prepared the way for us and then have died—in a sense, for us. We die, in turn, so that others may live. The tragedy of a single individual becomes, in the balance of natural things, the triumph of ongoing life.[22]

Nuland tries to give meaning back to death and dying with this naturalism, and I do not discount the possibility that some of his audience may be persuaded. Certainly it is to Nuland's credit that he makes a case for practicing medicine in a way that is calibrated to the personal needs of dying patients. But his naturalism is a two-edged sword. It may rightly criticize modern medicine's betrayal of the patient's need for meaning in the process of dying, but it can also undercut the value of personal life—and in doing so open the way for managed death and state-managed experimentation on the dying. In the passage just cited, we find Nuland shifting his concern away from the individual to the survival of the species and the ecosystem, reducing the human being to an epiphenomenon of the natural order and thus depersonalizing death. What Nuland reveals about his personal history and sensibilities suggests that he would likely be opposed to

Dr. Kevorkian's new science of obitiatry, but there is nothing in the sort of naturalism he propounds that is incompatible with such experimentation.

The Culture of Death

Our deep aversion to and obsession with death in contemporary Western culture attest to its power over us. Indeed, it has become our preeminent taboo, and many of us have come to view it as an ultimate power, a godlike thing. Yet, as with all things we fashion into gods, we have managed to overcome our fear of death enough to seek to manipulate it for our own purposes, to summon it to provide a solution for our personal and social problems. We have overcome our aversion to death enough to get comfortable with using it to get rid of criminals, to end unwanted pregnancies, and, increasingly, to relieve the misery of illness and injury. Through our own choices and predilections, we have fashioned a culture of death.[23]

Many secular moderns remain unaware of the fact that they are submerged in this culture of death. The contemporary secular imagination typically prides itself on its affirmation of life and is quick to dismiss the biblical imagination as morbid and otherworldly. But in fact, the secular imagination is formed by fictional and nonfictional stories that leave the impression—even the conviction—that death lurks everywhere and encompasses all of life, whereas the biblical imagination is formed by stories in which death is subject to a God who redeems his sin-damaged creation and renders death a contingent rather than an ultimate reality.

Secular moderns cling to the belief that they can celebrate life at the same time they embrace a culture of death. Some argue that they can best embrace life by putting an end to the lives they no longer value. But in making such a determination, they do not give enough consideration to the darkness that death casts over life whatever the use to which it is put. In *Rabbit, Run,* John Updike describes Harry Angstrom as someone "who has no taste for the dark, tangled, visceral aspect of Christianity, the *going through* quality of it, the passage *into* death and suffering that redeems and inverts these things, like an umbrella blowing inside out."[24] Moderns flirt with death as an answer to their problems, but, like Harry Angstrom, they refuse to look directly at death and see the darkness. They are unwilling to face the truth about sin and evil, unwilling to acknowledge that it is beyond the power of the physician, abortionist, euthanist, or executioner to provide the cure and the salvation they really seek.

Updike says that Harry Angstrom lacks "the mindful will to walk the straight line of paradox. His eyes turn toward the light however it glances into his retina."[25] The faith that Harry yearns for demands that he be honest about his mortal condition and willing to give himself up to God's care. Then he might begin to experience grace and have hope even when death intrudes. Living in the 1950s, Harry is not yet a child of the post-Christian era, and he still finds some traces of his Lutheran upbringing influencing his reaction when his wife accidentally drowns their baby daughter. It is darkly ironic that the child died in water, for "it occurs to him, what no one has mentioned, [that] the child was never baptized." Harry fears that the death of his daughter holds no promise of salvation. I take this message from Updike's story: If more people faced death in the presence of God as Harry does at just this moment, they might begin to recover from the *thanatos* syndrome. At least there might be fewer abortions, fewer executions, fewer homicides, and a greater reluctance to turn to physician-assisted suicide and euthanasia as solutions to the problems of chronic pain and terminal illness. Sadly, Harry turns away from his tentative encounter with God and (as we find in *Rabbit Redux*) goes back to Ruth for sex and escape. Sadly, too, our society is likewise turning away from any sort of encounter with God at virtually every critical juncture and choosing instead the *thanatos* syndrome and the embrace of redemptionless death.

Conclusion

The attitudes toward death in contemporary Western society pose a serious challenge to traditional Christian teaching on the subject. To the extent that these attitudes have infiltrated the Christian community, they have provoked a crisis of faith for many. Even among those who profess to have a biblical faith there is confusion about the meaning of death. Death is becoming the ultimate concern of all those who lack the mediation of the sacred and transcendent in their lives, religious and nonreligious people alike. Such people tend to fall into slavery either to a stultifying and debilitating dread of death or to the comforting illusion that life is for the living and death is for the dying. They become victims of a great spiritual emptiness. I do not believe that humanistic naturalism of the sort proposed by Sherwin Nuland is capable of calming these deep fears, reversing the denial, or filling the emptiness. But I do believe that a Christian theological vision of death can offer the meaning for which we yearn as we face both life and death.

NOTES

Robert L. Wilken: "Tradition and Trust"

1. See John Burnaly, *Amor Dei: A Study of the Religion of St. Augustine* (London, 1938).
2. Augustine, *Confessions* 10.6.
3. Hilary of Poitiers, *De Trinitate* 1.8.
4. Cited in Peter Gay, *The Enlightenment, an Interpretation: The Rise of Modern Paganism* (New York, 1966), 212.
5. Alasdair MacIntyre, *Whose Justice? Which Rationality?* (Notre Dame, IN, 1988), 6.
6. David Tracy, *Blessed Rage for Order: The New Pluralism in Theology* (New York, 1975), 6–7.
7. Cited in Cleo McNelly Kearns, *T. S. Eliot and Indic Traditions* (Cambridge, 1987), 3.
8. Matthew Arnold, "Preface to the First Edition of Poems (1853)," in *Poetry and Literary Criticism of Matthew Arnold,* by A. D. Culler (Boston, 1961), 212.
9. Charles Wood, *The Formation of Christian Understanding: An Essay in Theological Hermeneutics* (Philadelphia, 1981), 76.
10. Wolfhart Pannenberg, *Systematische Theologie,* vol. 1 (Göttingen, 1988), 7.
11. Augustine, *De Vera Religione* xxiv.45 in *Augustine: Earlier Writings,* trans. John H. S. Burleigh, The Library of Christian Classics (Philadelphia, 1953), 247.
12. Thomas Aquinas, *Quaestiones quodlibetales,* ed. P. Mandonnet (Paris, 1926), 155.
13. Gregory of Nyssa, *Contra Eunomium* 1.155–160, ed. Werner Jaeger (Leiden, 1960), 73–75. For English translation, see *Nicene and Post-Nicene Fathers,* Second Series (Grand Rapids, n.d.), 5:50–51.
14. Janet Martin Soskice, *Metaphor and Religious Language* (Oxford, 1985), 154.
15. Soskice, *Metaphor,* 159.
16. Dante quotations come from *Paradiso* 5.8 and 7.59–60, in *The Divine Comedy of Dante Alighieri,* trans. Allen Mandelbaum (Berkeley, 1982), 38, 58.

Robert Royal: "Christian Humanism in a Postmodern Age"

1. A different form of this story appears as the frontispiece to Luc Ferry and Alain Renaut, *French Philosophy of the Sixties: An Essay on Antihumanism,* trans. by Mary H. S. Cattani (Amherst: University of Massachusetts Press, 1990).

2. On the biochemical improbabilities of Darwinism in its classic formulation, see Michael J. Behe, *Darwin's Black Box: The Biochemical Challenge to Evolution* (New York: Free Press, 1996).

3. See Thomas Pangle, *The Ennobling of Democracy: The Challenge of the Postmodern Age* (Baltimore: Johns Hopkins University Press, 1991), 31.

4. G.K. Chesterton, *Chaucer* (New York: Sheed and Ward, 1956), 26. Though a late text in the original edition (1932), this passage echoes a sentiment that may be found in varying forms throughout Chesterton's whole oeuvre.

5. From Martin Heidegger, "The Thinker as Poet," in *Poetry, Language, Thought* (New York: Harper and Row, 1971), 9.

6. George Steiner, *Martin Heidegger* (Chicago: University of Chicago Press, 1978), 15, 131, and 146.

7. See, for example, Rorty's *Contingency, Irony, and Solidarity* (New York: Cambridge University Press, 1989).

8. See Philippa Foote, "Nietzsche's Immoralism," *New York Review of Books,* June 13, 1991, 18–22. For Foote, Nietzsche fails on several counts, not least because he denies anything but self-created truths: "There have been many attempts to see [in Nietzsche's promotion of self-creation] an inspiring call to a kind of joyous paganism that would leave us with all that is best in morals. Can this be sustained? I think not, just because of Nietzsche's attack on the universalism in morality. He insists that there are no kinds of actions that are good or bad in themselves, and this has, it seems, a fatal implication for the teaching of justice." Even the claims that Nietzsche's endless talk about inferiors and superiors, and the way he countenances some men looking down on others, together with his own readiness to sacrifice— to write off—the 'mediocre,'" confirms the impression that justice gets short shrift in his scheme of things. . . ."(20)

9. See my "Human Nature and Unnatural Humanisms" in *From Twilight to Dawn,* ed. by Peter Redpath (South Bend, IN: University of Notre Dame Press, 1990).

10. Jacques Derrida, *The Other Heading: Reflections on Today's Europe* (Fr. title: *L'autre cap*) Pascale-Anne Brault and Michael B. Nass, trans. (Bloomington: Indiana University Press, 1992).

11. Robert Royal, *1492 and All That: Political Manipulations of History* (Washington, D.C.: Ethics and Public Policy Center, 1992).

12. On this point, see James Brown Scott, *The Spanish Origins of International Law* (Washington, D.C.: Georgetown University Press, 1928).

13. See, for example, the terminological distinctions drawn by Albert Borgmann, *Crossing the Postmodern Divide* (Chicago: University of Chicago Press, 1992).

14. *Saints and Postmodernism: Revisioning Moral Philosophy* (Chicago: University of Chicago Press, 1990).

15. George Steiner, *Real Presences,* (Chicago: University of Chicago Press, 1989).

16. Ibid., p.3.

17. Susan Shell, "Preserving the Humanities," address to the Madison Center Conference on the Humanities, Washington, D.C., 1989.

18. Iris Murdoch, *Metaphysics as a Guide to Morals* (New York: Allen Lane, 1993), 202.

19. G. K. Chesterton, *Heretics* (New York: John Lane Company, 1909), 304–305. The original date of publication was 1905.

Robert Coles: "Freud and God"

1. The political implications of that mental activity are obviously enormous. Even elementary school children use presidents and prime ministers and kings and dictators, and not least the flag, in a continuing effort to establish loyalties, preferences, a sense of place, affiliation and purpose. And, of course, our political leaders reciprocate, trying to connect themselves (their names, faces, messages and slogans) with the personal as well as material aspirations of as many people as possible.

2. Simone Weil struggled long and hard with her own mind's considerable capacity to speculate about the world. The sections on "Illusions," "Idolatry" and "Decreation," in *Gravity and Grace* show her shrewdly aware of how anxious we are to use reverie and fancy in order to catch hold of meaning—and not only, she insisted, the uneducated or the overly emotional. Her fierce espousal of "decreation," awesomely severe and frightening even to many of those who love her ideas, can be regarded as an all but impossible attempt to remove what she felt to be the barriers of the imagination from her contemplation of God. She is, in contrast, much more relaxed about her (and everyone else's) imagination when she writes about science and its connection to our fantasy life—in, for instance, "Classical Science and After."

Wendell Berry: "Christianity and the Survival of Creation"

1. Psalms 24:1. (All biblical quotations are from the King James Version.)
2. Leviticus 25:23.
3. John 1:3.
4. Job 34:14–15.
5. Philip Sherrard, *Human Image: World Image* (Ipswich, Suffolk, England: Golgonooza Press, 1992), 152.
6. George Herbert, "Providence," lines 41 and 44, from *The Poems of George Herbert,* ed. by Helen Gardner (London: Oxford University Press, 1961), 54.
7. Dante Alighieri, *The Divine Comedy,* trans. by Charles S. Singleton, Bollingen Series LXXX, and *Inferno,* canto XI, lines 46–48 (Princeton, NJ: Princeton University Press, 1970).
8. Dante Alighieri, *Inferno,* canto XI, lines 109–11.
9. William Blake, *Complete Writings,* ed. by Geoffrey Keynes (London: Oxford University Press, 1966), 160.
10. Kathleen Raine, *Golgonooza: City of Imagination* (Ipswich, Suffolk, England: Golgonooza Press, 1991), 28.
11. 1 Kings 8:27.
12. Acts 17:24 and 28.
13. Matthew 18:20.
14. Isaiah 1:13–17.
15. Romans 1:20.
16. Deuteronomy 33:13–16.
17. Matthew 16:26.
18. William Shakespeare, *Macbeth,* ed. by Kenneth Muir (Cambridge, MA: Harvard University Press, 1957), V, v, lines 13, 26–28, 49.

19. Ananda K. Coomaraswamy, *Christian and Oriental Philosophy of Art* (New York: Dover, 1957), 98.

20. Walter Shewring, *Artist and Tradesman* (Marlborough, MA: Paulinus Press, 1984), 19.

21. Herbert, *The Poems of George Herbert,* 54.

22. June Sprigg, *By Shaker Hands* (Hanover, NH: University Press of New England, 1990), 33.

23. Ananda K. Coomaraswamy, *Selected Papers,* vol. 1 (Princeton, NJ: Princeton University Press, 1977), 255, 259.

24. Coomaraswamy, *Christian and Oriental Philosophy of Art,* 99.

25. Dante, *Paradiso,* canto XIII, lines 121 and 123.

26. Mark Twain, *Adventures of Huckleberry Finn,* in *Mississippi Writings* (New York: Library of America, 1982), 626.

27. Matthew 5:44.

28. George MacDonald, *A Time for Trumpets* (New York: Bantam Books, 1984), 458.

Andrew Kimbrell: "Second Genesis"

1. "Life Industrialized" (editorial), *New York Times,* February 22, 1988.

2. Langdon Winner, *Autonomous Technology* (Cambridge: MIT Press, 1967).

3. Gregory S. Butler, "George Grant and Modern Justice," *Humanitas,* Vol. 4. No. 2. Spring 1990, p.1.

4. Quoted in Virginia Morris, "Human Genes Not So Special," *New Haven Register,* 28 August 1988.

5. Francis Fukuyama, "The End of History?" *The National Interest,* 16 (Summer 1989), 3–18.

Vigen Guroian: "The Culture of Death"

1. Felix Salten, *Bambi: A Life in the Woods* (New York: Minstrel Books, 1988), 162.

2. Salten, *Bambi,* 187–88.

3. Arthur McGill, *Suffering: A Test of Theological Method* (Philadelphia: Westminster Press, 1982), 50.

4. John Updike, *The Poorhouse Fair* (New York: Fawcett Crest, 1958), 121.

5. Updike, *The Poorhouse Fair,* 115.

6. Updike, *The Poorhouse Fair,* 123.

7. William F. May, "The Sacral Power of Death in Contemporary Experience," in *On Moral Medicine: Theological Perspectives in Medical Ethics,* ed. Stephen E. Lammers and Allen Verhey (Grand Rapids, MI: William B. Eerdmans, 1987), 175.

8. John Cheever, "The Death of Justina," in *The Stories of John Cheever* (New York: Ballantine, 1980), 507.

9. Cheever, "The Death of Justina," 513.

10. Cheever, "The Death of Justina," 515.

11. Geoffrey Gorer, *Death, Grief, and Mourning* (Garden City, NY: Doubleday, 1965), 195.

12. Gorer, *Death, Grief, and Mourning,* 196.

13. Paul Griffiths, "Titian in Paris: The Venice Biennial," *New Yorker,* August 2, 1993, 70.

14. John Updike, *Rabbit, Run* (New York: Ballantine, 1960), 83, 279.

15. Philippe Ariès, *Western Attitudes Toward Death: From the Middle Ages to the Present,* trans. Patricia M. Ranum (Baltimore: Johns Hopkins University Press, 1974), 104.

16. Ariès, *Western Attitudes Toward Death,* p. 105.

17. Ariès, *Western Attitudes Toward Death,* p. 106.

18. Ariès, *Western Attitudes Toward Death,* p. 106.

19. Ariès, *Western Attitudes Toward Death,* p. 107.

20. Sherwin B. Nuland, *How We Die: Reflections on Life's Final Chapter* (New York: Alfred A. Knopf, 1993), 255.

21. Nuland, *How We Die,* 265.

22. Nuland, *How We Die,* 267.

23. In the following discussion of the culture of death, I develop a number of important insights mined from Peter J. Rega, "The Culture of Death," *Baltimore Sun,* 13 December 1994, p. 19A.

24. Updike, *Rabbit, Run,* p. 218.

25. Updike, *Rabbit, Run,* p. 218.

26. Updike, *Rabbit, Run,* p. 269.

PERMISSIONS

Annie Dillard, "Holy the Firm," reprinted from *Holy the Firm,* New York: HarperCollins, 1977. © Annie Dillard 1977. Reprinted by permission of the publisher.

Richard Rodriguez, "Credo," reprinted from *Hunger of Memory,* Boston, David R. Godine, Publisher, Inc. 1982. © 1982 by Richard Rodriguez. Reprinted by permission of the publisher.

Gerald Early, "Faith and Fatherhood, " reprinted from *Daughters: On Family and Fatherhood,* Reading, MA, Addison Wesley Longman, Inc., 1994. © 1994 by Gerald Early. Reprinted by permission of the publisher.

Kathleen Norris, "Exile, Homeland, and Negative Capability," reprinted from *The Cloister Walk,* New York, G.P. Putnam's Sons, 1996. © 1996 by Kathleen Norris. Reprinted by permission of the publisher.

Robert L. Wilken, "Tradition and Trust: The Role of Memory in the Christian Intellectual Life," originally published as "Memory and the Christian Intellectual Life," reprinted from *Reasoned Faith,* ed. Frank F. Birtel, New York: Crossroad Publishing Co., 1993. Reprinted by permission of the publisher.

Leon R. Kass, "What's Wrong with Babel?" was originally published by *The American Scholar,* Volume 58, Number 1, Winter 1988-89. Reprinted by permission of the author.

Robert Royal, "Christian Humanism in a Postmodern Age," was written for this collection.

Robert Coles, "Freud and God," originally published in *The Virginia Quarterly Review,* is reprinted from *The Mind's Fate,* Second Edition, Boston, Little, Brown and Co. © 1975, 1995 by Robert Coles. Reprinted by permission of the publisher.

Virginia Stem Owens, "Faith, Perception, and the New Physics," reprinted from *And the Trees Clapped Their Hands,* Grand Rapids, MI: Wm. B. Eerdmans, 1983. Reprinted by permission of the author.

Robert W. Jenson, "How the World Lost Its Story," originally published in *First Things,* October, 1993. Reprinted by permission of the author.

Glenn Tinder, "Can We Be Good Without God?" was originally published in *The Atlantic Monthly*, December 1989. Reprinted by permission of the author.

Os Guinness, "Tribespeople, Idiots, or Citizens?" reprinted from *The American Hour,* New York, The Free Press, 1993. Reprinted by permission of the publisher.